Contaminated Land

Contaminated Land

The Practice and Economics of Redevelopment

Paul M. Syms *MPhil, PhD, FSVA, ACIArb*

Principal
Paul Syms Associates, Cheshire

and

ISVA Visiting Professor of Land and Property
Sheffield Hallam University

Blackwell
Science

© 1997 by
Blackwell Science Ltd
Editorial Offices:
Osney Mead, Oxford OX2 0EL
25 John Street, London WC1N 2BL
23 Ainslie Place, Edinburgh EH3 6AJ
350 Main Street, Malden
  MA 02148 5018, USA
54 University Street, Carlton
  Victoria 3053, Australia

Other Editorial Offices:

Blackwell Wissenschafts-Verlag GmbH
  Kurfürstendamm 57
  10707 Berlin, Germany

Zehetnergasse 6
A-1140 Wien
Austria

First published 1997

Set in 11/14pt Bembo
by DP Photosetting, Aylesbury, Bucks
Printed and bound in Great Britain
by Hartnolls Ltd, Bodmin, Cornwall

The Blackwell Science logo is a trade mark of Blackwell
Science Ltd, registered at the United Kingdom Trade
Marks Registry

DISTRIBUTORS

Marston Book Services Ltd
PO Box 269
Abingdon
Oxon OX14 4YN
(*Orders:* Tel: 01235 465500
          Fax: 01235 465555)

USA
Blackwell Science, Inc.
Commerce Place
350 Main Street
Malden, MA 02148 5018
(*Orders:* Tel: 800 759 6102
          617 388 8250
          Fax: 617 388 8255)

Canada
Copp Clark Professional
200 Adelaide Street, West, 3rd Floor
Toronto, Ontario M5H 1W7
(*Orders:* Tel: 416 597-1616
          800 815-9417
          Fax: 416 597-1617)

Australia
Blackwell Science Pty Ltd
54 University Street
Carlton, Victoria 3053
(*Orders:* Tel: 03 9347-0300
          Fax: 03 9347-5001)

A catalogue record for this title is available from
the British Library

ISBN 0-632-04134-X

Library of Congress
Cataloging-in-Publication Data

Syms, Paul M.
    Contaminated land: the practice and economics of
    redevelopment/Paul M. Syms.
        p.   cm.
    Includes bibliographical references (p.   ) and index.
    ISBN 0-632-04134-X
    1. Land use–Government policy–Great Britain.
    2. Reclamation of land–Government policy–Great
    Britain.   3. Soil pollution–Great Britain.
    4. Environmental risk assessment–Great Britain.
    I. Title.
    HD596.S95   1997
    333.73—dc21
                                        97-1051
                                        CIP

Acknowledgements

Crown copyright is reproduced with the permission of the Controller of Her Majesty's
Stationery Office.

The quotation on page 1 from *Months in the Country* is reproduced by kind permission of the estate of the late Brian Redhead and of Ebury Press.

Contents

Preface

In writing this book I have attempted to take a 'non-technical' approach to what is a highly complex and technical subject. Whilst acting as the development consultant on a number of urban regeneration projects in the late 1980s and early 1990s, I found that it was often necessary to resolve contamination issues before the form of development and its value could be decided upon. Increasingly, it became necessary to form judgements as to the redevelopment potential of sites based on differing objectives and despite differing opinions. Potential investors and occupiers on occasions demanded that all contamination be removed from the site, contrary to engineering advice saying that containment within the site was perfectly adequate. Add to this a lack of certainty regarding legislation and government policies and it is understandable that many property developers, bankers and their advisors showed a marked reluctance to become involved in any land where contamination may be suspected.

In seeking to unravel some of the complexities I found myself confronted with an extensive body of literature, both academic and professional texts, dealing with subjects such as site investigations, sampling and testing regimes, soil treatment methods and waste management. Written mostly for engineers and environmental scientists, the existing works concentrated primarily on investigating, identifying and overcoming soil contamination, with scant attention being paid to the redevelopment of the land following treatment. Rarely, if ever, was any mention made of the economic and valuation issues surrounding the redevelopment of contaminated land.

Some of the North American professional literature considered the valuation aspects of contamination, especially proximity and stigma effects. For the most part, however, this tended to concentrate on issues such as the valuation impact of bad neighbour uses being located close to residential areas, or the damage caused by contamination migrating from one site to another, and did not really focus on redevelopment issues. I decided therefore to write a book which would assist those many individuals involved in the redevelopment process, from developers and construction professionals to investors, property valuers to bankers, regulatory authorities and the occupiers or users of completed developments.

The book is divided into four sections, the first of which discusses soil contamination, what it is, how it occurs and some of the possible harmful effects. This section also considers the ways in which contaminants may travel, as well as legislative approaches and the extent of the problem. The second section deals with technical issues, such as site investigations and soil treatment methods, together with the 'risk based' approach to the remediation of contaminated land. In Section 3 attention is turned to the redevelopment and valuation issues, using a number of case studies and describing the results of recent research. Section 4 addresses the issues of satisfying regulatory authorities and the potential users of contaminated sites that they are 'suitable for use'.

Where appropriate checklists have been included, to assist individuals dealing with the day to day issues of contaminated land to adopt the right course of action, or to ask the relevant questions of other professionals or landowners. Although the book is intended primarily as a professional text, it is hoped that it will also be of interest to those involved in education and research concerning land contamination and other environmental subjects.

The contribution made by a great number of people in producing this work is gratefully acknowledged. Almost 200 people participated in the research project described in Section 3. They came from a wide variety of professional disciplines but had one interest in common, namely the use and re-use of land. The contribution made by other people, from non-property related disciplines, enabled an assessment to be made as to how members of the public might perceive land contamination issues. I received assistance in respect of the legal and insurance aspects, in Chapter 12, from Stephen Sykes of the Environmental Law Group of solicitors Hammond Suddards and

Dr Marcel Steward of Sedgwick UK Risk Services Ltd. Their contributions are gratefully acknowledged.

I would like to thank my colleagues, John Storr and Geoffrey Marsden, at Sheffield Hallam University for their comments on the earlier versions of the work. Advice and comments were also received from many people in public and private sector organisations. My gratitude goes to Julia Burden, of my publisher Blackwell Science, for her confidence in the project and to my editor Dr Elizabeth Bates, for her thoroughness and searching questions. The most important thanks of all must go to my wife Janice for her constant support, patience and proof reading, throughout the four years of research which was required in order to produce this work.

The contribution of all concerned has been invaluable. I have tried to reflect their views in an unbiased way and to provide the reader with a comprehensive discussion of the issues surrounding the redevelopment of contaminated land. In the final analysis it is up to the reader to judge whether or not I have succeeded in this aim and I accept responsibility for any errors or omissions.

Note on legislation

When this book was being written it was expected that the new legislation affecting contaminated land in the United Kingdom would have come into effect shortly before publication. In the event, when the book went to press the legislation had not yet been implemented and the book describes the latest stages in the consultative process.

Paul Syms
Macclesfield
Cheshire
April 1997

Chapter 1
Introduction

'There are roughly 56 million people in this country and this country is roughly 56 million acres. If all things were equal we would have an acre each, plus perhaps a cow and a beanstalk.

But things are not equal. From the year dot to the year 1900 we built on two million of those 56 million acres. Between 1900 and 1950 we built on another two million acres. In other words, we covered as much land in the first half of this century as we had in all previous centuries.

And since 1950, in spite of, or perhaps because of, planning controls, we have gone mad. When the acres covered are added up at the end of the century they will have to publish them in hectares to make them look fewer...

For too long it was assumed that new development required green field sites. There are regions of Britain where, between 1950 and 1980, agricultural land was being built on at the rate of 100 acres a week. Then someone pointed out that developers could look inward as well as outward. Land which had been used once could be used again.'

(Brian Redhead, *Months in the Country*, 1992, pp. 25–6)

The re-use of land is not without its problems, but over the past two decades a considerable expertise has developed in tackling those problems. This book is concerned with the re-use of land that has previously been occupied for industrial purposes or has been affected by contamination arising out of human activities. The methods by which land is brought back into use, and the ways in which former industrial sites may be valued before and after redevelopment, are considered through the use of valuation models and case studies.

Although intended primarily for use by valuers and development surveyors, it is hoped that the book will be of interest to the members of other professions involved in the use and development of land. Town planners and environmental scientists may develop an understanding of the issues which affect the viability of development projects. Architects and engineers may come to appreciate the marketing and valuation aspects of the developments which they design. Bankers and lawyers may benefit from the 'non-technical' overview of contamination problems and their resolution.

The approach adopted in preparing the book has been to make it an easy to use reference for those people who are faced with the day to day question of how to deal with the problems presented by contaminated land. So as to assist this task the book has been arranged in four sections:

Section 1: Chapters 2–4   Background
Seciton 2: Chapters 5–8   Technical issues
Section 3: Chapters 9–11 Valuation and redevelopment issues
Section 4: Chapters 12–13 Satisfying users and regulators

Several chapters conclude with checklists, detailing some of the questions which need to be asked by those involved with the investigation, redevelopment and valuation of contaminated land.

A significant body of literature exists in respect of soil contamination, its causes, pathways, targets and methods of remediation, but most of this literature is of a highly technical nature and virtually incomprehensible to anyone other than an engineer or soil scientist. An important task was therefore to review the literature, in order to gain an understanding of the problem and then to distil it into a form which is readily understood by individuals in the 'non-technical' professions.

Part of the book is devoted to a research study, which endeavours to identify how the issues and problems associated with contaminated land are perceived by property practitioners. However, the intention was not simply to report upon research outcomes but also to suggest practical ways in which the redevelopment of contaminated land may be approached. The effects which different types of contamination, remediation methods and future uses may have on land value have been considered through the perceptions of individuals from diverse professions. The perception studies and actual contaminated land case studies have been used to develop a valuation model.

More than a dozen redevelopment case studies are discussed and recommendations made as to good practice in dealing with soil contamination on those sites. Valuation aspects are considered, both before and after redevelopment, in order to determine the extent to which there exists a diminution in the value of contaminated land which exceeds the cost to cure.

The background section of the book opens, in *Chapter 2*, with a discussion of the problem of soil contamination and its origins. *Chapter 3* defines contamination and looks at the industrial processes, many of which are still in use today, which have been responsible for land becoming contaminated. Also considered in *Chapter 3* is the nature of contaminative substances, their sources, the pathways by which they travel and the ways in which they affect their targets. Standards and guidelines are reviewed. The number and spatial extent of affected sites is discussed.

Considerable attention has been paid in recent years to the formulation of government policies designed to tackle the problems of contamination and pollution. Legislation and government policies are considered in *Chapter 4*.

The technical issues section is intended as a 'non-technical' review of contamination identification, treatment, and risks, which might be required by individuals in non-engineering or non-scientific disciplines in order to provide an adequate service to their clients. The approach has been to consider the scope of knowledge required by the general practice surveyor or valuer, so as to be able to identify the need for a site investigation and to advise upon the appointment of suitable consultants. The need for adequate site investigations and the ways in which these may be achieved are discussed in *Chapter 5*.

Once a site has been investigated and the extent of any contamination has been identified, treatment may or may not be required, and several alternative forms of remediation may be suitable. For the most part the approach to site remediation has been biased towards civil engineering solutions which can take many forms, according to the nature of the contamination, the geology and hydrogeology of the site, and the intended future use. The use of other forms of treatment has suffered from a degree of scepticism and their acceptance has been slow. Currently available methods, their suitability for use in redevelopment situations and their likely cost are considered in *Chapter 6*.

The process of property development and investment requires an assessment of the risks involved. The likelihood of increased risk is identified as a major influence in respect of the treatment and redevelopment of contaminated land. *Chapter 7* considers perceptions of risk and relates these to the development process.

The 'suitable for use' approach, favoured by British government policies, is discussed in *Chapter 8* in the context of determining risk. Risk assessment methods are described in this chapter. A very significant difficulty in tackling the problems of contaminated land has been the paucity of accurate data concerning past uses and the extent of contamination within individual sites. Linked to this has been an understandable reluctance, on the part of both existing landowners and prospective developers, to spend money on site investigation work.

Whilst the earlier parts of the book are focused primarily on historic issues and how to overcome the problems of land contamination, the chapters dealing with valuation and redevelopment considerations address present and future economic concerns. Issues of value are considered in *Chapter 9* and academic literature and professional guidance issued to valuers are considered. The extent to which valuers should become involved with environmental matters is discussed, especially as some members of the profession appear to hold diametrically opposed views. For example, one faction appears to believe that valuers should do no more than advise the client that the possibility of contamination has not been taken into account in preparing the valuation, whilst another faction believes that the valuer should endeavour to ascertain the cost of remediation and take cognisance of this when producing the valuation.

Only a limited amount of academic literature concerned with the subject of contaminated land has been produced in the UK, although there is a substantial body of literature in the United States. A great deal of practical knowledge is available regarding the remediation and redevelopment of such sites. The majority of valuers have not had much direct involvement in site reclamation, with the advice regarding treatment options being regarded as the responsibility of civil engineers and environmental scientists. *Chapters 10 and 11* consider the impact which different forms of site treatment and end uses may have on the redevelopment process.

In the light of greater environmental awareness, and with an increasing range of options becoming available for the treatment of contaminants, valuers need to improve their knowledge so as to be able to provide proper advice as to the valuation implications relating to soil remediation alternatives. Landfilling with contaminated wastes is regarded by many as being environmentally unacceptable, suitable landfill sites are also reducing in number and the costs involved are increasing, including the imposition of a levy in the Landfill Tax. Developers must therefore give the fullest consideration to all available options and the valuer has a role to play in ensuring that the most appropriate decisions (based on present technical knowledge) are reached by their clients.

Sellers of contaminated sites may seek to ensure that they are absolved from any future liability in respect of contamination arising out of past industrial activities, whilst buyers will undoubtedly seek to ensure that they have been provided with the fullest possible information regarding the inherent problems. Both parties may have difficulty in obtaining insurance cover to minimise their risks. Issues concerning the sale, transfer and insurance of contaminated land are considered in *Chapter 12*.

Reaching agreement with regulators regarding site investigation procedures and remediation methods is likely to increase in importance. *Chapter 13* considers the issues involved in satisfying planning and public health officers, as well as the environment agencies, as to the viability of remediation proposals without losing sight of the economic aspects of redevelopment projects. A summary of findings from the research and the conclusions derived therefrom is contained in *Chapter 13*, together with recommendations to be followed as to 'good practice' in respect of the redevelopment of contaminated land.

Section 1
Background

Chapter 2
The Problem and its Origins

Throughout the late 1970s and early 1980s, the demand for land as the raw material of property development encouraged the re-use of former industrial sites. These sites were redeveloped for a variety of purposes but there was no concerted effort on the part of property developers to ensure that land should be re-used before further areas of virgin land were consumed. Redevelopment tended to occur in areas where there was little or no alternative. The 'urban regeneration' of these areas therefore came about as a matter of necessity rather than development or planning policy, although some encouragement was given to the redevelopment of old industrial sites through the enactment of the Inner Urban Areas Act 1978 (HMSO, 1978).

In some cases the redeveloped sites were retained in industrial use as new 'industrial estates', but instead of supporting new manufacturing industries, these estates very often consisted of warehousing and distribution centres, providing far fewer employment opportunities than the old industries which they replaced. The demand for new industrial premises reached a peak in 1980, accompanied by the abandonment of older industrial sites as manufacturing industry underwent a process of 'down-sizing' and modernisation. Proximity to motorway junctions became an important factor in terms of industrial location. In a survey by Adams (1986), motorway access was perceived as being of greater importance than proximity to city centres, airports and rail facilities. Land use criteria, such as a ready supply of raw materials and access to markets, diminished in importance as a result of the globalisation of industry, and so the traditional manufacturing areas of the inner cities fell into a state of dereliction (Figure 2.1).

Fig. 2.1 Old machinery bases and oily residues remain after demolition of a former engineering works.

In bringing these derelict areas back into use, site preparation generally consisted of little more than demolition of old buildings and structures and the grubbing up of floorslabs. Frequently the old foundations were left in place, provided that they were not likely to cause a hindrance to the new development, and service pipework and ducts were simply cut off, left to remain under the new buildings. Investigations were undertaken by structural engineers to ensure that sites were capable of supporting the steel portal framed buildings which became the standard form of construction for these new estates. Unless, however, the sites were obviously contaminated by some odorous or visibly unpleasant wastes, little thought was given to the chemical composition of materials left behind from the former uses.

Investors in these new industrial estates included pension funds and property companies, as well as companies purchasing for their own occupation. Many of the new developments were on sites which had been used previously for purposes such as coal yards, chemical works, textile mills and engineering works, and they may still have what Patchin (1988, p. 7) referred to as 'ecologic and economic time-bombs' buried beneath them. The investors gave little or no thought to the possibility that they may have been acquiring properties affected by contamination and with potential future problems. That is not to suggest that the new developments were in any way unfit for the purposes for which they were intended. In the majority of cases contamination left behind by the past industrial uses was safely contained beneath floors, service yards and car parks, and may be expected to remain so for the economic life of the building.

As few of these developments from the 1970s and 1980s are nearing the end of their economic life, they are more likely to pose problems for future generations than to constitute a 'short term' problem. There are, however, many other industrial sites which have fallen into disuse and have not been redeveloped. The lessons of the past must therefore be learned, if these sites are to be brought back into economic use.

The contaminated land problem

Although the existence of land contamination had been recognised by government, environmentalists, and engineers, it was not generally perceived by the surveying profession to be a problem of any significance until the late 1980s and early 1990s. In consequence, scant consideration was given to the valuation aspects of a problem which was not even acknowledged to exist.

The relatively recent awakening of awareness amongst the surveying profession was evident from comments made by Malcolm Grant, Professor of Land Economy, University of Cambridge, in Spring 1992.

'We've only recently come to understand both the extent of the problem of contaminated land and its implications. So far as extent is concerned, we are told that there are several thousand sites in Britain which are contaminated, although that judgement does not carry with it the second judgement which is that they should be cleaned up, or the third judgement which is to what level they should be cleaned up. So it's a multi-layered problem. But it's been brought home to us particularly that our previous safeguards, as we understood them, and particularly the planning system, hasn't operated as effectively as we might have hoped. We have had instances of redevelopment being carried out, particularly on closed landfills, without anybody appreciating at the time that it was a closed landfill and without proper engineering work being in place to deal with the continued process of decomposition underground.'

(Grant, 1992, p. 16)

The subject of contaminated land was addressed by Parliament, in a critical report by the House of Commons Select Committee on the Environment in 1990, the 'Rossi Report' (Environment Committee, 1990). This report made a number of detailed recommendations intended to strengthen the framework of legislation and environmental standards to reduce pollution risks and to facilitate the reclamation of land for new uses. The government response (DoE, 1990a), presented to Parliament in July 1990, recognised the report as a valuable contribution to the debate on contaminated land but perceived a number of problems in implementing its recommendations.

The Government's White Paper 'This Common Inheritance: Britain's Environmental Strategy' which followed in September of the same year (DoE, 1990b) stated that contamination of land by chemicals and waste products is hard to define and measure exactly, although surveys suggested that 50% of the derelict land in the UK might be contaminated and that contamination is also found on other, non-derelict, land.

The Environmental Protection Act 1990

It was the Environmental Protection Act 1990 (HMSO, 1990), which came into force at the beginning of 1991, that first alerted valuers to the fact that the possibility of contamination may have a serious adverse effect on property values. Section 143 of the Act introduced proposals for the setting up of registers of land and buildings where industrial processes of a potentially contaminative nature had been, or were still being, carried out. The full implications of the legislation were not immediately apparent from reading the section itself and it was not until a consultation paper was published in May 1991 that developers and valuers were alerted to the possible effects of the proposals on property values.

Following abandonment of the Section 143 registers in March 1993, there was a feeling of relief amongst developers, surveyors, and valuers that the registers were no longer to be compiled. Lawyers had increased the number of environmental type questions in their pre-contract enquiries and bankers exercised extreme caution over the financing of development projects on potentially contaminated sites. The possibility that legislation could result in environmental liabilities running into billions of pounds forced banks to reconsider their lending policies. Many pension funds and other investors, such as insurance companies, were not prepared to take the risk of investing in land which might be affected by contamination, for fear of future liabilities. They resolved not to become involved with contaminated land, or even 'suspect' land, at any price.

Property developers, including those who had previously under-taken developments on former industrial sites, decided to adopt a more cautious attitude than hitherto and the valuation profession pondered over how to reflect actual or possible contamination when estimating values or giving advice to clients. Taken altogether, it now seems likely that the proposal to introduce registers, followed by their abandonment, had a detrimental effect on the process of urban regeneration in the short term but it also had the effect of heightening awareness in respect of contamination.

There can be little doubt that the professional press, and the media generally, made too much of the register issue, using headlines such as 'Beware, contaminated site' (Chartered Surveyor Weekly, 1991) to report upon legislative proposals. Nevertheless, it is probably fair to say that the government could not have introduced the proposal at a less appropriate time. The property market was in the worst recession since the 1930s and it was feared that the introduction of registers would depress property values even further. Some valuers were of the opinion that values would be seriously damaged by the government's proposed register of potentially contaminated land and that the asset values of some whole classes of property (used for particular purposes specified in the register) would be reduced to nil or negative values. In other cases values would be significantly reduced, with the effect of rendering some properties virtually unsaleable and having an adverse effect on the balance sheets of businesses owning those properties.

Whether or not values would have fallen to the extent that was feared can now only be a matter for conjecture. The whole subject of land contamination and its effect on property values is under-researched in the United Kingdom and this book aims, in a small part, to redress the balance. A chronology of events which affected the valuation of contaminated land and, to some extent, influenced the formulation of Government policy is set out in Box 2.1.

Box 2.1 Chronology of significant events affecting the valuation of contaminated land – January 1991 to September 1996.

January 1991	The Environmental Protection Act 1990 brought into effect, having received the Royal Assent in October 1990.	The Act contained provision, in Section 143, for the compilation of 'Public registers of land which may be contaminated'
May 1991	A consultation paper 'Public Registers of Land which may be Contaminated' published jointly by the Department of the Environment and the Welsh Office. Regulations for the registers to come into effect 1 April 1992.	The registers intended as records of fact, containing details of historic uses as well as present uses, once entered on the registers removal of property details would not be allowed. In respect of blight on property values 'the Government takes [sic] the view that, in all but the very short term, it is better for everyone concerned to be aware of possible contamination'.
May 1991	The consultation paper included Annex C: SCHEDULE OF CONTAMINATIVE USES.	This schedule contained 16 groups of industrial and other operations which were deemed to be potentially contaminative. The groups were divided into 42 sub-groups affecting between 80 and 100 industries.
March 1992	Government announced that implementation of the regulations for the new registers would be delayed.	This was due to comments that the proposed registers would affect an unacceptably large area of the country and have an adverse affect on property values at a time when markets were depressed.

Box 2.1 *Continued.*

July 1992	Draft Statutory Instrument ENVIRONMENTAL PROTECTION, published by the Department of the Environment and the Welsh Office.	The land uses to be included in the proposed registers reduced to eight specific industries, affecting only 10-15% of the land area covered by the original proposal. Removal of properties from the registers would still not be allowed and Government reserved the right to add other uses in the future.
March 1993	The registers proposal was withdrawn by Government.	Decision made in the light of continued opposition to the registers, an interdepartmental review of contaminated land policies to be undertaken.
October 1993	Valuation Guidance Note 11, Environmental factors, contamination and valuation, published by the RICS.	The first guidance on the valuation of contaminated land published by the valuation profession in the UK, based on the earlier Guidance Note and Background Paper by the International Asset Valuation Standards Committee (TIAVSC).
March 1994	The consultation paper 'Paying for our Past' published by the Department of the Environment and the Welsh Office.	Intended to gather the informed and structured views of interested parties on the key issues arising out of the review set up in March 1993.
November 1994	Policy document 'Framework for Contaminated Land' published by the Department of the Environment and the Welsh Office.	Outcome of the Government's Policy Review and Conclusions from the Consultation Paper 'Paying for Our Past'. Restated the fact that the Government is committed to sustainable development and that there is an already established modern and effective regime for action to deal with future pollution. So far as the treatment of contaminated land is concerned the Government is committed to the 'suitable for use' approach.
January 1995	'Land Contamination Guidance for Chartered Surveyors' published by the RICS. (RICS, 1995a)	Intended to embody 'best practice' but not mandatory. The use of 'Land Quality Statements' recommended.

Box 2.1 *Continued.*

July 1995	The Environment Act 1995, received Royal Assent (1995)	The provisions of the Environmental Protection Act 1990 amended by the addition of a further 32 pages (26 Sections) of legislation dealing with contaminated land. Also contained the framework for the establishment of an Environmental Agency for England and Wales and a Scottish Environmental Protection Agency.
December 1995	Guidance Note 2, Environmental Factors, Contamination and Valuation, together with amendments to Practice Statements 2.2.2, 4.14, 6.3 and Appendix PSA 3, published by the RICS as part of the new Appraisal and Valuation Manual, effective from 1 January 1996 (RICS, 1995d).	Use of the Practice Statements now mandatory in respect of valuations undertaken by members of the RICS, the Incorporated Society of Valuers and Auctioneers (ISVA) and the Institute of Rating, Revenues and Valuation (IRRV). The guidance takes account of the Environment Act 1990 legislation changes and practice experience, but will be subject to further revision once Parliamentary Guidance is issued under the legislation.
January 1996	Technical guidelines for dealing with contaminated sites, due to be published January 1996, delayed by Government	Draft guidelines due to be issued late February or early March, followed by a period of consultation.
February 1996	Working draft of the Statutory Guidance issued.	Consultation guidance due 'after Easter' to be followed by a three month consultation period. New regulations expected to be in force January to April 1997.
June 1996	Second working draft issued.	Takes account of comments made in respect of the first working draft. Public consultation to follow 'shortly'.
September 1996	Public consultation draft of Statutory Guidance published.	Responses to public consultation draft requested by Wednesday 18 December 1996.
December 1996	Second report on contaminated land by the House of Commons Select Committee on the Environment.	Several concerns and recommendations in respect of the draft Statutory Guidance.

Sources: various, including informal comment from the Department of the Environment

Economic value in the context of contaminated land

Any 'real property' used in connection with a manufacturing business has a value, although that value may not be readily realisable in the open market. It may instead be deduced by reference to the contribution which the property makes to the income of the business. The value may also be apportioned between the land and the buildings or structures. An apportionment may be made arbitrarily by the owners of the business, or by reference to market transactions in respect of comparable land in the same locality, or by deduction of the *depreciated replacement cost* of the buildings and plant from the total value.

Economic circumstances may render the property redundant. Demand for the products produced by the business may decline to such an extent that it is no longer viable to continue in production. New methods of production may supersede those currently in use and the buildings or plant may be incapable of adaptation at reasonable cost. The availability of raw materials may be extinguished, or no longer be economically obtainable. Market centres may change and the increased costs of transport to market may render the goods uncompetitive. All of these events will affect the value of the property.

In economic terms, value is the price which would be paid for the highest and best use of the property which, in a free market, would be determined through the forces of supply and demand. Such a free market does not exist in the United Kingdom as the uses to which real property may be put are determined by town planning legislation. The price to be paid for real property will be influenced in either a positive or a negative manner by the permitted town planning uses. The economic value may therefore come to be regarded as 'the highest and best use as adjusted by the permitted use or uses'.

Whilst an industrial property continues to be used for manufacturing purposes, the buildings and structures have a value which can be calculated. Following the cessation of production, it is quite possible that the buildings and other structures may be totally unsuited to any alternative use. This may be due to obsolescence brought about by age or economic factors, or the buildings may be unsuitable for alternative use due to the nature of the manufacturing processes previously carried out. The buildings, structures and plant may thus be transformed from being valuable assets into costly liabilities.

Some scrap or salvage value may be realisable from the buildings and structures, after the costs of demolition or dismantling have been deducted. A problem may remain if, following removal of the above ground appurtenances, the land itself is left damaged by former manufacturing activities. Such damage may take the form of underground building foundations, machine bases, abandoned services, storage tanks and contamination or pollution arising out of spillages or the inadequate disposal of residues from the former manufacturing processes. Expenditure will have to be incurred in rectifying the damage before any value for a new or alternative use can be realised.

In such circumstances, the value of the highest and best use is the price which would be paid by a willing buyer to a willing seller, in an open market, subject to town planning controls, after deduction of the lowest cost attributable to overcoming the damage to the land. An additional element of risk is introduced to the valuation process by virtue of the fact that the land itself is damaged, or may have suffered damage. The risk arises out of the need to quantify the cost of site treatment required to ameliorate such damage. The full extent of damage is unlikely to be visible to the valuer upon inspecting the property, indeed the visual appearance may be one of an undamaged site if it has been 'grassed over' following demolition of the buildings or other structures (Figure 2.2). Even if information is available from other professionals, in order to assist the valuer, the full extent of the damage and thus the cost of treatment may not become known until such time as the redevelopment has been completed.

A factor additional to the financial cost of treating the contamination lying in or on a damaged site is the disquiet arising from the presence of contamination, which may be engendered in the minds of both the occupiers of neighbouring properties and other individuals, including valuers and potential developers or occupiers. The concerns of such individuals may be attributable to the real or perceived risk of actual harm. In either case the disquiet has the potential to affect the desirability of the site for redevelopment purposes and thereby has an impact upon the value of the land. This potential impact on value, which exceeds the cost of treatment, has

Fig. 2.2 An investigation team, in full protective clothing, using a 'window sampler' to explore for mustard gas canisters on an apparently 'greenfield' site. (Source: AEA Technology plc.)

been defined as 'stigma' (Patchin, 1988, p. 12), although Wilbourn (1996) has stated that, in his experience, 'it is not possible to define a level of stigma discount'.

One purpose of the research described in the later chapters of this book has been to ascertain whether deduction of the cost of treatment, on its own, is the correct approach to be adopted in the valuation of land damaged by former industrial uses, or whether any additional allowance should be made to reflect 'stigma' and to identify a method by which the value of contaminated land may be ascertained. In situations where land has been contaminated or polluted by past industrial activities, the approach of 'highest and best use net of lowest amelioration costs' may be inappropriate in ascertaining the true value of the land. For a valuation of a contaminated or formerly contaminated property to be undertaken, it is also necessary to take account of a number of other factors which are specific to such properties. These include; governmental policies on the treatment of contamination, emanating from both the United Kingdom and Europe, the attitudes and perceptions of potential occupiers and investors in such properties towards any long term liabilities and the availability, or otherwise, of financial incentives to assist in the treatment of damaged land.

Checklist

Industrial estates

- Check whether the estate is built on land previously used for industrial purposes.
- If built on previously used land, are site investigation reports and details of any remediation or containment work available?
- Does the information provided and/or the work carried out appear adequate? If not, further technical advice may be required.

Contaminated Land Registers

- Check whether the local authority compiled a draft register under Section 143 of the EPA 1990, or has any other list of potentially contaminated sites.
- Check whether there is any evidence of land or property values being adversely affected as the result of past or present industrial activities.
- Check whether the property is included in a Register of Contaminated Land under Part II A of the EPA 1990.

Contaminated Land

- What is the value of the 'highest and best' use for the site, assuming that it is capable of redevelopment?
- Is any reduction in value attributable to the existence of contamination, or is it caused by some other factor, e.g. economic obsolescence of the buildings?
- Does it appear that the site value may be adversely affected by 'stigma' attaching to the present or former use?
- Consider whether or not contamination may have been concealed as a result of the 'greening over' of the site.

Chapter 3
Land Contamination: Sources and Effects

Defining contaminated land

'Contaminated land is one of the many complex issues to be addressed by all those involved in ensuring protection of human health and the environment. It should be considered both in terms of its prevention and as part of the overall assessment of land for a variety of purposes and users.'

(Denner, 1991).

In spite of this statement by an official in the Department of the Environment, no standard definition exists in respect of contaminated land, although a legal definition was introduced for the first time in the Environment Act 1995. The problem of definition is perhaps not surprising given that the contamination of land can itself take many different forms.

Contamination and pollution are often regarded as synonymous and it is therefore appropriate to start by defining what is meant by the word 'contamination' before considering effects upon land and its value. The Collins English Dictionary supports the argument that contamination and pollution are synonymous, with the following definitions:

'**Contamination:** the act or process of contaminating or the state of being contaminated.

Contaminate: to make impure, especially by touching or mixing; pollute.

Pollute: to contaminate, as with poisonous or harmful substances.'

The Royal Commission on Environmental Pollution considered the problem of defining contaminated land and attempted to do so by distinguishing between 'contamination' and 'pollution' in the following way:

> 'Pollution can be defined as the introduction by man into the environment of substances or energy liable to cause hazards to human health, harm to living resources and ecological systems, damage to structures or amenity, or interference with legitimate uses of the environment. Substances introduced into the environment become pollutants only when their distribution, concentration or physical behaviour are such as to have undesirable or deleterious consequences. For comparison, contamination can be defined as the introduction or presence in the environment of alien substances or energy, on which we do not wish or are unable to pass judgement on whether they cause, or are liable to cause, damage or harm. Contamination is therefore a necessary, but not sufficient, condition for pollution.'
>
> (RCEP, 1984)

In practice, most approaches to land contamination seem to imply that land is polluted and not merely contaminated. This may be attributed to the fact that it is harder to exercise the 'judgement' required in the Royal Commission's definition of contamination, with the result that the public, local authorities, and others prefer to use the definition of pollution, which is seen as being more positive.

A term which is frequently used, especially in American literature, to describe land which has been used previously, is 'brownfield'. This term is often regarded as being synonymous with contaminated land but this may not necessarily be the case. No official definition of 'brownfield' exists in the United Kingdom but an attempt was made in 1994 at defining such sites as being:

> '... any areas of land which have previously been the subject of man-made or non-agricultural use of any type. This would include industrial uses such as chemical works, heavy engineering, ship-building and textile processing, together with unfit housing clearance sites and docklands, both inland and coastal, as well as mineral extraction and those used for landfill purposes.'
>
> (Syms, 1994a, p. 63)

Whether or not such land is also 'contaminated land' will depend upon the propensity of any materials in the soil, or groundwater, to cause 'significant harm', which is referred to later.

The term 'brownfield' in the United Kingdom context is probably more closely associated with the Department of the Environment's definition of 'derelict land' which is regarded as being 'land so damaged by industrial or other development that it is incapable of beneficial use without treatment' (DoE, 1986a, p. 2). The word 'treatment' in the context of 'derelict land' may include, for example, the removal of underground obstructions such as old foundations and redundant services, or the consolidation of fill material, rather than any works of decontamination.

In contrast to the definition of 'derelict land', the Department of the Environment in its evidence to the House of Commons Select Committee on the Environment defined 'contaminated land' as 'land which represents an actual or potential hazard to health or the environment as a result of current or previous use' (Environment Committee, 1990).

These two definitions make it clear that, for official purposes, 'contamination', 'pollution' and 'dereliction' all arise out of human activities. Naturally occurring contamination, such as the emission of radon from certain geological formations and methane from peat, falls outside the definitions and is thus excluded from consideration in the definitions. It is also implicit from the definitions that both contamination and dereliction are seen as having a direct relationship with land use, previous, current or future.

The Department of the Environment's definition of contaminated land was criticised by a number of witnesses giving evidence to the Environment Committee, who pointed out that land which contained toxic chemicals would not be classed as contaminated if no use was proposed for the site. In other words, if at the end of its working life a chemical plant was simply to be closed and its boundaries secured, above and below ground, with no redevelopment proposed, then the site would not be classed as contaminated.

Mike Smith (the original secretary of the government's Inter-departmental Committee on the Redevelopment of Contaminated Land), when giving evidence to the Committee, stated that:

'It is not surprising that the Department would wish to limit the definition [of contaminated land] because the acceptance of the broader definition would mean that substantial parts of some urban areas would have to be classified as contaminated – as indeed they are.'

(Smith, 1990)

The Environment Committee expressed concern that, by defining contaminated land narrowly and solely in relation to end use, the Department of the Environment might be underestimating a genuine environmental problem and misdirecting effort and resources.

The description of the circumstances leading to the contamination of land, produced by the Interdepartmental Committee on the Redevelopment of Contaminated Land in 1983, is somewhat longer than the definition given to the House of Commons Environment Committee in 1990 but is nevertheless consistent in referring to future land use:

'The use of land for industrial purposes or for waste disposal may result in chemical contamination which can restrict or prevent subsequent redevelopment because of immediate or long-term hazards to human health (directly or indirectly), to plants, to amenity, to construction operations, or to any buildings and services.'

(ICRCL, 1983)

The linkage between contamination and land use continued to be government policy, as evidenced by preliminary conclusion number 4A.5 of the consultation paper *Paying for our Past* (DoE, 1994a). It stated that one of the objectives for dealing with contaminated land could be to improve sites in line with the 'suitable for use' approach where hazards are tackled as and when the private sector decides to develop land, or public authorities prepare land to promote development. This was subsequently confirmed as government policy in *Framework for Contaminated Land* (DoE, 1994b) and is in marked contrast with the approach adopted in the Netherlands, where the policy adopted by government was that the standard of treatment should be the same, regardless of end use, an approach known as 'multifunctionality'. It should, however, be noted that in the Netherlands soil is considered to be a resource, although returning contaminated soil to multifunctional use may take a long time, perhaps even longer than one generation.

The British Standards Institution, in its *Draft Code of Practice* (BSI, 1988) on the identification and investigation of contaminated land, offered the following definition:

'. . . land that contains any substance that when present in sufficient concentration or amount presents a hazard. The hazard may
(a)   be associated with the present status of the land
(b)   limit the future use of the land; and
(c)   require the land to be specially treated before use.'

Dr Mary Harris pointed out that definitions of this type have been challenged by the Department of the Environment and that a new operational definition of contaminated land had been proposed by the Department:

'(i)   Land which because of its former uses now contains substances that give rise to the principal hazards likely to affect the proposed form of development, and which
(ii)   Requires an assessment to decide whether the chosen development may proceed safely or whether it requires some form of remedial action, which may include changing the layout or form of the development.'
(Beckett and Simms, 1984; Harris, 1987)

Harris also commented that the exact form of these, apparently similar, definitions not only has repercussions for the estimation of the scale of the problem but also provides some insight into how various authorities regard the subject of contaminated land.

One definition which appears to have received fairly widespread acceptance defines contaminated land as:

'Land that contains substances that, when present in sufficient quantities or concentrations, are likely to cause harm, directly or indirectly, to man, the environment, or on occasions to other targets.'
(Smith, 1985)

This definition has been adopted by the NATO Committee for Challenges to Modern Society (NATO CCMS), the Welsh Development Agency (Welsh Development Agency, 1993), and The European Group of Valuers of Fixed Assets (TEGOVOFA, 1988). It should, however, be pointed out that a report by Harris et al published by CIRIA in 1995, defined contamination and pollution as follows:

> '**Contamination:** The presence in the environment of an alien substance or agent, or energy, with the potential to cause harm.
> **Pollution:** The introduction by man into the environment of substances in sufficient quantity or concentration as to cause harm to human health, harm to living resources and ecological systems, damage to structure or amenity, or interference with legitimate uses of the environment.'
>
> (Harris et al, 1994)

As may be seen, most of these definitions depend upon the concept of 'harm' when seeking to define contaminated land and this is also the case with the Environment Act 1995, which defined contaminated land as being:

> 'any land which appears to the local authority in whose area it is situated to be in such a condition, by reason of substances in, on or under the land, that –
> (a) significant harm is being caused or there is a significant possibility of such harm being caused; or
> (b) pollution of controlled waters is being, or is likely to be, caused;'

'Harm' is defined in the 1995 Act as meaning 'harm to the health of living organisms or other interference with the ecological systems of which they form part'. In the human context, this is intended to include harm to property. The word 'significant' is not defined in the Act and its use 'in the main definition of contaminated land narrows its scope considerably' (Denner and Lowe, 1995), which may not be acceptable to environmental lobbyists.

A definition of 'significant harm' has been proposed by the Department of the Environment and is discussed in Chapter 4. The definitions of contaminated land and significant harm have not yet been tested in practice and will no doubt be tested in the courts in due course. For valuers and their clients, such as the potential developers of contaminated sites, the test may not be whether the contaminants in the soil are at such concentrations as to result in the site being classified as 'contaminated' within the legal definition, but rather whether the site will be acceptable for funding and investment purposes.

The causes of contamination

By the 'strictest' definition almost any activity of man has the potential to cause contamination.

> 'The presence of contamination in land does not, however, mean that for a particular purpose, and in the specific conditions of a site, that the contamination has reached an action level where remediation or risk reduction actions are necessary.'
>
> (RICS, 1995a)

This would appear to confirm agreement with the Environment Act 1995 definition and it may be that valuers only need to be concerned with contamination which has the potential to pollute and cause damage to living beings or the environment.

Land may become contaminated as a result of a variety of human activities, and the polluted soil may result in problems for centuries to come. The mineral and metal extractive industries, together with their associated processing activities, are known to cause soil contamination. Manufacturing industry is also a contributor to land contamination, often resulting from the use of processes and practices which would not comply with current environmental standards. Some industries are still contributing to the problems of environmental pollution in the United Kingdom, although stricter town planning and environmental controls should ensure that their potential to exacerbate the problems of contaminated land is minimised in future.

Extractive, mineral processing, and manufacturing industries are by no means the only causes of land contamination. Landfilling and accidental occurrences, such as spillages and pipeline ruptures, are also major contributors. Other activities, such as steel-making, coal-fired electricity generating stations and coal gasification plants have added to the problems of soil contamination as a result of airborne emissions, although these are now more rigorously controlled. Leaking underground storage tanks from petrol filling stations, transport depots and even private dwellings, may contribute to the contamination problem, and this is seen as a major issue in the United States.

A significant part of the problem is one of treating, in a relatively short period of time, the contamination left behind by previous generations on sites which have been used for a variety of purposes. Very often several uses may have subsisted on a single site, both over time and at the same time as each other. Most probably little or no documentation will exist as to the processes employed and the materials manufactured or stored on the site, especially where industrial activities have existed for centuries.

Case study 3.1: Former dockyard at Woolwich

A site investigation at a former dockyard in Woolwich, adjacent to the south bank of the River Thames, revealed that several different stages of development had taken place on the site since the early 16th century, with at least three types of piled foundations existing on top of each other. The ground level had been built higher at each development stage through the importation of a variety of fill materials, the slipways and docks had also been filled. Following closure of the dockyard in 1869 the site was used by the army as a storage depot until about 1926, when the site was sold into various ownerships. Subsequent uses included a sugar refinery, a food storage depot and the recovery of metals from cables. Fly tipping had taken place and the site was contaminated by a wide range of chemicals from its previous uses. Landfill gas was being produced, with high concentrations of methane. Not one but several different problems on the same site.

As shown by this example case study, contaminated land has a history but is not simply an historical problem. The management of contaminated land is therefore a twofold process, requiring consideration of remedial works for land already contaminated, and the implementation of appropriate management and environmental standards so as to minimise future contamination.

Several attempts have been made at identifying those activities which have the potential to cause contamination. The list produced by the Department of the Environment in connection with the registers proposed to be introduced under Section 143 of the Environmental Protection Act 1990 is an example. The Schedule of Contaminative Uses contained in Annex C of the Department of the Environment's consultation paper (DoE, 1991a) would have resulted in vast areas of the United Kingdom being classed as 'contaminated', whereas the subsequent list of only eight uses was woefully inadequate in identifying the extent of the problem. Harris (1987) produced a list of 18 'contaminating' industries, the Interdepartmental Committee on the Redevelopment of Contaminated Land cited 13 examples of the types of sites on which contaminants may be found (ICRCL, 1987) and the Environment Committee (1990) identified 19 activities as being the 'most common contaminative uses'. Many, but not all, are similar to those contained in the other lists.

The Department of the Environment has produced profiles for more than 50 industries, see Box 3.1, giving information on the types of contamination that may be associated with the particular activities and factors that affect the presence of contaminants, as well as their mobility.

Box 3.1 Industries for which profiles have been produced by the Department of the Environment.

- Airports
- Animal and animal products processing works
- Asbestos manufacturing works
- Ceramics, cement and asphalt manufacturing works
- Chemical works: coatings (paints and printing inks) manufacturing works
- Chemical works: cosmetics and toiletries manufacturing works
- Chemical works: disinfectants manufacturing works
- Chemical works: explosives, propellants and pyrotechnics manufacturing works
- Chemical works: fertiliser manufacturing works
- Chemical works: fine chemicals manufacturing works
- Chemical works: inorganic chemicals manufacturing works
- Chemical works: linoleum, vinyl and bitumen-based floor covering manufacturing works
- Chemical works: mastics, sealants, adhesives and roofing felt manufacturing works
- Chemical works: organic manufacturing works
- Chemical works: pesticides manufacturing works
- Chemical works: pharmaceuticals manufacturing works
- Chemical works: rubber processing works (including manufacturing of tyres and other rubber products)

Box 3.1 *Continued.*

- Chemical works: soap and detergent manufacturing works
- Dockyards and dockland
- Engineering works: aircraft manufacturing works
- Engineering works: electrical and electronic equipment manufacturing
- Engineering works: mechanical engineering and ordnance works
- Engineering works: railway engineering works
- Engineering works: shipbuilding, repair and shipbreaking, including naval shipyards
- Engineering works: vehicle manufacturing works
- Gasworks, coke works and other coal carbonisation plants
- Metal manufacturing, refining and finishing works: electroplating and other metal finishing works
- Metal manufacturing, refining and finishing works: iron and steelworks
- Metal manufacturing, refining and finishing works: lead works
- Metal manufacturing, refining and finishing works: non-ferrous metal works (excluding lead works)
- Metal manufacturing, refining and finishing works: precious metal recovery works
- Oil refineries and bulk storage of crude oil and petroleum products
- Power stations (excluding nuclear power stations)
- Pulp and paper manufacturing works
- Railway land
- Road vehicle fuelling, service and repair: garages and filling stations
- Road vehicle fuelling, service and repair: transport and haulage centres
- Sewage works and sewage farms
- Textile works and dye works
- Timber products manufacturing works
- Timber treatment works
- Waste recycling, treatment and disposal sites: drum and tank cleaning and recycling plants
- Waste recycling, treatment and disposal sites: hazardous waste treatment plants
- Waste recycling, treatment and disposal sites: landfills and other waste treatment or waste disposal sites
- Waste recycling, treatment and disposal sites: metal recycling sites
- Waste recycling, treatment and disposal sites: solvent recovery works
- Profile of miscellaneous industries, incorporating:
  charcoal works; dry-cleaners; fibreglass and fibreglass resins manufacturing works; glass manufacturing works; photographic processing industry; printing and bookbinding works.

Following on from earlier research, a list of 30 uses, regarded as being 'most prevalent' in resulting in land contamination, has been adopted by the RICS in its current guidance on the valuation of properties affected by contamination, (see Chapter 9). In spite of the fact that the RICS list is less comprehensive than the Department of the Environment profiles, it is considered that the list fairly represents those uses which have the greatest potential to cause serious contamination. These are therefore seen as the uses most likely to have an impact in valuation terms and which should be taken into full account when considering development proposals.

The contaminants which may be found on a site will vary according to present or former activities and, where sites have been used for a number of different purposes, it must be remembered that different types of contamination may remain from those earlier uses. The valuer or intending developer therefore needs to take account of the full history of any site under consideration.

Parry and Bell (1987) described a number of different types of contaminated sites and the activities which had the potential to cause contamination. It is possible that not all of the earlier uses will have been adequately documented, if indeed any documentary evidence remains, and it is therefore quite possible for sites to contain contaminants which are totally unrelated to the present, or last known, use of the land. The types of contaminants found on industrial sites include: heavy metals, found at sites scrapyards, sewage works and tanneries; organic compounds, including chlorinated solvents from chemical industries; asbestos, from power stations and other industries; combustible substances and flammable gases, which may originate from gasworks and former waste disposal sites.

Detailed consideration of the nature and origin of contaminants, the pathways by which they travel and the manner in which they may affect their targets, is beyond the scope of this book, although some understanding of the subject is required and will be discussed in the next section. A fuller consideration of a number of the most commonly occurring contaminants, their sources and principal hazards has been presented by Haines and Harris (1987). Kruus et al (1991) have provided an introduction into the ways in which chemicals enter the environment, whilst Sax and Lewis (1989) have described the dangerous properties of more than 20 000 industrial materials. For present purposes, however, consideration has been limited to those contaminants most likely to be found as a result of the activities listed in Box 3.1. These include those contaminants set out in Box 3.2.

At the present time, no mandatory standards for site remediation or contaminant concentrations exist in the United Kingdom and it is understood that there is no intention to introduce such standards within the foreseeable future. The Interdepartmental Committee on the Redevelopment of Contaminated Land (ICRCL) has published

Box 3.2 Major contaminants and where they may be found.

Contaminant	Industry or Land use
1) Metallic contaminants	
Arsenic	Timber treatment, dyestuffs manufacture, glass, paint, textiles and explosives
Cadmium	Plastics, paint, mining and smelting. Scrapyards, (from discarded batteries)
Chromium	Mines and smelters, metallurgy industries, power station ash, sewage sludge, timber preservation, pigments, leather tanning, plating
Cobalt	Pigments, metallurgy industries, hospitals
Copper, nickel, zinc	Mining and smelting, paint, plating, glass
Lead	Mining and smelting, foundries, manufacturing industries, pigments, batteries, plating, anodising and galvanising works, fungicides, sewage sludge, landfills
Magnesium	Fireworks manufacture
Mercury	Mining and smelting, paints, plastics, glass, pulp and paper production, fungicides, foundries, iron and steelworks, plating, anodising and galvanising
Uranium	Nuclear industries
2) Inorganic contaminants	
Cyanide	Waste disposal, metal treatment and finishing, gasworks
Sulphates	Waste disposal, gasworks
3) Organic contaminants	
Phenols	Chemicals manufacture and storage, gasworks, waste disposal, manufacture of paper, plastics, rubber, solvents, paints and wood preservatives. Iron and steel manufacture.
Coal tars and polycyclic aromatic hydrocarbons (PAHs)	Gasworks, chemicals manufacture and storage, combustion of coal, wood and other organic materials.
Oils	Transport and processing of crude oil and related products, animal fats and vegetable oil from food manufacture, soap manufacture
PCBs	Transformers, capacitors, inks, fire retardants, hydraulic and lubricating systems.
4) Asbestos	Railway land, heavy engineering, waste disposal, asbestos related manufacture, scrapyards, power stations
5) Combustible materials	Waste disposal, mining, gasworks, oil refining and storage
6) Gases	
Ammonia	Iron and steel manufacture, coal gas production, refrigerant units
Carbon dioxide	Filled dock basins, waste disposal, iron and steel works, organic decomposition
Methane	Landfills, coal mine gas

Sources: Haines and Harris (1987); Applied Environmental Research Centre, (1994)

guidance notes on several aspects of reclaiming and redeveloping sites used for specific industries, for example, gasworks sites (ICRCL 18/79, 1986) and landfill sites (ICRCL 17/78, 1990).

So far as contaminant concentrations are concerned, ICRCL Guidance Note 59/83 (1987) identifies a number of common contaminants, in respect of which it suggests trigger concentration threshold values, based on mg/kg in air-dried soil, above which levels remediation may be needed. These threshold values are based on two groups of 'planned uses'; domestic gardens and allotments, and parks, playing fields and open space. For phytotoxic contaminants, threshold values are given for any uses where plants are to be grown.

For a number of contaminants both threshold and action values are given, differentiating between two groups of uses; domestic gardens, allotments and play areas, and landscaped areas, buildings and hard cover.

'If all sample values are below the threshold concentrations then the site may be regarded as uncontaminated as far as the hazards from those contaminants are concerned, and the development may proceed. Above these concentrations, remedial action may be needed, especially if the contamination is still continuing. Above the action concentrations, remedial action will be required or the form of development changed.'

(ICRCL 59/83, 1987)

It must be stressed that the ICRCL publications are only intended as guidance but there is sometimes a tendency for people to interpret the threshold concentrations in ICRCL 59/83 too rigidly and propose, or even embark upon, remediation programmes which are out of all proportion to the risks involved. The guidance note states that all values are for concentrations determined on 'spot' samples based on an adequate site investigation and it cautions that the table of values 'is invalid if reproduced without the conditions and footnotes'. The Department of the Environment is in the process of publishing a series of Contaminated Land Research Reports, including one entitled 'Collation of Toxicological Data and Intake Values for Humans', due to be published in spring 1997 which may replace, or at least supplement, the existing guidance.

Pathways and targets

Holdgate (1979) advanced the concept of pollution pathways and suggested that all pollution events have certain characteristics in common as shown in Figure 3.1:

- the *existence* of a pollutant
- the *source* of the pollutant
- the *transport* medium (air, water or soil)
- the *target* in terms of the organisms, ecosystems or items of property affected by the pollutant

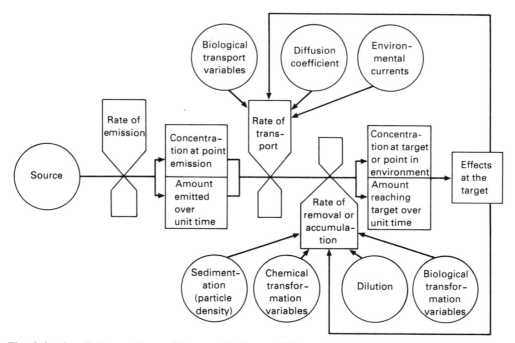

Fig. 3.1 A pollution pathway. (Source: Holdgate, 1979 p. 46.)

This simple model may be developed through varying degrees of sophistication, which may include considering the rate of emission of the pollutant from the source and the rate of transport from source to target. Chemical and physical transformations which the pollutant undergoes, either during transport or after arriving at the target, together with the amounts reaching the target, movement within the target to sensitive organs, and quantification of the effects, may all be taken into account. Detailed knowledge of the technical, chemical and biological aspects as to how pollutants travel and affect their targets are beyond the scope of knowledge required by most people involved with the redevelopment of contaminated land. A broad understanding of the transmission mechanisms involved is, however, important as it can assist in determining the extent to which a property may be impaired.

Beckett (1993a) provided a simplified development of Holdgate's pollution pathway concept, describing it as a chain of inter-linked relationships -

Previous and/or present use → Contamination → Hazard → Target → Protection

The extent to which contaminants are potentially harmful to human beings, to flora, fauna and the wider environment, depends largely on how they occur, their degree of concentration, the methods by which they travel and the nature of the detrimental effects on their targets. The extent of any detrimental effect is also of importance, in view of the government's definition of 'significant harm', discussed in Chapter 4, which is based on the identification of specific environmental risks. For any such risks to be present it is proposed that the following elements must exist:

(1) *a source* – the presence on the land of a substance, or substances, with the potential to cause harm or water pollution ('potential pollutant')
(2) *a receptor* or target – the presence of something which could be harmed by that pollutant or controlled waters which could be polluted
(3) *a pathway* or a number of pathways by which the receptor could be exposed to the pollutant.

(DoE, 1996)

It is therefore necessary to examine the relationships between the contaminants, the means by which they cause harm and their relevance to different existing and potential land uses. Box 3.3 illustrates the linkages between several main contaminants, the methods by which they cause harm and the possible nature of that harm to potential targets.

Box 3.3 Contaminants, hazard pathways and harmful effects.

Contaminant	Hazard pathway	Harmful Effects
Heavy metals	Ingestion	May cause respiratory cancers, emphysema and other lung disorders, kidney disfunction. Birth defects (teratogenecity)
Organics	"	
Asbestos	Inhalation	Asbestosis (a scarring of the lungs), mesothelioma (cancer of the lining of the chest and abdomen), lung cancer
Metal dusts	"	Respiratory cancers and other lung disorders
Toxic gases	"	May cause breathing difficulties and may be carcinogenic
Acids and alkalis	Skin contact	Can cause burning
Organics (e.g. phenols)		May be carcinogenic and/or teratogenic
Some metal salts (e.g. chromates)		May cause irritation
Zinc, copper, nickel	Phytotoxicity	Can stunt plant growth, cause discoloration, shallow root system and dieback
Sulphates		
Landfill Gas		
Sulphate/Sulphides	Building material degradation	Can corrode and accelerate the weathering of services and structural components
Organics (e.g. oils, tars, phenols)	"	
Acidity	"	
Carbonaceous matter, including PAHs	Fires	May be carcinogenic, cause liver damage and/or teratogenicity
Sulphur wastes (spent oxide)	"	May cause burning or irritation on skin contact
Gases	"	May cause breathing difficulties and lung defects
Landfill gas	Asphyxiation	May cause breathing difficulties and lung defects
Landfill gas	Explosion	May cause breathing difficulties and lung defects

Box 3.3 *Continued.*

Carbon monoxide	Inhalation	Can affect the cardiovascular system and the central nervous system
Sulphur dioxide	Inhalation	Can affect lung function
Nitrogen oxides (NO_2 & NO)	Inhalation and deposition	Can affect the rspiratory system and cause damage to aquatic and other ecosystems

Sources: Beckett (1993a); Alloway and Ayres (1993); Sax and Lewis (1989), Haughton and Hunter (1994); and DoE (1994c).

It should be stressed that the harmful effects of the types of contaminants set out in Box 3.3 will vary significantly according to type and degree of concentration. The table should therefore be regarded as a general summary, designed to prompt those persons involved in the valuation and development of land to make further enquiries if references to the listed substances are made in any site investigation report or schedule of materials used on a site. A more comprehensive list of contaminants, their harmful concentrations and adverse effects on their targets may be found in Barry (1991). Box 3.4 indicates those hazards from Box 3.3 which may pose a threat according to the use carried out, or proposed, on a site to be valued or developed.

One aspect of soil contamination which should be of particular concern to valuers, and to intending developers, is the potential for some types of contaminants to spread or leach for considerable distances from the location at which the contaminants are buried, or the polluting incident has occurred. Consider, for example, the problem caused by a leaking drum of a dense non-aqueous phase liquid (DNAPL), such as lubricating oil, buried in the unsaturated (vadose) zone of the subsurface soil, as shown in Figure 3.2.

The example in Figure 3.2 illustrates a situation where the downward migration of the leaking lubricating oil is initially halted by an impermeable clay lens, until such time as the liquid overspills the lens into the surrounding sands and gravels. The permeability of the adjacent soils allows the oil to be distributed more widely, both with the flow of the groundwater and with the geology of the site, until it reaches the bedrock and penetrates any fissures, causing widespread contamination. Therefore valuers and developers need to have regard not only for the potential of contaminants to migrate from the site with which they are concerned but also the possibility of

Box 3.4   Land use and hazard links.

Proposed use	Principal hazards that may pose a threat
Residential with gardens	All
Residential without gardens (i.e. flats, etc.)	All except phytotoxicity or ingestion
Allotments/market gardens	Phytotoxicity and skin contact
Agriculture:	
Arable	Phytotoxicity
Grazing	Phytotoxicity and ingestion
Public open space/amenity/recreational	Phytotoxicity and skin contact
Commercial (e.g. offices, retail)	Building material degradation, fires, explosion
Light industry (e.g. warehouses, factory units)	Building material degradation, fires, explosion
Heavy industry	Building material degradation, fires

Source: Beckett (1993a)

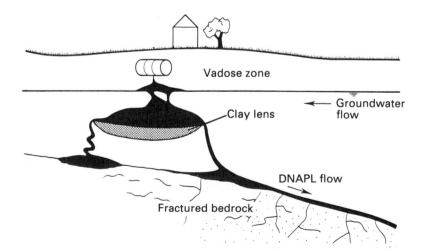

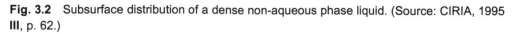

Fig. 3.2   Subsurface distribution of a dense non-aqueous phase liquid. (Source: CIRIA, 1995 **III**, p. 62.)

inward migration from adjoining or nearby sites which may be contaminated. This aspect is considered further in Chapter 5 when addressing the requirements for site investigations.

The extent of the pollution problem

There is comparatively little literature on the subject of reclaiming and redeveloping derelict and contaminated sites. For the most part, published works address the technical issues and pay little attention to the financial issues involved, for example Cairney (1987) and Fleming (1991). Even where such issues are considered (Haines, 1987; Ironside, 1989), the authors appear to confine themselves to a discussion of the availability of public sector finance to go towards the cost of site reclamation. It is of course very true that, without public sector support in one form or another, many site reclamation projects would fail to come to fruition. However, in many cases, the private sector input is of equal or greater importance.

Derelict or contaminated sites have previously been used for a wide range of purposes, often over a period of many centuries. During this time the use may well have changed and quite often buildings may have been constructed over the remains of earlier developments. Fleming (1991) has commented that the state of such land is often so poor as to be unsuitable for continued use or re-use without major land engineering works. The Department of the Environment adopts a similar view in its definition of derelict land as 'land which has been so damaged by industrial and other development that it is incapable of beneficial use without treatment' (DoE, 1986a).

Taking the United Kingdom as a whole, dereliction is not widespread, although the problem of derelict land is by no means insignificant. Kivell (1987) noted that, according to a survey by the Department of the Environment, the total area of dereliction in England had increased from 43 300 hectares in 1974, to 45 700 hectares in 1982. This increase occurred despite major programmes of reclamation which dealt with 17 000 hectares during the same time period. By 1988, however, the equivalent study indicated a reduction to 41 456 hectares (DoE, 1991b), whilst the 1993 Survey (DoE,

1995) reported a further reduction to 39 600 hectares of land being recorded as derelict in England. Table 3.1 sets out the changes in the amount of derelict land in England between 1974, 1988 and 1993, under the different categories used in preparing the study.

Table 3.1 The composition of derelict land in England.

Type of dereliction	Stock (ha)	1974 (%)	Stock (ha)	1982 (%)	Stock (ha)	1988 (%)	Stock (ha)	1993 (%)
Spoil heaps	13 118	30.3	13 340	29.2	12 015	29.0	9 191	23.0
Excavation and pits	8 717	20.1	8 578	18.8	6 186	14.9	5 807	15.0
Military	3 777	8.7	3 016	6.6	2 624	6.3	3 275	8.0
Railway	9 107	21.0	8 210	18.0	6 650	16.0	5 615	14.0
Other	8 554	19.8	12 539	27.4	13 981	33.7	15 702[1]	40.0
Total	43 273	100.0	45 685	100.0	41 456	100.0	39 600	100.0

[1] The 1988 and 1993 surveys included separate figures for Mining subsidence and General Industrial Dereliction, which had been included within the 'Other' category in the earlier surveys. In 1993 the area of land identified as suffering from General Industrial Dereliction amounted to 9749 hectares, or 25% of the total area.

Source: Kivell (1987); Department of the Environment (1991b); Department of the Environment (1995)

Taken as a percentage of the total area of England, this is equal to only 0.31%, but it is still 150 times the area of the City of London, where so many property investment decisions are made. It should also be borne in mind that not all derelict land can justify reclamation. For example, in the 1988 study only 32 010 hectares (77%) were considered to justify reclamation, although by 1993 some 34 600 hectares (87%) were considered to justify reclamation. From Table 3.1 it can be seen that spoil heaps, arising from mineral extraction and other industrial processes, account for the largest area of dereliction. Many of these sites, especially those of a metalliferous nature, are considered to be so badly contaminated, or in such remote locations, as to not justify reclamation.

The survey of derelict land provides only a small part of the overall picture. There are many other sites which are still in use, or may be semi-derelict, which suffer from the same instability or contamination problems as those sites which are officially classed as derelict. Kivell cited as an example Stoke-on-Trent which, in 1984, identified 332 hectares of derelict land, but added 291 hectares of potential dereliction (where existing industrial activity is [sic] expected to cease shortly, leaving behind land which is unsuitable for use without treatment). A further 538 hectares was classed as neglected land (at present uncared for, untidy and in a condition detrimental to the environment) (Kivell, 1987).

Although the quantity is unknown, of the 34 600 hectares of derelict land justifying reclamation and the industrial land still in use, it is believed that a very significant percentage is contaminated. This contamination, lying in or on the ground, takes many forms: heavy metals, PCBs and coal tars to name but a few. Recent estimates suggest that 50 000–100 000 sites may be considered to be contaminated, affecting perhaps 50 000 hectares. Only a small proportion of these, however, are likely to pose an immediate threat to public health or the environment (Hobson, 1991).

The 1988 survey provided details of the post-reclamation use of almost 12 000 hectares of derelict land which was reclaimed between 1982 and 1988 (Table 3.2). A similar analysis was provided in the report on the 1993 survey (Table 3.3).

Table 3.2 Derelict land reclaimed and brought back into use, 1982–88; the use of land after reclamation (hectares).

Land use	By local authority with grant	By local authority without grant	By other agencies[2]	Total
Industry	901	44	622	1 567
Commerce	118	11	460	589
Residential	294	79	675	1 048
Sub total (hard end use)	1 313	134	1 757	3 204
Sport and recreation	793	96	251	1 140
Public open space	3 078	251	475	3 804
Agriculture/forestry	1 282	199	1 212	2 693
Sub total (soft end use)	5 153	546	1 938	7 637
Other	289	103	736	1 128
Total	6 755	783	4 431	11 969

[2] Including private sector developers and commercial organizations

Source: Department of the Environment (1991b)

Table 3.3 Derelict land reclaimed and brought back into use, 1988–93; the use of land after reclamation (hectares).

Land use	By local authority with grant	By local authority without grant	By other agencies	Total
Industry	579	54	687	1 319
Commerce	120	18	518	656
Residential	89	16	816	922
Sport and recreation buildings	82	17	82	181
Other development	281	60	301	643
Sub total (hard end use)	1 152	165	2 404	3 721
Agriculture	226	4	607	837
Forestry/woodland	561	5	51	617
Public open space	1 269	103	192	1 564
Outdoor recreation	906	133	336	1 375
Nature conservation	180	54	94	328
Sub total (soft end use)	3 142	299	1 280	4 721
Total	4 293	465	3 684	8 442

Source: Department of the Environment (1995)

As can readily be seen, local authorities play a major role in the reclamation of derelict land, accounting for the reclamation of 35% of land reclaimed for hard end uses and 73% of land reclaimed for soft end uses in the most recent survey. It should be noted however that the local authority percentages in the latest survey are down from 45% and 75% respectively in the previous survey, against an overall decline of 29% in the amount of land reclaimed. The area of land reclaimed and brought back into use by other agencies, which includes private sector developers and investors, is therefore of considerable importance, representing many millions of pounds worth of development projects.

Whilst the Department of the Environment reports provide a useful insight into the extent of the derelict land problem in England, they do not cover the whole of the United Kingdom, nor do they provide information in respect of the redundant industrial land still controlled by manufacturing companies and not officially classified as 'derelict'.

'John Handley, professor of land reclamation at Manchester University, suggests that there are 270 square miles (699km^2) of derelict, disused and neglected land in Britain, made up of about 150 000 individual brownfield sites.'

(Richards, I. 1995)

Based on his experience of investigating previously used land in many parts of the world, Ivor Richards suggests:

'that the Pareto Principle (after the Italian economics professor, whose Parkinson-like laws, apply to all manner of activities) will hold good throughout Britain's 270 sq.miles (699km^2) of brown sites.'

Therefore, according to Richards in adopting the Pareto Principle, 80% of the total area 'is likely to have few problems and could be prepared for redevelopment using conventional civil engineering techniques' (Figure 3.3). So far as the remaining 54 square miles (140km^2), Richards suggests that 80% 'is probably contaminated or presents serious engineering problems, but could be made ready for

Fig. 3.3   Derelict it may be, but is it contaminated? Not all derelict sites are contaminated and not all contaminated sites are derelict.

redevelopment economically through existing techniques', whilst the remaining land 'is likely to be too contaminated or problematic for any commercial development' (Richards, I. 1995).

Therefore, if Richard's estimates are accepted, a total area of 14 000 hectares (34 594 acres) of land in either present or past industrial use throughout Britain could be affected by contamination. Coincidentally, the area of contaminated land in Britain, calculated by Richards, is almost identical to the area of land in England (34 600 hectares in 1993) considered to justify reclamation (DoE, 1995). Whether or not this is a reasonable estimate of the extent of the problem is open to debate. In practice the full extent of the problem is impossible to assess and, as stated in the consultation paper *Public Registers of land which may be contaminated* (DoE, 1991a), the cost of requiring investigation of all sites suspected of containing contamination 'would be prohibitively expensive'. The British Government has therefore sought to limit the extent of the problem in the form of words used to define contaminated land, as discussed in this chapter, and such attempts are still continuing, as described in Chapter 4.

Checklist

Contamination and pollution

- Is it possible to distinguish between contamination and pollution?
- Check the nature of any possible risks from the site.
- Are the contaminants and associated risks the result of human activities, or have they occurred naturally?
- Is the land 'suitable for use' in relation to its existing or proposed purpose?
- Check whether new contamination, or pollution, is being caused by current activities on the site.

Potentially contaminative land uses

- Is the land used for a purpose for which the Department of the Environment has published an industry profile?

- Check the nature of any contaminants that are most likely to be found on the site as a result of the existing land use or any previous land uses.
- Check whether there are any potentially contaminative activities occurring within the vicinity of the site, say within a one kilometre radius.
- Do a source, receptor (or target) and a pathway all exist?
- Is there any recorded, anecdotal or visual evidence of harmful effects having been caused as a result of activities on the site or within the vicinity?

Chapter 4
Legislation and Policies

The values ascribed to properties by valuation professionals, and the decisions taken by property developers as to whether or not a contaminated site should be redeveloped, will be influenced by their individual perceptions of land contamination issues. Those perceptions will be affected by a number of factors, such as personal experience, training and press comment. Government policies in respect of liabilities for the registration and treatment of contaminated sites will also influence the perceptions of property market actors. Similarly, as was demonstrated by the response to the registration proposals contained in Section 143 of the Environmental Protection Act 1990 (HMSO 1990), the perceptions of property market actors concerning adverse impacts may be so strong as to result in a complete re-evaluation of Government policies. Legislation and government policies can therefore be expected to play an influential role in the redevelopment of contaminated land.

As noted in Chapter 2, it was not until after the publication of a consultation paper concerning the proposed preparation of registers of land which had been subjected to 'potentially contaminative uses' that valuers were alerted to the implications of Section 143 of the Environmental Protection Act 1990. Prior to this time valuers were unlikely to take account of industrial contamination when preparing valuations of industrial land and buildings. They would, however, have been expected to make provision for the cost of overcoming abnormal ground conditions, demolition and the removal of plant and equipment where appropriate. Such cost allowances may incidentally have resolved any contamination issue and the valuer would not have been expected to make an additional allowance to cover unknown matters or 'stigma'. Unless specifically instructed by clients, valuers were not usually expected to undertake searches of local authority or other records which might contain details of contamination.

Government policies in the United Kingdom

According to the consultation paper, *Public Registers of Land which may be Contaminated* (DoE, 1991a), the main purpose of registers of potentially contaminated sites was to alert local authorities, landowners and potential purchasers to the possibility of contamination, and to indicate the types of contamination to be expected. They were not however intended to be registers of actual contamination as this would have required local authorities to investigate many of the sites considered for inclusion. This would have been prohibitively expensive and taken many years to complete. There were also technical reasons why registers of actual contamination were impracticable, as the compilation of such registers would have involved the setting of highly complex standards for both site investigations and treatment methods, covering all types of contaminants and soils.

Notwithstanding the fact that the Government's consultation paper stressed that the registers were not intended as records of actual contamination, the press and professional bodies immediately referred to them as the 'Contaminated Land Registers' and expressed serious concern over the possible blighting effect on property values. The question of blight had been considered in the consultation paper but the Government took the view that, in all but the very short term, it would be better for everyone concerned to be aware of possible contamination. This would ensure that appropriate investigations were carried out on a basis of knowledge. Such an approach completely ignored the emotive reaction of householders whose homes were, for example, built on the sites of former town gasworks, or the shareholders of industrial companies, the activities of which were to be classified as 'potentially contaminative' in nature. All of these people could see the value of their investments being severely reduced, even to negative figures.

A further point of concern was the intention that, even if it could be proved that a registered property was free from contamination, or had been 'cleaned up', removal from the register was not to be allowed. This was because the registers were intended as records of historical fact concerning past uses, although provision was made for the results of any site investigations or 'clean up' operations to be recorded on the registers.

The schedule of contaminative uses, annexed to the consultation paper, covered 16 groups of industrial activities, divided into 42 sub-groups, plus demolition operations. If all of the activities and profiles described in the schedule are taken into account, then up to 100 industrial, or quasi-industrial, activities could have been affected by the proposals.

The view which came to be generally adopted by the valuation profession was that the impact on values of premises used for the scheduled purposes, or built on land previously used for any of those purposes, could be so detrimental as to render the properties virtually unsaleable. It was feared by the land contamination group of the RICS Asset Valuation Standards Committee that the registers would result in some property assets of big companies having negative values, with a resultant adverse impact on the total asset value of the companies concerned. The proposed list of 'contaminative uses' also included a number of 'high street' trades such as dry cleaners, printers and electrical repairers. From an investment point of view, the inclusion of these 'high street' uses was seen as having a potentially catastrophic impact on the values of many purpose built shopping centres.

So great was the outcry against the proposed registers that the Government was forced to reconsider the way in which Section 143 was to be brought into operation. The majority of the written responses received by the Department of the Environment, in respect of the consultation paper, were actually in favour of the concept of registers but the strength of the minority opposition, including the Royal Institution of Chartered Surveyors, the British Property Federation and the National Farmers Union, was such that there was no real alternative but to reconsider the scope and operation of the registers.

A Ministerial decision was taken to reduce the area of land likely to be subject to registration to between 10% and 15% of that which would have been included under the schedule contained in the consultation paper. This was achieved by deleting uses from the schedule until the required reduction in land area had been obtained. Once uses relating to certain vested interests had been removed, such as those on the 'high street' and land used for agriculture and railways, further deletions were made on an arbitrary basis until the required reduction was obtained.

The result of the reconsideration, intended to reduce the area of land affected by the proposals, was published in July 1992. This took the form of a revised schedule of eight very specific uses, attached to the draft regulation (DoE 1992a) which was intended to bring the legislation into effect. It was still intended that once on the register a property could not be removed, but provision was made in the draft for landowners to be notified of the intention to include their premises in the register and to have the opportunity to appeal as to matters of fact regarding past or current uses. Furthermore the registers were to be divided into two parts: Part A containing details of premises where nothing was known other than past or present use; Part B containing details of premises where site investigation or remediation works had been undertaken. However, no criteria were laid down defining the nature of the works to be undertaken for properties to be included in Part B. Therefore the testing of a single sample, or the introduction of a thin cover layer over contaminated material, could have been sufficient to qualify a site for inclusion in Part B, notwithstanding the fact that the work undertaken was totally inadequate.

Rather than removing the opposition to the proposed registers, the draft regulation had precisely the opposite effect and even more letters of objection were received by the Department of the Environment than had been received in respect of the original consultation paper. A view within the property profession was that by reducing the scheduled uses to only eight specific industries, these were perceived by the Government as being the most contaminative of all industrial processes. Therefore, in the opinion of some valuers, land and buildings currently or previously used for these purposes could be expected to have nil, or even negative, values. To make matters even worse, the letter which accompanied the draft regulation stated that 'The Government has it in mind to extend the list of uses by further regulations in due course in the light of experience' (DoE, 1992a), thus potentially condemning other groups of properties to the same fate at some future date. As much as anything else, it was this uncertainty that brought increased opposition, even from those members of the valuation profession who had previously been in favour of the registers.

In the face of such opposition to the proposed registers, the Government announced in March 1993 that they were to be abandoned (Howard, 1993) and that an interdepartmental review of contaminated land policies was to be undertaken. This review resulted in the publication of a further consultation paper *Paying for our Past* (DoE, 1994a) and the outcome of the review was published in a report *Framework for Contaminated Land* (DoE, 1994b), followed by the Environment Act 1995 (HMSO, 1995). So far as contaminated land is concerned, the Environment Act 1995 brought two major changes:

- amendment of the Environmental Protection Act 1990, with the introduction of new legislation relating specifically to contaminated land,
- the establishment of an Environment Agency with responsibility for England and Wales, and a Scottish Environmental Protection Agency.

The legislation is expected to come into effect during 1997, following the publication of Parliamentary Guidance, and the agencies have taken over responsibility for the functions previously undertaken by the National Rivers Authority, Her Majesty's Inspectorate of Pollution and the Waste Regulation Authorities.

Prior to the establishment of the two environment agencies, the main control for ensuring contaminated land was not used for any unsuitable purposes had been through the planning system. This operated through controls or conditions placed on the use of land for a particular purpose. The conditions could also stipulate the nature of remedial work required to be undertaken as part of the development permission. The fact that only incomplete records exist of former land uses means that this system of control is not very satisfactory, especially in the light of increasing pressures for land to be released for development purposes. It is therefore to be hoped that, in placing such widespread responsibility in the hands of a single agency, the new legislation will result in improved standards of record keeping.

Even though the Government failed to introduce registers of potentially contaminated land, a great deal of the information in respect of land and buildings affected by land contamination is in fact available. This can be used in order to arrive at informed decisions but diligent research is required on the part of valuers, developers, lawyers and other interested parties in order to obtain the relevant information, as described in Chapter 5.

A detailed consideration of the law relating to contaminated land was undertaken by Tromans and Turrall-Clarke in 1994, when they expressed the view that policy on contaminated land was at a sensitive and formative stage in both the UK and EC. This is particularly so in relation to registers, clean-up standards and the design of any liability regime. Graham (1995, p. 5) stated that the 'law relating to contaminated land is currently characterised by its uncertainty, and this creates a considerable challenge for all those involved in land'. This state of uncertainty has had to be reflected in the approaches adopted in research, as new legislation and case law may bring about significant changes over the forthcoming months and years.

Part II of the Environment Act 1995 (sections 57-60), which received the Royal Assent in July 1995, has brought a number of major changes to the law relating to contaminated land. These will only be introduced in stages, as a new Part IIA of the Environmental Protection Act 1990. The 1995 Act contains a total of 32 pages of new legislation in respect of contaminated land, introduced by way of amendment to the Environmental Protection Act 1990 through the insertion of 26 new clauses (78A to 78YC) into that Act. In addition, the 1995 Act repeals both Section 143 of the 1990 Act, the registers of potentially contaminative uses, and Section 61 of the Act, in respect of the duty of local authorities to inspect closed landfills. Neither of these Sections had been brought into force.

A 'working draft' of the statutory guidance to be published by the Department of the Environment was issued in February 1996 and was followed by a second draft in June and a public consultation draft in September 1996 (DoE, 1996). These drafts dealt with the definition and identification of contaminated land; the exclusion of persons otherwise liable to meet the costs of remediation and the apportionment of liability between parties deemed to be liable; the recovery of remediation costs and draft regulations to define special sites. The statutory guidance is intended to assist local authorities in the performance of their duties under Part IIA of the Environmental Protection Act 1990 in identifying and ensuring the remediation of contaminated land. Once approved by Parliament, this guidance will bring into effect the legislation on contaminated land.

Perhaps the most important part of the draft statutory guidance is the proposed definition of 'significant harm' which, in effect, gives force to the legal definition of contaminated land, as discussed in Chapter 2. This limits the scope of the legislation, as referred to by Denner and Lowe (1995), and was probably the most difficult aspect to agree between the consultees involved in the 'working draft' stages. In each of the 'working draft' documents the definition was altered and further changes were made in the public consultation document on the draft statutory guidance. The public consultation document was published shortly before this book went to press and this defined 'significant harm' in the following way:

'Only harm which is both
(a) to receptors of the type listed in Table A, and
(b) within the description of harm specified for that type of receptor in that table,
should be regarded as significant.'

The draft statutory guidance also sets out the conditions which need to be satisfied in order that a local authority may determine that there is a 'significant possibility of significant harm' being caused within a timescale decided by the local authority. The draft guidance was considered by the House of Commons Select Committee on the Environment in October 1996. It expressed concern over the possible 'blighting' effect of the guidance and the burden imposed on local authorities in respect of both financial and human resources. The Royal Institution of Chartered Surveyors, in its evidence to the Select Committee, also criticised the draft guidance for its lack of 'plain English'. The Local Authority Associations, in their evidence, concluded that:

'whilst recognising that any system to deal effectively with this legacy [of past pollution of land] will be complicated ... the provisions of both the Act and guidance as currently written will not achieve their objective of dealing with contaminated land so as to protect the public health and the environment.'

Table A

Type of receptor	Description of harm
Human beings	Death, serious injury, cancer or other disease, genetic mutation, birth defects, or the impairment of reproductive functions. Disease is to be taken to mean an unhealthy condition of the body or some part thereof.
Any living organism or ecological system within any habitat notified under section 28, declared under section 35 or designated under section 36 of the Wildlife and Countryside Act 1981[1], any European Site within the meaning of regulation 10 of the Conservation (Natural Habitats etc) Regulation 1994[2] or any habitat or site afforded policy protection under paragraph 13 of Planning Policy Guidance Note 9 on nature conservation or Planning Guidance (Wales): Planning Policy (that is Conservation, potential Special Protection Areas and listed Ramsar sites).	Harm which results in an irreversible or other substantial adverse change in the functioning of the habitat or site. (In determining what constitutes a substantial adverse change, the local authority should have regard to the advice of English Nature, Scottish Natural Heritage or the Countryside Council for Wales, as the case may be, and the requirements of the Conservation (Natural Habitats etc) Regulations 1994.)
Property in the form of livestock, of other owned animals, of wild animals which are the subject of shooting or fishing rights or of crops.	Death, disease or other physical damage such that there is a substantial loss in their value. For this purpose, a substantial loss should be regarded as occurring when a substantial proportion of the animals or crops are no longer fit for the purpose for which they were intended. In many cases, a loss of 10% of the value can be regarded as a benchmark for what constitutes a substantial loss.
Property in the form of buildings, where the 'building' has the meaning given in section 336(1) of the Town and Country Planning Act 1990, that is, 'building means any structure or erection, and any part of a building ... but does not include plant or machinery comprised in a building'.	Structural failure or substantial damage. For this purpose, substantial damage should be regarded as occurring when any part of the building ceases to be capable of being used for the purpose for which it is or was intended.

[1] Sections 28, 35 and 36 of the 1981 Act relate to Sites of Special Scientific Interest, National Nature Reserves and Marine Nature Reserves, respectively.
[2] SI 1994/2716. Regulation 10 relates to Special Areas of Conservation and Special Protection Areas.

Source: DoE, (1996)

The Local Authority Associations also expressed the view that the legal interpretation and argument which will ensue 'will reduce the effect of the contaminated land regime even further', resulting in 'lengthy, complex and costly legal processes.' (Local Authority Associations, 1996).

The Department of the Environment invited comments to be submitted by no later than 18 December 1996 and, as this book went to press, it was expected that the legislation, including any revisions to the draft statutory guidance, would become effective in Spring 1997.

At the same time as the United Kingdom government has been reconsidering its policies in respect of contaminated land, other European countries have been reviewing their policies, in the realisation that the full extent of the problem, in accordance with the 'strictest' definition of contaminated land, may be greater than had been realised. A number of these policy reviews are described in the following section.

Policies in other European countries and regions

'Many countries are developing approaches to deal with contaminated land. Many of the issues are common and there are benefits in collaborative work and exchange of information.' (Denner et al, 1995). The fifth International Conference on Contaminated Soil was held in Maastricht, Belgium in November 1995 and provided a forum for such an exchange of information. Most of the policy outlines described in this section are based on papers presented at that conference and may therefore, to some extent, reflect the views of the individual authors rather than confirmed government policies.

Germany

In Germany the 'clean-up' of contaminated land has historically been tackled through the use of liability orders administered by the different *Länder* under the soil protection provisions contained in various types of legislation. As a result, the approaches differed quite significantly throughout the country and in order to establish nationally uniform criteria a draft Federal Soil Conservation Act was published in August 1995 and was due to come into force during 1996. The legislation is intended as a framework law encompassing waste, building codes, building regulation, emission control, nature conservation, regional planning and statistics; with three main objectives:

- elimination of the proliferation of lists on soil values,
- removal of blockages in respect of urban and economic development,
- the prevention of future contamination.

The 'polluter pays' principle will apply and a 'suitable for use' approach is to be adopted in respect of soil treatment, with only one licence being required in respect of proposed remediation operations. The federal legislation will seek to encourage cost effective clean-up in preference to low cost remediation and aims to reduce pressure on greenfield sites by keeping contaminated land in beneficial use. The possible effect of land contamination in putting 'a block on urban and economic development' is recognised and uniform standards are seen as providing 'investors with a measure of legal security and make it easier to calculate the risks involved in soil damage' (Sanden, 1995).

The Netherlands

Soil 'clean-up' policy in the Netherlands has evolved through three distinct phases. In 1982 the contaminated soil problem was perceived as being associated with landfills and gas works. However in 1987 it was 'realised that general industrial sites should be added' (Deelen, 1995). By 1995 it had come to be accepted by the government that the problem was in fact one of diffuse pollution, with social processes coming to a standstill. In describing the effect of these three phases Dr A. Deelen, Deputy Director in the Department of Soil Protection (part of the Netherlands Ministry of Housing, Spatial Planning and the Environment), cited the case of the City of Maastricht:

- in 1982 there were 52 known cases of contaminated soil in the city,

- by 1987 the number of identified sites had increased to 175,
- in 1995 there existed widespread diffuse contamination affecting an unknown number of sites.

Recognition of the widespread nature of the problem has led to a reconsideration of Dutch policy on contaminated land, treating soil as a capital asset, and recognising that the country 'will have to learn to cope for many years with the problem of soil pollution' (Deelen, 1995). This change has brought with it a moderation of the 'multifunctionality' approach to the treatment of contaminated land, under which all sites affected by contamination had to be remediated to the same standard of 'cleanliness', regardless of proposed future use. Instead the current policy has three main 'strategy lines':

- Strategy Line 1; spread the financial responsibility and involve industry on a voluntary basis, for example, an individual petrol filling station may be unable to afford the cost of remediating its own contamination and therefore the problem should be tackled by the industry as a whole – the sustainable quality of soil should be seen as a social responsibility.
- Strategy Line 2; improve the returns of tackling soil pollution, using public/private sector partnerships to increase the number of sites remediated, encourage the wider use of in-situ biological treatments and the re-use of slightly contaminated soil, for example in roads and embankments, in preference to landfill disposal – changing to function orientated soil management.
- Strategy Line 3; government concentration on designing and implementing standards and regulations changing to one of government becoming an active participant and co-investor, seeking 'win-win' solutions in which all participants derive benefits in spite of conflicting interests.

Finland

In a rather less industrialised country such as Finland it may be that the 'problems are known to a large extent and authorities have become more and more involved' (Sappänen, 1995). A contaminated sites survey was completed in 1994, excluding military and nuclear sites, which identified 25 000 suspected contaminated sites, including sawmills, wood impregnation sites, waste disposal sites and scrap yards. It is estimated that possibly as many as 90% of the identified sites may be contaminated.

'Some legislation exists in Finland but amendments may be needed' (Sappänen, 1995). A handling policy was implemented by the State Council in 1988 and a Waste Act has been in force since 1 January 1994. The need for a systematic approach has been recognised and the polluters pay for treatment so far as is possible to enforce, failing which it is the responsibility of the site owner, although the state can step in if the owner is unable to pay. Links have been established between waste management and strategic land use planning. Future soil pollution has been banned, a site survey and information on any remedial actions undertaken must be provided to purchasers and to the authorities. Permits are required in respect of remediation works and fees are to be charged from 1996 for the disposal of contaminated soil to landfill.

Belgium

In Belgium there is regional responsibility for contaminated soil and in October 1995 a new Soil Remediation Act came into force which applies to Flanders, the Northern region of the country. Under the terms of this Act OVAM, the Public Waste Agency, is charged with the task of identifying affected sites and compiling a register of contaminated soils. The Agency also has the power to step in and 'clean-up' contaminated land in default of action by the site owner and recover appropriate costs.

The 'polluter pays' principle applies, as does the BATNEEC principle (Best Available Technique Not Entailing Excessive Cost). There are provisions to protect the innocent landowner under which the costs will be borne by the government, which will then seek to recover the expenditure from the original polluter.

When land is to be sold, a certificate must be obtained from OVAM in respect of the contamination situation. If any contamination found on the site is historic, i.e. before 29 October 1995, remediation may not necessarily be required but severe penalties will be imposed if the contamination has occurred since the Act came into force. The policy in Flanders may therefore be described as a 'pragmatic approach towards historic contamination but seeking to ensure that new pollution does not occur' (van Dyck, 1995).

Austria

The Law for Clean-up of Contaminated Sites (Altlastensanier-ungsgesetz in German (ALSAG)) was enacted in Austria in July 1989.

> 'This law creates a legal basis for detection and evaluation of potentially contaminated sites. Old waste sites and industrial facilities, which might be injurious to the environment, are to be considered as potentially contaminated sites.'
>
> (Weihs, 1995)

The law provides for the establishment of a register of con-taminated sites, the first or 'detection' stage of which appears not dissimilar to the registers proposed for England and Wales under Section 143 of the Environmental Protection Act 1990, in that it seeks to identify 'potentially contaminated' sites. Unlike the Section 143 proposal, this detection stage is followed by an assessment pro-cedure, in three phases:

- the preliminary assessment phase, during which the priorities for investigation of the potentially contaminated site are established,
- the risk assessment phase, to determine whether or not treatment is required at that time,
- a classification phase, when priorities for treatment are determined and the urgency of treatment is documented.

Upon completion of the assessment stage, the contaminated sites are divided into three priority categories, using the same evaluation factors as used in the preliminary assessment, but redefined to reflect the results of the investigation. On 1 January 1995 the Austrian register comprised 1759 potentially contaminated sites with 111 of those sites identified as actually contaminated (Weihs, 1995). The total number of contaminated sites in Austria is expected to be around 5000 to 10 000. (Kasamas, 1995)

In addition to the registers ALSAG provides the legislative structure for dealing with contaminated sites in Austria including:

- the creation of public funds through the levy of charges in respect
  of the disposal of certain types of waste to landfill, waste export
  and the temporary storage of wastes for periods exceeding one
  year,
- a nation-wide uniform distribution of the funds created to stimulate voluntary activities at contaminated sites, 80% of the funds
  are assigned to support site remediation with the remaining 20%
  being used to fund additional site investigations to complete risk
  assessments,
- the responsibilities of the different authorities in the programme,
- liabilities and enforcement procedures under the environmental
  laws.

The Austrian system is therefore one of encouraging land owners to
'clean-up' their sites through the allocation of public money derived
from the management of wastes which might otherwise have the
potential to create further contamination. The guidelines for funding
should encourage co-operation between the public authorities and
the potential responsible parties (PRPs). 'The prospect of financial
support should encourage property owners to come forward to
report PCS [Potential Contaminated Sites] for subsequent risk-
assessment or to realize remedial measures at the site voluntarily'
(Kasamas, 1995).

Summary of European policies

It would appear that throughout Europe there is developing a
widespread acceptance that the remediation of contaminated land is a
long term problem, and that treatments should be selected on the
basis of suitability for use. The 'clean-up' of contaminated land to a
uniformly 'clean' state may not always be a realistic proposition and
regard needs to be paid to the cost-effectiveness of any treatments
proposed.

Where registers have been introduced, these would seem to go further than was proposed in the United Kingdom in terms of the evaluation of the actual state of contamination affecting registered sites. That the polluter should pay for the treatment of contamination would seem to be fairly widely accepted as a principle but the extent to which that principle is enforced in respect of historic contamination would seem to vary significantly from country to country. Approaches also differ in the extent of protection offered to the 'innocent landowner' and those who are unable to pay for the cost of treatment.

Conclusion

The definition of 'significant harm' contained in the draft statutory guidance published by the Department of the Environment in September 1996 (DoE, 1996) effectively limits the scope of the contaminated land legislation and would appear to be similar in approach to the policy definition offered to the House of Commons Select Committee on the Environment in 1990. Therefore, it would seem that having proposed to introduce legislation which would have identified a large number of industries as potential contaminators, the Department of the Environment has turned full circle in its policy thinking by applying a narrow definition to contaminated land.

Such a pragmatic approach is perhaps not unreasonable, given Mike Smith's evidence to the 1989/90 Select Committee that 'acceptance of the broader definition would mean that substantial parts of some urban areas would have to be classified as contaminated – as indeed they are.' (Smith, 1990) The test must surely be to determine whether or not any actual risks exist and the likelihood, or otherwise, of those risks causing harm to human health or the wider environment. The draft statutory guidance to local authorities has, in narrowly defining contaminated land, created the possibility of a blighting effect in respect of 'grey area' land which is affected by elevated levels of contaminants in the soil but is not legally classed as 'contaminated'.

Other countries throughout Europe are coming to realise that it is not practical to 'clean-up' all of the contamination which remains from historic industrial or other man-made activities. Every effort should be made to avoid future contamination, although this may need to be considered through cost/benefit analysis, with the treatment of historic contamination being determined on the basis of risk assessment and the most serious hazards given the highest priority.

Whether or not the legal definitions of contaminated land and significant harm will be accepted in the context of redevelopment, remains to be seen. Investors in property, whether for owner occupation or income production, tend to take a 'long term' view of their commitment and may seek greater reassurance than that contained in the definitions proposed by the Department of the Environment. This aspect is considered further in Sections 3 and 4 of the book.

Checklist

Significant harm

- Consider whether the contamination represents 'significant harm' in accordance with Part IIA of the Environmental Protection Act 1990.
- Does the source of the contamination still exist and is it causing new contamination?
- If 'significant harm' is not being caused at the present time, is there potential for such harm to be caused in the future?
- What are the targets, or receptors, most likely to be at risk from the contamination?
- Is the present owner responsible for having caused the contamination, or can the previous owner or occupier of the site be held liable?
- Has any action been taken by the local authority, or the Environment Agency, to classify the site as 'contaminated land' or as a 'special site'?

Section 2
Technical Issues

Chapter 5
Locating and Identifying Contamination

The first four chapters have provided an introduction to the problems associated with the redevelopment of contaminated land. They serve to demonstrate the need for detailed knowledge to be obtained in respect of ground conditions, and for values to be adjusted in the light of that knowledge. Adequate knowledge of ground conditions, especially the presence and extent of any contamination, can only be obtained through a properly designed and executed site investigation. A well designed investigation consists of a number of clearly defined stages, and whether or not it is necessary for all of these stages to be undertaken in order for the developer to be sufficiently informed will depend upon site specific circumstances and the type of development proposed. Similarly, where a valuation is required, the extent of any site investigation will depend upon the information provided by the client, the purpose of the valuation, site specific circumstances and the nature of the instructions given to the valuer.

Whether or not general practice surveyors and valuers should undertake site investigation will depend on their training and experience, but generally speaking, work of this nature will be outside their sphere of competence. There are, however, members of the surveying profession who view this area of work as an opportunity to provide clients with a more comprehensive service, whilst others believe that surveyors should adhere more closely to their traditional roles.

For the majority of surveyors and valuers, site investigations will involve the appointment of specialist consultants. It is therefore appropriate for the general practitioner to have some knowledge about the subject of site investigations, so as to be able to advise clients on the appointment of suitably qualified and experienced consultants. The level of knowledge should be sufficient for general practice surveyors to prepare briefs upon which the specialist consultants may be invited to submit their proposals and to be able to advise clients as to the strengths and weaknesses of those proposals.

Locating and identifying contamination invariably involves a number of parties, and at the outset, the only adviser employed by the landowner or the intending developer may be the general practice surveyor or valuer. Amongst the other parties who will need to be involved in the investigative process, or may have an interest in its outcome, are the following:

- a specialist consultant or sub-consultant if the main consultant lacks contamination expertise,
- a specialist contractor experienced in the investigation of contaminated land,
- a specialist laboratory equipped to undertake appropriate chemical analyses if the ground investigation specialist contractor does not have such in-house facilities,
- the regulatory and statutory bodies who are not party to the contract but whose requirements may have to be complied with under the contract,
- the landowner, if not the client, and adjoining landowners/users etc.,
- the public who may be affected by on-site works and may have an interest both in the nature of any contaminants found on the site and any future development proposals.

(Source: after CIRIA, 1995, **III**, p. 26)

If the valuer or surveyor is to assume management responsibility for the location and identification of contamination, or is to advise the client on the appointment of suitable consultants, he or she will need to take account of a number of issues. These will include defining the roles and responsibilities of the various members of the professional team, obtaining any necessary consents, and taking account of any legal constraints, insurance requirements, health and safety considerations, environmental protection and long-term monitoring.

Most, if not all, of these issues will need to be addressed in the invitations to tender issued to specialist consultants and contractors.

The appointment of suitable specialists is vital to the success of the project, and in procuring specialist advice two main options are available:

- Use of a professional adviser, with the separate employment of a contractor(s) for physical work, testing and reporting as required.
- Use of a single contract covering specialist advice, physical investigation, testing and reporting.

(Source: CIRIA, 1995, **III**, p. 27)

The decision as to which option is selected will depend upon different considerations such as, the size and complexity of the project, the previous experience of the lead consultant, the individual preference of the client and the availability of suitable personnel. Whichever option is selected, competitive tendering will probably be used in making the final choice of the consultant(s) and/or contractor(s) to be appointed.

> 'This has the potential disadvantage that costs can assume greater importance than technical sufficiency, but it can be operated successfully provided the tender list is restricted to a few firms able to tender on an equal footing.'
>
> (CIRIA, 1995; **III**, p. 28)

The selection of suitable consultants is often of fundamental importance to the success of a redevelopment project, as inappropriate advice or inadequate supervision may result in substantial losses being incurred. Cost considerations alone should not therefore be the only criteria which determine the selection of consultants and it is recommended that the tender list should contain no more than three firms of equal standing, in terms of both reputation and capability. The firms should be asked to provide detailed proposals in response to a brief, which needs to be designed in such a way as to facilitate comparison between proposals.

Site investigations

The subject of site investigations has been considered by many authors, including Lord (1987), McEntee (1991), Smith (1991) and

Beckett (1993a). The Department of the Environment has commissioned reports containing guidance on the investigation and sampling of contaminated land (DoE, 1994c and d), the Welsh Development Agency has produced a comprehensive manual on the remediation of contaminated land (Welsh Development Agency, 1993), a substantial part of which is devoted to the subject of site investigations, and Scottish Enterprise has published its *Requirements for contaminated land site investigations* (Scottish Enterprise, 1993). The Construction Industry Research and Information Association has published guidance on the 'best practice' for site investigation and assessment (CIRIA, 1995 **III**), as part of a comprehensive review of remedial treatment for contaminated land. A number of conference papers have also considered the issues involved, including Fletcher (1992), Ferguson (1993), Waters (1993) and Crowcroft (1994).

This chapter attempts to summarise, in a non-technical manner, the procedures to be followed in ascertaining if a site is contaminated. It is intended to assist landowners, valuers and development surveyors when considering the appointment of specialist consultants to undertake site investigation work. Perhaps the most succinct advice given to those contemplating a new development is set out in the ICRCL guidance note 59/83 (ICRCL, 1987) which stresses that 'The aim therefore should always be to check whether a site is contaminated before deciding on the form of development'. The outcome of such a check may raise important valuation issues, as the nature and extent of any contamination may influence the developer in making changes to the type of development proposed. For example, an intended residential development may be replaced by a decision to retain the site in industrial use, and may even result in the developer deciding not to proceed with acquisition of the site.

Any site investigation must be sufficiently comprehensive, so as to present a reasonably accurate picture of the site condition, and not a misleading impression as described in some of the case studies in Chapters 9 and 10. In order therefore to satisfy the principles of good practice and to achieve the objective of the investigative process, the site investigation should be designed with a view to:

- determining the nature and extent of any contamination of soils and groundwater on the site,

- determining the nature and extent of any contamination migrating off the site into neighbouring soils and groundwater,
- determining the nature and extent of any contamination migrating into the site,
- determining the nature and engineering implications of other hazards and features on the site, for example, expansive slags, combustibility, deep foundations, storage tanks,
- identifying, characterising and assessing potential targets and likely pathways,
- providing sufficient information (including a reference level to judge effectiveness) to identify and evaluate alternative remedial strategies,
- determining the need for, and scope of, both short- and long-term monitoring and maintenance,
- formulating safe site working practices and ensuring effective protection of the environment during remedial works,
- identifying and planning for immediate human health and environmental protection and contingencies for any emergency action.

(CIRIA, 1995, **III**, p. 9)

In addressing these objectives the topics of interest for the investigation of contaminated land may be classified into six main groups:

- physical site conditions
- likely contaminants
- extent and severity of contamination
- effects on users
- potential for environmental harm
- hazards during construction

(after Hobson, 1993, p. 34)

Hobson suggested that the process of site investigation,

'essentially involves the construction of a theoretical "model", which can be used to assess the condition and behaviour of the ground, and the mechanisms and processes that lead to hazards and other effects'.

(Hobson, 1993, p. 34)

Existing records, including previous site investigations and visual observations must be used to construct an initial model, so as to facilitate an assessment of both the likely nature of any treatment which may be required and the suitability of the site for the proposed after use. The model should define:

- natural geology and topography
- modifications, mining and other alterations
- filled and disturbed areas
- locations of potentially contaminating activities
- historical and modern drainage paths
- services and other constraints

(Hobson, 1993, p. 40)

The model may then be refined in the light of an investigative programme. The site investigation must therefore be designed in such a way as to provide the information required by the project, taking account of physical and other constraints, and the data produced must be capable of logical interpretation.

'As the principal means of gathering data to assess risks and select, design and implement remedial action, it is essential that site investigation is carried out according to good practice principles. It is an iterative process involving the collection and evaluation of information on both the site and its setting. There are at least two distinct phases: the first phase, preliminary investigation is non invasive by nature; the second phase uses invasive ground investigation techniques and may be termed the main investigation.'

(Welsh Development Agency, 1993, p. 3.1)

Depending upon site specific circumstances, it may be appropriate to introduce an exploratory investigation between the preliminary and main investigations. This may involve a limited on-site investigation,

'intended to confirm initial hypotheses about contamination and site characteristics, and to provide additional information to aid design of detailed investigation(s), including health and safety etc. aspects.'

(CIRIA, 1995, **III**, p. 12)

It may be possible to combine the investigative work relating to contamination with a site investigation designed for other purposes, for example a geotechnical investigation required for foundation design, but the differing objectives should not be allowed to come into conflict with each other. It should also be stressed that many of the procedures involved in site investigation of contaminated sites, especially associated with invasive work, are potentially hazardous to the health of the operatives involved, and to the wider public. Health and safety issues must therefore be taken into account in the design of any site investigation and specific advice in relation to contaminated land is provided by the Health and Safety Executive (Health and Safety Executive, 1991).

The precise nature of any site investigation will be determined by specific conditions and, in many instances, by budget allocation. However, 'the importance of undertaking a thorough desk study prior to the field-work cannot be overstressed' (McEntee, 1991, p. 67). The main components of the two phases of site investigation may be summarised as shown in Box 5.1.

Box 5.1 Main phases and components of site investigation.

Phase 1	Phase 2
Preliminary investigation	**Main investigation**
Historical study	Inspection and testing
Site characterisation	Ground investigation
Site reconnaissance	Sampling and analysis
	Supplementary investigation

Source: Welsh Development Agency (1993, p. 3.2)

Although the two stage site investigation described above may be desirable, such an investigation may not always be necessary, or even feasible. For example, in circumstances where the subject property is to remain in industrial use and a valuation is required for asset or security purposes, a preliminary investigation may suffice, although it must be recognised that the results obtained from such an investigation may, on occasions, be at variance to those obtained from a subsequent main investigation.

Even when redevelopment is intended, existing operational constraints and a desire to limit potentially abortive expenditure may mitigate against a full site investigation. In such cases it may be appropriate to consider commissioning a preliminary investigation plus an exploratory investigation, designed so as to take account of information provided by the preliminary stage and operational constraints. This intermediate stage may be followed by additional work to complete the main investigation, thus creating a three stage investigation.

When sites are vacant and immediate redevelopment is proposed and the intending developer is not in a competitive bidding situation for the site, the two stage site investigation approach should be recommended. The additional expenditure at this stage may influence decisions regarding the site, and reduce the risk of unforeseen costs at a later stage.

When competitive bidding situations are intended or envisaged, it may be appropriate for the vendor to at least commission a preliminary investigation and possibly also an exploratory stage investigation. If the presence of contamination is indicated, the vendor should make available the information obtained to all prospective purchasers in order that they may submit their bids on an equal footing. Whether or not further work is required will then depend on the nature of the development, the findings of the vendor's investigation and whether the consultant is prepared to provide a warranty to the purchaser.

Preliminary investigation

Historical study

Referred to by McEntee (1991, p. 64) as a 'desk study' and 'generally confined to an inspection of the available geological records', the historical stage of the investigation cannot in reality be undertaken by a researcher sitting at a desk, nor should it be confined solely to geological data. The information needed for an historical study of a potentially contaminated site will have to be obtained from many different sources, including those listed in Box 5.2.

Assembly of the information available from the sources in Box 5.2 should provide an understanding of the stages of development which have taken place on the site. This is most important in situations where sites have been used for different purposes and have probably

Box 5.2   Information sources for historical study.

Source	Materials
Local library	Maps, current and historic Books, journals Newspaper records and magazine articles
Ordnance Survey	Current and superseded maps
National map libraries	Various maps
British Geological Survey, universities, and local bodies, e.g. Greater Manchester Geological Unit	Geological maps and memoirs Well and exploration records Hydrogeological records
British Coal	Mining records
Minerals Planning Authority	Mineral extraction records
Public utilities	Location of services
Local authorities	Town planning registers, and enforcement notices
Present and previous owners, occupiers and users	Details of activities and processes carried out Plans and photographs
Environment Agency and Water undertakings	Surface water run-off Outfall details Licensed waste disposal activities River details
Drainage authorities	Surface water drainage and improvement schemes
Aerial photographic libraries	Historical and modern photography

changed hands on several occasions throughout the period of their industrial use.

Even sites which have been used for the same purpose, or have been in the same ownership, throughout their period of use 'may also have been subject to a succession of enlargements and extensions, often bearing no relation to later layouts on the site' (McEntee, 1991, p. 67). It is therefore most important that a comprehensive historical study is undertaken, even if the present owner is adamant that the site was a greenfield when production commenced fifty years earlier. Waste products may have been disposed of, quite legally, for example to the public sewer, but the practice may have been discontinued years ago, leaving behind a latent problem. Parts of the site may have been raised and levelled using contaminated materials, now hidden under buildings or yard areas (Figures 5.1a and 5.1b).

Much of this information may be available in the valuer's files or those of the architect, where they have acted for the company over a number of years. Alternatively, relevant documents may be found in the records of the site owner, and where possible should be summarised in the site investigation brief.

Site characterisation and reconnaissance

Once the historical study has been completed, or even whilst it is still under way, it is important to characterise the public health and environmental context. This will enable the critical hazard or source, pathway and target scenarios to be identified and assessed. A number of factors, both internal and external to the site, need to be considered at this stage, as shown in Box 5.3.

The purpose of a site reconnaissance is to check the information obtained from documentary evidence and to add further detail. (Hobson, 1993, p. 42) It is suggested that wherever possible the valuer and the person(s) responsible for the past management and maintenance of the site should accompany the site investigation specialist on the site reconnaissance. This is especially beneficial in cases where any of these individuals have any knowledge of previous landfilling activities, wastes disposal procedures and other potentially contaminative activities.

'A visual assessment of the site may disclose evidence of unrecorded events and activities, particularly those which post-date available records, e.g. fly-tipping' (Welsh Development Agency, 1993, p. 3.4). Site reconnaissance should not be carried out unless a desk study has indicated that it is safe to do so. Before commencing the reconnaissance it is advisable to sub-divide the site into identifiable areas of interest, say by former uses or by topography, and to mark up the site plan with points of interest, possibly by use of an overlay. Hobson (1993, p. 42) suggested that:

'the reconnaissance should, wherever possible, be conducted on foot and it is usually best to walk around the perimeter of the site first, before inspecting the central area and points of detail. This gives an understanding of the overall scale of the site and allows landmarks to be easily located.'

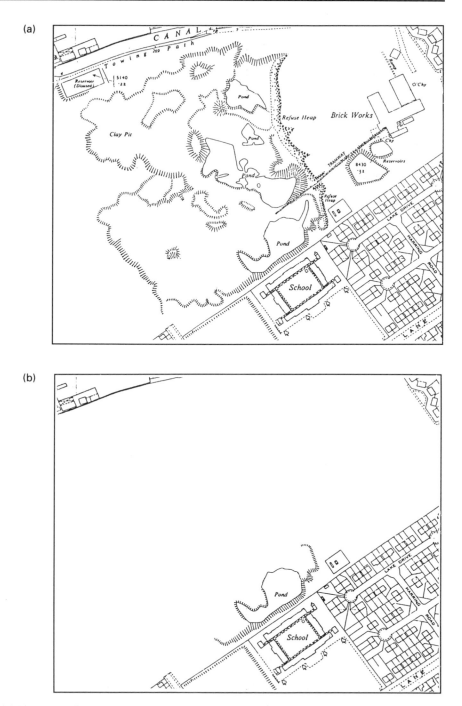

Fig. 5.1 (a) Map published in 1951; (b) map published in 1971. Comparison between older and more recent maps can provide a good indication of past activities on the site. In this case the former brick pits had been filled with household refuse and other material. (Based on Ordnance Survey.)

Box 5.3   Factors for consideration in a site investigation.

Human beings – those who currently live or work on the subject property, or by whom it was previously occupied, and those who will use the property in the foreseeable future. This includes building operatives who will be employed on the site during the construction phase of any proposed development and any casual visitors to the site, including trespassers. In the case of residential developments, special consideration needs to be given to the possible ingestion of surface material by young children, known as '*pica*' syndrome.

Geology, soil and surface material – particular consideration needs to be given to the potential for any contamination to be carried away from the site through the ground, or from its surface by humans (for example on the soles of shoes or on vehicle tyres), by animals, birds and invertebrates.

Surface and ground water quality – the existence of any potable water supplies in the vicinity of the property needs special consideration, in respect of the potential of contaminants to cause pollution. Even if there are no potable supplies of concern and the only surface or ground waters are already contaminated to such an extent that contaminants leaching from the subject property are unlikely to make any significant difference, the possibility that a pathway may exist needs to be considered. For example, a decision may be taken at some future date to 'clean up' an affected water course, say following closure of the major polluter, and riparian owners may be faced with having to meet part of the cost.

Climate and air quality – including the possibility of the deposition, or 'fall out', of contaminants from the manufacturing processes undertaken on the subject property, on to other properties lying downwind of the site and also the possibility that any contamination found on the property might originate from upwind of the site.

Flora and fauna – in particular are any species being adversely affected by conditions on the site, or emanating from within the locality? Conversely are any species thriving on the site conditions? Consideration also needs to be given to the possibility of finding rare or endangered species on the site, the existence of which may mitigate against the use of certain types of remediation methods, such as total removal of contaminated material, and in favour of other, *in situ*, methods. The ability to use the site for the proposed after use may also be affected, with a resultant impact on value.

Cultural heritage – this can cover many different aspects of the former, or even present, uses of a property and its suitability for alternative uses in the future, including use of the site for a fairground or more modern activities, such as off-road 4x4 driving.

Landscape – regard needs to be paid to any discontinuities between the landscape of the subject property and the surrounding area; these may, for example, indicate areas of unrecorded filling of the site. Landscape may also be important in considering the likelihood of contaminants migrating on to the subject property from other industrial activities in the vicinity.

Box 5.3 *Continued.*

> **The built environment and services** – the historical study should have provided information as to the past development of the property and the characterisation stage should include consideration as to how these might impact on its continued use and/or redevelopment.
>
> **Regulatory framework** – consideration must be given to any regulations affecting the particular industry carried out on the site, as well as to more general legislation dealing with the control of pollution, and health and safety. The impact of Local Plans, both those currently in force and any proposed changes, affecting not only the property itself but also the surrounding area, needs to be taken into account. For example, it may be proposed that land adjoining the property be allocated to a potentially contaminative use.
>
> **Interaction between any of the above** – none of these factors should be considered in isolation but they should be used to build up a composite understanding of the property, so as to assess the likely significance of any contamination and thereby provide essential background information in order to determine the most appropriate response.

Preliminary report

Completion of the reconnaissance stage should enable the Preliminary Investigation Report to be prepared. This should describe all completed work, report on the findings, and include a summary of those hazards, pathways and targets likely to be most important at the site. Recommendations for future action should be made at this stage, and where possible, an indication provided as to any remediation work which may be required. The theoretical model, described by Hobson (1993) should be adjusted and refined in the light of the information obtained and prospective developers would probably expect the model to include an estimate of likely treatment costs, possibly based on a 'worst case' scenario.

At this stage the preliminary report should be submitted to the client and, where appropriate, to the other members of the professional team, with advice as to whether or not the main investigation should be undertaken. The brief to the consultants and their terms of appointment should provide for the possibility of the investigation being terminated following submission of the preliminary report. This is in case the degree of contamination identified is beyond that which the developer is prepared to consider and the decision is taken not to continue with the project. In situations where only a valuation is required, the information provided from the preliminary investigation should be sufficient either to enable the valuer to complete his or her valuation, or to determine the extent of any additional information, or exploratory investigation, which may be required.

Main investigation

Ground investigation

The principal objectives of any investigation, where contamination is suspected, must be to determine the nature of the contaminants present on the site, their likely behaviour, spatial distribution and volumetric extent. Assuming that the decision is taken to proceed with the main investigation, the preliminary investigation may be regarded as a type of 'screening device' or filter which should have the effect of enabling a worthwhile and cost effective main investigation to be designed. To omit the preliminary stage and proceed directly to a main investigation may be regarded as foolhardy, and may well result in potential contaminants being overlooked. Such an omission may necessitate partial repetition of the invasive investigation and increased costs.

Before commencing with the ground investigation some further inspection and testing may be required, to refine the hazard identification and assessment from the preliminary stage and to assist in the design of the main investigation programme. This may take the form of an exploratory phase between the preliminary investigation and the main investigation, as referred to previously, or it may even involve an extension of the site reconnaissance stage. The amount of work needed at this stage will depend to a large extent on the nature of the previous, and current, activities on the site, the size of the site and its complexity. A plan will need to be prepared under the Control of Substances Hazardous to Health Regulations 1988 (COSHH) and consideration may need to be given to a Construction Design and Management (CDM) plan.

Sufficient detail is needed for:

- assessing health and environmental hazards and risks
- evaluating financial and technical options for the subsequent development if one is planned
- selecting and planning any remedial work

- designing the works
- ensuring safe working for personnel on-site
- ensuring health and safety of the public
- assessing requirements for both short- and long-term monitoring

(CIRIA, 1995, **III**, p. 19)

Ferguson (1993) stated that each site must be judged individually, taking into account the available information and the objectives of the investigation, but sampling is usually designed to answer three key questions

- which hazardous substances, if any, are present in the soil?
- do contaminant hotspots exist on the site, and if so where?
- what size and shape are the hotspots, if they exist?

(Ferguson, 1993)

No ground investigation can guarantee to locate all contaminants which may exist within a site and to quantify their extent and volume. The objective of an investigation should be to assess, with a reasonable degree of certainty, the likelihood of any contamination being present, the nature of the contaminants themselves and the media within which they are located. The information thus obtained can then be used in selecting the appropriate method, or methods, of treatment and designing the programme of remediation. Therefore the ground investigation must be sufficiently comprehensive, so as to achieve these objectives.

'A decision needs to be made on the largest hot-spot that could be accepted or dealt with economically if it were missed in sampling. This critical hot-spot size is an important design parameter'

(DoE, 1994d, p. 2).

Deciding upon the economics of the sampling pattern may involve the development team in preparing sensitivity analyses for several different options and may well necessitate some consideration being given to alternative site layouts, should the extent of contamination be greater than envisaged. In general, however, an under-designed site investigation has the potential to result in unexpected costs during the development period and an increase in the timescale of the project.

Three main sampling patterns are discussed in the contaminated land literature and these are shown in Figure 5.2.

The mathematical theories attaching to the different patterns are beyond the scope of this book but interested readers may wish to refer to Bell et al (1983), Lord (1987), Ferguson (1993) and DoE (1994d). Efficient sampling must, however, satisfy four conditions:

(1)   It should be stratified, that is the area under investigation should be partitioned into regular sub-areas.
(2)   Each stratum, or sub-area, should only contain a single sampling point.
(3)   The investigation should be systematic.
(4)   The sampling points should not be aligned with each other.

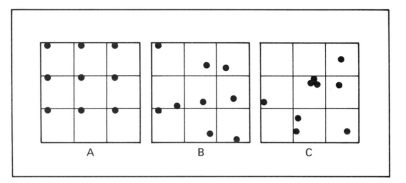

Fig. 5.2 Common sampling patterns for site investigations. A = square grid; B = simple random; C = stratified random. (Source: DoE, 1994d.)

None of the three most commonly used sampling patterns shown in Figure 5.2 satisfy all of the above conditions. The square grid and simple random patterns satisfy all but condition 4, whilst stratified random patterns satisfy all but condition 3. The main disadvantage of the square grid pattern, in particular, is in respect of its reduced ability to detect elongated hot-spots where the long axis runs parallel to the grid axis. The herringbone sampling pattern, Figure 5.3, overcomes this disadvantage, satisfies all four design conditions and is easy to set out on site.

Sampling patterns assume that any contamination is likely to be generally distributed throughout the site. However, the preliminary investigation may have provided sufficient data to enable the location

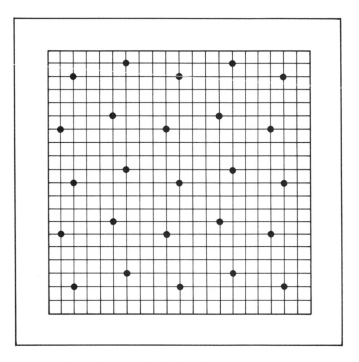

Fig. 5.3 Herringbone sampling pattern. (Source: DoE, 1994d.)

of possible contaminants to be determined with a reasonable degree of accuracy. It may therefore be appropriate to design the sampling pattern, for at least part of the site, with the specific objective of confirming the boundaries of hot-spots. Investigation of the remaining site area should not however be ignored, in case there are other hot-spots which were not identified during the preliminary investigation, and to ascertain whether there has been any migration of contamination. The ground investigation may therefore comprise a mixture of specifically targeted trial pits or boreholes (Figure 5.4) with others conforming to a grid or herringbone pattern.

The British Standards Institution's *Draft for Development* 175 (BSI, 1988) gives the minimum number of sampling points required, according to different site areas, in order to have a 95% probability of locating one contaminated sample from a contaminated area of a minimum specified size (Table 5.1). ICRCL Guidance Note 18/79 (ICRCL, 1986) recommends a grid spacing of 10–25 metres for small sites and a 25–50 metres grid spacing for larger sites. On a 1 hectare (1 ha = 10^4 m^2) site a 10 metre grid would give a probability of only 63.4% of finding a total contaminated area of 100 square metres (i.e.

Fig. 5.4 An auger drilling rig in use for site investigation. (Source: AEA Technology plc.)

the size of the grid) (Hobson, 1993, p. 47). For gas works and similar sites, sampling densities of 20–50 trial pits per hectare are suggested by the Department of the Environment for suspected hot spot areas (DoE, 1987), with 5–10 trial pits per hectare elsewhere.

The ground investigation should be designed in such a way as to characterise the contamination present within the site with respect to:

- lateral and vertical extent
- chemical composition and concentration
- physical characteristics (e.g. volatility, solubility)
- biological characteristics (e.g. pathenogenicity, degradation potential)

(Source: Welsh Development Agency, 1993, pp. 3.11–3.12)

Design of the ground investigation must therefore take account of any constraints which may prevent adequate characterisation. This is

Table 5.1   Minimum area of contamination located by BSI DD175 sampling frequency.

Area of site (hectares)	Recommended number of sampling points	Minimum contaminated area to provide one contaminated sample at a 95% confidence level (m^2)
0.5	15	905
1.0	25	1129
5.0	85	1732

one aspect to which the surveyor should pay particular attention when analysing site investigation proposals and reports. For example, if the preliminary investigation has indicated the presence of fill material with depths of up to five metres, and a trial pit investigation is to be undertaken, then it is of no use employing a wheeled excavator with a maximum reach of only three metres; but even leading consultants have been known to make such an error. Trial pits located in fill material need to be excavated down to natural undisturbed ground so as to facilitate the taking of samples from below the fill, to determine whether or not the contamination is mobile. A report which contains phrases such as 'natural ground was not found in trial pits numbers...' or 'the excavator was unable to penetrate to the full depth of the fill material' is of limited use and it may be necessary for further investigation work to be undertaken, at additional expense, and a possibility that further disturbance of the ground will cause a more widespread distribution of the contaminants. Similarly, the design of the sampling and testing procedures must be sufficiently rigorous to maximise the likelihood that any possible contaminants will be identified.

Sampling and analysis

In many cases, the site investigation for contamination will be undertaken at the same time as, or even as part of, a wider investigation designed to ascertain the geotechnical, geological, hydrological and hydrogeological attributes of the site. Whilst it may be possible to combine the different aspects into one investigation, the sampling requirements and techniques may be different. The actual method used to carry out the ground investigation may be determined by criteria related to the other aspects of the investigation, rather than by the nature of contamination, and some compromises may be necessitated. For most forms of contamination, a trial pit or trench investigation is likely to be most appropriate, as these methods facilitate visual inspection of both the contaminants and the media within which they are contained (Figure 5.5). For volatile contaminants, however, trial pits and trench methods are inappropriate, due to the problems of sample collection, and a borehole investigation will produce better results. Other forms of investigation include hand sampling of surface materials (to depths of about 0.5 metre), dynamic probes and soil gas surveys. Whatever method is used, however, there is a chance that something will be missed. Therefore it is important for there to be a logical justification to the sampling plan, at least qualitatively if not quantitatively.

At least three samples should be taken at each sampling location, from near the surface (150–200mm depth), the depth of greatest concern and a random intermediate sample (BSI, 1988) and the consultants' proposals should include testing at least this number. In addition it is advisable, on sites which have been subjected to fly tipping, to take at least one sample from each discrete tipped load (Figure 5.6), and from within trial pits, to sample any materials which

Fig. 5.5 Trial pit excavation, using a tracked excavator to examine fill material. Vegetation can flourish on contaminated sites; buddleias in particular are quite common.

appear not to conform to the general nature of the ground. When the site investigation is being designed, it is essential that an anticipated testing programme is formulated and appropriate sample sizes selected for each material to be sampled. It should also be borne in mind that the testing programme and sampling may need to be refined as the investigation proceeds.

Fig. 5.6 Sampling illegally tipped chemicals of unknown origin can be extremely time consuming and costly. (Source: AEA Technology plc.)

Health and safety regulations must be adhered to, especially when taking samples from trial pits and trenches, which may need to be shored up if the sampling method requires the investigator to enter the pit or trench. All data obtained during the investigation must be accurately recorded and in a manner that can be understood later. If this is not done, the value of the entire investigation will be seriously reduced. The sampling method must ensure that material of interest is sampled, which includes any contaminants and the background media, and that the sample remains stable until analysed. The state of the sample must also be compatible with the method of analysis to be used.

Lord (1987), McEntee (1991), Smith (1991) and Hobson (1993), provide a comprehensive review of analytical techniques which may be used for the testing of potential contaminants. Analysis may take place both on-site and in the laboratory, and the location of testing will quite often be determined by site-specific circumstances. For example, on-site testing may be required:

(a) To support health and safety remedial measures by indicating the presence say of toxic vapours or acidic liquids etc.

(b) Because immediate measurement of contaminant is the only way to quantify its concentration, i.e. because of its instability, volatility etc.

(c) To speed up analysis of site materials, i.e. by having immediate analytical response.

(d) To reduce the costs of analysis, i.e. by avoiding transport costs.

(Lord, 1987, p. 89)

Throughout all stages of the site investigation quality control is of the utmost importance.

'The methods and techniques used must be standardised so that reproducible results are obtained both between sites and within the same site; reference to published sampling and analytical protocols and the use of NAMAS (National Measurements Accreditation Service) accredited laboratories will help to ensure these requirements are met.'

(Welsh Development Agency, 1993, p. 3.17).

Supplementary investigation

Good planning and working practices during the main investigation will almost certainly reduce the likelihood of a supplementary investigation being required, but logistical and phasing constraints may dictate that further work is undertaken. The extent of any supplementary work will be site specific and may arise as the result of the discovery of contaminants, during laboratory analysis, which were not previously expected. It may also be that part of the site was unavailable during the main investigation because it was still operational or in another ownership, although it should normally be possible to allow for this type of situation through phasing of the main investigation.

Any supplementary investigation must be subject to the same quality and safety standards as the main investigation, and may comprise some or all of the same types of works carried out in the main investigation. In situations where supplementary investigations are unavoidable, the additional work should be specifically targeted, for example with the objective of obtaining further information about a specific contaminant or to investigate a particular area of the site in more detail.

Supplementary investigations such as obtaining larger samples of contaminants and media, may also be required in order to assist in the design and selection of remedial works. They may also involve pilot studies of treatment processes, or in-situ testing of ground bearing capacities (see McEntee, 1991).

The report

The outcome of the investigative process should be a report which is readily understandable by the 'non-technical' client, the other members of the professional team and the appropriate regulatory authorities. A high standard of presentation is therefore important and the report should describe the various stages of the work undertaken, together with the findings obtained and any assumptions which may have been made.

Within the constraints of the site and available information, the report should indicate the location of those parts of the site affected by contamination and identify the nature of those contaminants. Potential pathways and targets should be described and the report should clearly define the options available to the client. The availability of contaminants, relative to actual or possible targets, should be considered. Perceived risks should be evaluated, and when it is noted during the investigation that environmental harm is still occurring, recommendations should be made in respect of immediate actions required to prevent further harm.

Plans should be included in the report which clearly detail the work which has been undertaken, differentiating between trial pits, trench excavations, boreholes and other forms of invasive work. The locations of all sampling points should be shown. Sampling criteria adopted by the site investigator should be stated, together with the selection criteria used for sample analysis. This is especially important when not all of the samples taken from the site are subjected to chemical analysis, or where some samples are only tested for specific contaminants, for example Total Petroleum Hydrocarbons (TPHs).

Ideally the report should include a plan which indicates the spatial extent of any contamination found on the site, distinguishing between contaminants. Sketch sections, showing any filled areas and the dispersion of contaminants in the soil, may also be appropriate.

The report should conclude with firm recommendations, regardless of whether or not immediate redevelopment is proposed, and advice in respect of future monitoring. An executive summary should be provided, together with a table of contents, a schedule of documents consulted and a bibliography.

Checklist

Site investigation

- Check whether any site investigation work has been undertaken.
- Decide whether existing site investigation information is sufficiently comprehensive and whether it is still relevant.
- Consider whether adequate technical expertise is available within the existing team, or if specialist consultancy advice will be required.
- What specific objectives need to be set for the site investigation?
- Find out if any other form of investigation, for example geotechnical, is proposed to be undertaken at the same time as the soil contamination investigation.
- Check the records of the site owner or operator for any relevant information.

- Check whether or not it will be possible to gain access to the entire site for the duration of the main investigation.
- Consider whether the site investigation proposals provide for an adequate degree of invasive work to ensure a reasonable chance of encountering any contamination which may be present.

Chapter 6
The Treatment of Contaminated Soil

The purpose of this chapter is to consider the options available to an intending developer and to discuss a number of soil treatment methods currently available or being developed in the United Kingdom. The suitability of different soil treatment methods in preparing contaminated land for redevelopment will also be considered. It is not intended as a detailed critique of current technologies but is intended as an overview and a discussion as to the suitability of the processes for redevelopment purposes. For a more detailed discussion of soil treatment methods, readers are referred to Martin and Bardos, 1996.

It is unlikely that the selection of a suitable treatment method will be a straightforward decision and many different issues will probably have to be considered (Figure 6.1). The factors which will influence the decision making process in the choice of remedial strategy and design, may be grouped under nine category headings as shown in Box 6.1.

It is likely that in selecting a treatment method or methods for a site, the developer will have to consider the available options in terms of their appropriateness under the nine categories listed in Box 6.1 and these may have markedly different effects on the final decision.

Selection of available options

Any urban renewal project will almost certainly bring with it a multiplicity of problems. It should always go without saying that

Fig. 6.1   Is it worth redeveloping or not? The selection of appropriate remediation methods will have a significant impact on the viability of a redevelopment project.

Box 6.1   Factors affecting the decision making process.

> **Legal**   This would include international, national and local legislation, as well as any legal requirements as to 'clean-up' standards. Town planning conditions and contractual obligations, and issues such as waste disposal and health and safety requirements would also be included in this category.
>
> **Political**   Which would include present and future government policies, together with public and 'corporate' perceptions. The speed of any response, as well as any possible criminal or civil liabilities, would have to be taken into consideration. The timing of redevelopment, its end use, and its phasing relative to other activities on and around the site would be of significant importance, as too would be the selection of treatment methods.
>
> **Commercial**   The value of land before and after treatment would be of the greatest importance to any intending developer and may have a direct influence on the selection of treatment methods, with 'high' technology being compared to 'low' technology methods, especially if any relatively untried methods are to be considered. Possible fluctuations in value would also have to be considered. The specification of any 'clean-up' requirements and the volumes of materials requiring treatment are major factors in determining commercial viability. The type of contract and the availability of collateral warranties, or guarantees from contractors must be considered, together with the time available to undertake the work and the physical space available. If material is to be removed from site for disposal, transport and landfilling or off-site treatment, costs need to be taken into account. Cash flow requirements and the likelihood of commercial success are of over-riding importance to the project.

Box 6.1 *Continued.*

Geographic The proximity of the site to domestic dwellings and other 'sensitive' structures, such as hospitals, will need to be considered. Ease of access to the site is important, especially if the remediation option calls for the removal of large volumes of material through potentially sensitive areas. The presence of any other polluted sites in the vicinity must be taken into account.

Environmental The proximity of the site to an aquifer or other controlled waters; these may not be polluted at present but may be placed at risk during the remediation works. The hydrogeology of the site and its surroundings, together with any nearby extraction points will need to be considered, as too will local weather conditions.

Engineering Existing groundwater levels, whether a producing aquifer or not, and the soil type, especially its homogeneity, may directly influence the selection of suitable treatment methods. The volumes of materials to be treated may rule out some treatment methods as uneconomic, either because there is insufficient material to justify setting up costs, or because the volumes are too great to be handled with available plant or by currently developed processes, within the timescale allowed. The availability of plant and equipment may also exclude some treatment methods.

Health and Safety The toxicity of the contaminants and any side effects of the proposed treatment method(s), including noise, dust, vibration and odour, will be a primary concern. The presence of any underground or overhead services will need to be taken into account, as well as the handling requirements of the materials, including special clothing and equipment.

Managerial The availability of suitably experienced remediation companies and the ease with which the project can be managed will need to be considered. Quality control and assurance procedures will need to be established and agreed with the appropriate regulatory authorities.

Technical The limitations of treatment methods and their application will need to be assessed, as too will the specification of treatment criteria and analytical methods. The availability of proven methods will need to be compared with new technologies and confidence limits defined. Treatment monitoring will have to be specified, with the objective of producing an auditable report of the works undertaken.

Source: based on Ellis (1992)

when contemplating the redevelopment of a site which has previously been used for some other purpose, great care should be taken so as to overcome any problems which may remain hidden from sight. Fleming (1991, p. 1) observed that in an industrialised community such as Europe, 'much of the land used for redevelopment has a history of previous uses' and he went on to point out that 'the state of such land is often so poor as to be unsuitable for continued use or re-use without major land engineering works'. The cost of such works will, in very many instances, have a significant impact upon the viability of a redevelopment project. 'Such costs may be far in excess of the reclaimed value of the land and a potentially successful urban regeneration project may be tipped from profit into substantial loss.' (Syms, 1993, p. 307)

In the absence of public sector grants and the unwillingness, or inability, of the polluter to meet the cost of soil remediation, the high costs associated with reclaiming contaminated sites may simply result in ever increasing areas of industrial dereliction and eyesores across the landscape of the United Kingdom. According to Haughton and Hunter (1994), 'there is evidence that environmental degradation may be a key contributory element in instigating and maintaining a spiral of urban decline, influencing the investment intentions of industrialists'. The authors also expressed the view that, 'the legacy of environmental external costs such as contaminated land and derelict buildings imposes further costs on those attempting to break out of the downward spiral of urban change, whether through reindustrialisation or residential, leisure or commercial usage.' (Haughton and Hunter, 1994, p. 59).

Before a decision can be taken in respect of site options, investigation work needs to be undertaken and a risk assessment prepared, so as to ensure that contaminants are safely contained and are not likely to present an environmental hazard in the future. A range of options should be considered, perhaps from doing nothing, except possibly monitoring the situation, up to a full remediation programme aimed at making the site suitable for any future uses which may be envisaged.

When considering a 'do nothing' approach, it may be found that the hazard risks are such that it is not safe to leave the site in its untreated state and that some work of partial treatment or containment is required. The 'do nothing' option should not therefore be regarded as a 'no cost' option. Such measures may fall short of returning the site to a developable state, at least in the short term. Bardos (1993b) has considered the process constraints on innovative soil treatment technologies and Bardos and van Veen (1995) have studied 'extensive' treatment methods which are discussed later in this chapter.

Assuming that the 'do nothing' approach is unacceptable then the options available to a developer or landowner seeking to extract an economic return from a contaminated site may be either:

(1) excavate and remove the contaminated material for safe containment on or off the site or for treatment, or
(2) leave the contamination where it is and contain or treat it in-situ.

In order to be able to decide which of these options is most appropriate and then to identify the technical aspects of any possible treatments, it is necessary to consider the factors set out in Box 6.2.

Box 6.2 Factors to be considered when selecting remedial measures for contaminated sites.

- present and intended topography and relation of site levels to surrounding areas, roads, etc.
- adjacent land areas (e.g. proximity of buildings and current and future uses)
- surface drainage, adjacent water courses, groundwater levels and movement, underlying aquifers
- propensity of site for flooding, etc.
- location of existing services
- maximum depth of excavation required for services or foundations (major services, especially sewers, usually have to be installed at considerable depths and this inevitably means digging into the contaminated materials even if all the other work can be kept within any clean cover material laid over the site)
- the consequences of settlement within any imposed clean soil cover and settlement of the underlying ground due to imposed loads from cover or buildings, or for other reasons
- the safety of workers and neighbours during site works
- environmental impact of site works
- the significance of a future pollution incident on the site (e.g. acid spill)
- effect of building works (e.g. foundations and services) on any completed reclamation works
- the significance of any future site works (e.g. extensions to buildings, repairs to services)
- possible or any planned future changes of land use
- safety of workers engaged in future site works
- need for long-term monitoring
- need for long-term maintenance
- who is going to be responsible in the long term for monitoring, maintenance and enforcement of any regulatory controls on what may be done on the site?

Source: Smith (1993, p. 27)

Removal and containment methods

Soil clean-up was defined by Armishaw et al (1992) 'as treatment to remove, stabilise or destroy contaminants'. Such treatments would not usually include landfill and containment systems, the methods most frequently used in the United Kingdom, as on their own these are not true clean-up techniques. Nevertheless, they are widely used and are of considerable importance in the context of redevelopment and value; they are therefore considered first.

The excavation of contaminated material should be regarded as a process which precedes the disposal or treatment of contaminants and not as a treatment method in itself. Post-excavation options may include:

- off-site disposal to a suitably licensed facility,
- controlled disposal of contaminated material on-site to a licensed depository or pursuant to a licensing exemption,
- treatment of the contaminants present in the excavated material to permit reuse or reduce disposal requirements.

(CIRIA, 1995, **V**, p. 1)

Excavation and disposal

For many intending developers, the first and most obvious solution will appear to be simply to excavate the contaminated material for deposition elsewhere. Redevelopment can then take place at the reduced level, or the excavated material may be replaced with clean imported fill, see Figure 6.2. 'Off-site disposal to a licensed tip has been by far the most widely used reclamation solution' (Beckett and Cairney, 1993, p. 74) but the authors noted that 'this situation is changing' due to the fact that 'suitably licensed tips are now scarcer and more expensive'.

The objective of the excavation and disposal method may be to either totally remove the contamination from the site, so far as this is physically possible, or to reduce the concentration of the contaminants and their accessibility to potential targets to an acceptable level of risk. In situations where the source and physical distribution of the contamination can be readily identified, say as the result of a

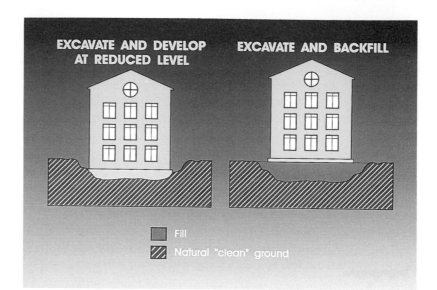

Fig. 6.2 Contaminated material may be removed and new buildings constructed at the lowered ground level or, alternatively, the excavated material may be replaced with clean fill so as to enable redevelopment at the original, or a new, ground level.

single polluting incident, total removal of the contaminated material may be the best solution and may also be financially viable. If however the contamination has been occurring over many years, is widespread throughout the site and is heterogeneous, total removal of the affected material may be both unnecessary and prohibitively expensive. The alternative solution may be to consider on-site disposal, but it should be noted that any on-site disposal operation must:

- be appropriately approved, in terms of planning permission and waste management licensing,
- comply with all waste regulation, planning, environmental and occupational health and water quality protection requirements specified in planning or licensing conditions or general legal requirements,
- be of a design and construction acceptable to the regulatory authorities,
- incorporate appropriate provision for monitoring and maintenance to ensure the long-term security of the deposit and the performance of any control measures.

(CIRIA, 1995, **V**, p. 3)

Failure either to comply with any of these requirements or to retain documentary evidence of such compliance, may result in a serious adverse impact on the value of the treated site and any subsequent redevelopment. The on-site disposal of contaminated material may also burden the developer, or a subsequent investor, with a long term monitoring obligation under a Waste Management Licence. This too may have an impact on the value of the site and its future as an investment.

A detailed site investigation and accurate classification of the in-ground materials can achieve significant reductions in disposal costs by facilitating the accurate identification of material for disposal. It may often be possible to identify visually the more contaminated materials and to separate them from less contaminated, or inert, materials when a site is excavated. The most heavily contaminated material which will attract the highest tipping charges when disposed of elsewhere, can be transported separately from that which is affected to a lesser degree, thus reducing the cost of site reclamation. Inert and slightly contaminated material may then be re-used on site, as demonstrated in some of the case studies described in Chapters 10 and 11.

The new buildings may either be constructed at the reduced level, or alternatively the original site levels may be reinstated or new levels created through the import of material to fill the voids left by the removal of contaminated 'hot-spots'. The import of fill material brings additional risks and it is essential that the imported material is subjected to chemical analysis to ensure that it is clean or inert before it is placed in the ground.

> 'The predictable decline in the amounts of off-site tipping has the significant advantage that it will remove the cheapest reclamation option and so make other newer techniques more cost effective. It also has the wider benefit of reducing the past policy of simply relocating environmental problems, and limiting the possible hazards when large volumes of contaminated soils are moved by road transport'
>
> (Beckett and Cairney, 1993, p. 74)

There are already signs that this is happening and that developers are less inclined towards the indiscriminate disposal of material to landfill.

Nevertheless, it is likely that the excavation and disposal method of treatment will play a significant part in the reclamation of contaminated land in the United Kingdom for the foreseeable future.

To some extent the use of landfills for the disposal of contaminated soil will be affected by the Landfill Tax, which came into effect on 1 October 1996. This tax is intended to discourage the indiscriminate use of landfills and to promote more ecologically favourable methods of waste disposal. Two rates of tax are applicable, a standard rate (in 1996) of £7.00 per tonne, which will cover most substances disposed of to landfills, and a lower rate of £2.00 per tonne for inert materials. Opponents of the new tax argue that, far from encouraging the use of ecologically desirable methods of waste disposal, the new tax will result in the increase of illegal waste disposal, or 'fly-tipping'.

So far as contaminated land is concerned, application can be made for an exemption certificate which if approved will exempt the contaminated material from the Landfill Tax. Developers will have to provide details about the contamination, and whether or not the activities leading to the pollution have ceased, together with details of the proposed development. A brief summary of the reason for reclamation is also required. The tax is administered by HM Customs and Excise, and if the application for an exemption certificate is refused, for example if the Customs and Excise experts consider that the contamination can be treated on site, an appeal can be made to a tribunal. Whether or not the new tax leads to further problems and litigation remains to be seen.

According to Armishaw et al, (1992, p. 31):

'The range of material types that are disposed of to landfill are generally considered to be very diverse and include the whole spectrum of soil types and particle sizes including construction and demolition debris. Similarly the range of contaminants that are landfilled is also broad, probably wider than for any other treatment method.'

Although not normally regarded as a treatment system, a properly designed landfill may facilitate attenuation of the contaminants, for example by adsorption or degradation, thereby reducing their toxicity. The principal mechanisms of attenuation are set out in Box 6.3.

Box 6.3   Principal types of attenuation mechanisms occurring in decomposing waste.

Process	Mechanism
Physical	Absorption, adsorption, filtration, dilution, dispersion
Chemical	Acid-base interactions, oxidation, reduction, precipitation, co-precipitation, ion-exchange, complex ion formation
Biological	Aerobic and anaerobic microbial degradation

Source: Department of the Environment (1986b)

Not all materials can be safely disposed of to landfills; polychlorinated biphenyls (PCBs) are very persistent in the environment and are unlikely to degrade through chemical or microbiological activity within an acceptable period of time. Cyanides are also unlikely to degrade when mixed with inert wastes, but have been found to degrade in the presence of organic material. Caution is also needed when disposing of arsenic, mercury, selenium, antimony, heavy metals, phenols, oily wastes and pesticides.

The problems associated with the disposal of contaminated soil to landfill may be divided into design/construction issues and long term uncertainties. From the developer's point of view, the ability to transfer any future problems to a third party in return for a pre-determined payment must be attractive, but the question must be asked as to whether or not the full legal liability has in fact been removed from the developer.

Clean cover and containment

'When large scale industrialization commenced and produced volumes of unwanted wastes, covering was often seen as the obvious answer to the problem. The wastes were tipped into whatever convenient hollows existed, capped with soil or hardcore, and usually became the foundations for later generations of the industrial activities.'

(Cairney, 1987, p. 144)

Whilst simple covers may have been adequate in terms of rendering the contaminants inaccessible to potential targets on or above the surface of the ground, they were unable to prevent migration of the contaminants sideways or downwards through the soil and especially did nothing to prevent the possibility of groundwater becoming contaminated. It follows, that if contaminants are to remain on site, close attention needs to be paid to the design of a suitable cover or containment system.

The design criteria for cover systems may be described in a few simple questions:

- What does a particular cover have to do?
- How long does it have to remain effective?
- What materials can be included in the cover?
- How can the design properties of these materials be defined?
- How is the design quantified?
- Have possible failure modes been checked and potential failure pathways been closed?
- How quickly can failure occur?
- Does the client clearly understand the design basis and any possible liabilities this could present?

(Cairney & Sharrock, 1993, p. 85)

The performance requirements of a particular cover will depend upon the proposed end use of the site and the mobility of the contaminants themselves. For example if all that is required is a clean site surface upon which no buildings are to be constructed and no services laid and the contaminants are limited in their mobility, then the design and specification of the cover is a simple matter. If, on the other hand, the intention is to prevent the upward migration of contaminants, then the design will have to include a capillary break layer. Similarly, if the intention is to prevent rainwater from reaching the contaminants, an impermeable barrier may need to be incorporated within the cover. The design of such covers requires a knowledge of the material properties of the cover materials and the contaminants to produce a satisfactory design.

Failure of the cover system is most likely to occur for one or more of the following six reasons:

- siltation of the pore voids in granular covers
- dessiccation, cracking of clayey covers

- chemical attack on a cover's materials
- settlement
- erosion
- human activities, whether permitted or not

In addition to the possible causes of failure listed above, other more site specific factors may need to be taken into account; according to Cairney and Sharrock (1993, p. 94) the most common of these would seem 'to arise from the location of buried services. If these are installed within the clean cover, later maintenance and repair should not pose a hazard' (Figure 6.3).

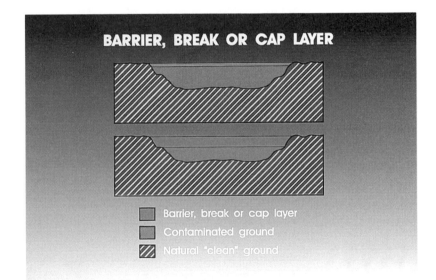

Fig. 6.3 A simple cover may be sufficient to prevent contaminants migrating to the surface of the site, but an increased depth of clean cover may be desirable to contain foundations and building services.

Sudden and catastrophic failure of a cover system is unlikely. Provided that the cover has been adequately designed and constructed it is unlikely to show signs of any failure for many years and even after failure it may be many months before the failure becomes apparent. The client, future users and investors in the property should be made aware that it is not a treatment system in itself (although some attenuation may occur) and the contaminants remain on the site in an untreated form.

Cover systems on their own are only of use where there is no risk of the contamination migrating in a sideways or a downwards direction. If migration is a possibility then it may be appropriate to incorporate a barrier system so as to ensure full containment or isolation of the contaminants (Figure 6.4).

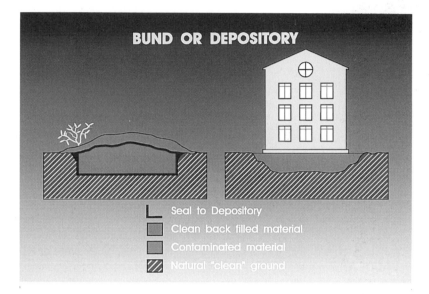

BUND OR DEPOSITORY

Seal to Depository
Clean back filled material
Contaminated material
Natural "clean" ground

Fig. 6.4 An alternative to off-site disposal may be the on-site containment of contaminants in a secure bund or depository. This may however have important valuation implications. A Waste Management Licence may be required and there may be Landfill Tax implications.

'In principle the containment system must completely surround the pollution source. That is there must be barriers above, below and around the source. For sites such as new landfills the barrier systems employed usually will be a combination of geomembranes, clay layers and drainage layers. For in-situ containment of existing contamination the most common procedure is some form of vertical barrier wall taken down to a natural geological aquiclude. The site may then be covered with a low permeability cover layer.'

(Jefferis, 1992, p. 59)

The ideal containment design would be one which ensured that no leakage of the contaminated material can occur but in reality this is an ideal which cannot be achieved or maintained. It may be necessary to consider three conceptual designs:

(a)   Design for total containment for a defined period. Thereafter no control.

(b)   Design for continuous controlled release to the environment.

(c)   Design for total containment with monitoring and built in procedures for recovery of the contained material or remedial if the containment fails.

(Jefferis, 1992, p. 59)

Many different forms of barrier system are currently available and their suitability will depend upon the nature of the contaminants to be contained as well as the ground in which they are to be installed. Several systems are listed in Box 6.4.

Box 6.4   Types of barrier systems.

Jet grouting – may be used to form both vertical and horizontal barriers by the injection of materials under pressure into pore spaces of permeable soils or rocks so as to create a barrier of low permeability.

Shallow cut-off walls – formed by excavating a narrow trench and inserting an impermeable membrane, which must reach an aquiclude.

Driven barriers – formed by driving steel sheet piles, or concrete or HDPE membrane elements into the ground.

Vibrated beam wall – a combination of the driven barrier and injected barrier methods.

Secant piling – often used in civil engineering to provide structural walls which also function as a cut-off, there may be problems in respect of the joint formation between the piles.

Slurry trench process – a trench filled with an appropriate fluid so that the trench can be kept open and excavated without collapse. The fluid must exert sufficient hydrostatic measure to maintain the stability of the trench and it must also not drain away into the ground to an unacceptable extent.

Treatment methods

Denner and Bentley (1991) provided an overview of clean-up technologies and, so far as process treatment methods are concerned, Armishaw et al (1992) and Bardos (1993a) have described five generic treatment categories. These categories were derived from the work into waste treatment processes which they had undertaken at Warren Spring Laboratory, a research laboratory formerly operated as an agency of the Department of Trade and Industry. It subsequently merged with the Atomic Energy Authority's laboratory at Harwell to form the National Environmental Technology Centre (NETCEN), now part of AEA Technology plc. The systems they identified were:

- Biological systems of soil treatment [which] depend on the biological transformation or mineralization of contaminants either to less toxic, more mobile forms or a form which is both mobile and less toxic. Biological processes can also be used to fix and accumulate contaminants in harvestable biomass.
- Chemical systems in soil treatment systems are used to destroy, fix or neutralize toxic compounds. Chemical processes do not necessarily destroy contaminants. Chemical processes of fixation have been grouped with solidification for convenience since solidification-based processes tend to be associated with stabilization processes and vice versa.
- Physical systems used in soil treatment are used to remove contaminants from the soil matrix, concentrating them in process residues requiring further treatment or safe disposal.
- Solidification systems are those which encapsulate the waste in a monolithic solid of high structural integrity. Solidification may or may not be accompanied by the destruction or stabilization of contaminants in the solidified mass.
- Thermal systems are those based on incineration, gasification, or pyrolysis at elevated temperatures.
    (Armishaw et al, 1992, pp. 27–28 and Bardos, 1993a, p. 37)

Within each of these generic categories there are numerous different types of treatment, some of which may be commercially available, whilst others are only at experimental or pilot study stages.

Biological systems

'Bioremediation is a process that uses soil's naturally occurring micro-organisms to decompose contaminants such as toxic or hazardous substances. Bioremediation works because most of the organic compounds that comprise hazardous wastes can be used as food by micro-organisms.'

(ENSR, 1992, p. 24)

The biological treatment of contaminated soils is primarily based on the actions of microbes to oxidise (metabolise) organic compounds and reduce them into their constituent parts, producing by-products such as cell matter, carbon dioxide, water and other inert materials. This may be caused by the action of a single micro-organism but more often will involve the interaction of two or more microbial species. Biodegradation can occur in a number of different ways but the success, or otherwise, of the treatment process will depend upon factors such as the chemical composition of the substance to be treated and the micro-organisms involved, as well as the chemical and physical environment within which they are located (for example, the environment may be either aerobic or anaerobic).

Not all contaminants are amenable to treatment by biological processes, although these are effective against a wide range of common contaminants provided that the correct conditions exist. Even some man-made (xenobiotic) compounds are amenable to treatment. It is therefore necessary to have a good understanding of the nature of the contaminants, their locations and concentrations before the appropriate biological treatment can be selected.

If the natural microbial community does not appear able to

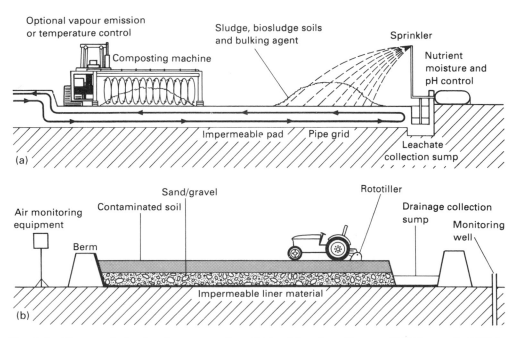

Fig. 6.5   Bioremediation by: (a) composting; (b) land farming. (Source: ENSR report, 1992.)

remove the site contaminants, it may be appropriate to investigate the feasibility of treating the site with non–indigenous/commercially available bacterial innoculants if biological treatment is still an option under consideration. Nutrients may also be added and it may be possible to modify the physical structure of the soil which will enhance the mass transfer of oxygen to the site of microbial activity.

Biological treatments can be undertaken *in situ* but for difficult soils, *ex-situ* methods may be preferred. The *in-situ* treatment of contaminated soil does not require excavation but may involve the addition of surfactants, or other agents, to water lying within or infiltrating the contaminant so as to increase its mobility. *Ex-situ* biological treatments, such as composting, require the excavation of the contaminated soil and its placement in a purpose designed treatment bed, where it may be mixed with a suitable bulking agent such as wood chips or sand, to aerate the material, and inoculated with water, nutrients and, if necessary, additional microbes (see Figure 6.5).

Chemical systems

Chemical treatment processes can alter hazardous constituents in waste streams to reduce their toxicity or mobility, or they may produce inert compounds from the original material. A wide range of chemical treatments may, in theory, be applied to the remediation of contaminated soil and these may be categorised according to the chemical processes involved, for example, oxidation, reduction, neutralisation, mobilisation, hydrolysis and polymerisation. Most chemical treatment processes require soil to be in a slurry form, or for the contaminants to be mobilised in a liquid medium such as groundwater, and they may therefore not be suitable for large scale use.

As with bioremediation, chemical treatments can be applied both *in situ* and *ex situ*. Although relatively few chemical processes have been used to clean up contaminated soils, they have been used more widely for cleaning of a wide range of other contaminated materials. Two chemical methods which have been used at hydrocarbon contaminated sites are:

- *in-situ* (chemical) oxidation
- ultraviolet–enhanced oxidation

(ENSR, 1992)

In some instances, chemical oxidants may be used to decompose or oxidise hydrocarbons in the subsurface. The process is similar to chemical burning and the oxidant is usually a dilute hydrogen peroxide solution, which is injected into the contamination through injection wells at carefully controlled rates. This method is beneficial where hydrocarbons are too highly concentrated, or are too toxic, for successful bioremediation.

Ultraviolet oxidation uses the injection of oxidants, usually hydrogen peroxide or ozone, either alone or together, to decompose the hydrocarbons chemically. The injected stream of material is passed through a bank of ultraviolet lamps to 'activate' the oxidisers. This very active solution rapidly attacks the hydrocarbons to produce carbon dioxide, water and chloride ions. Ultraviolet oxidation is only effective on clear aqueous streams but it is capable of destroying some chlorinated hydrocarbons. Pre-treatment may be needed in order to remove suspended solids, colloidal or other material which may plate the ultraviolet lamps, but a benefit of the system is that it does not produce any secondary waste streams. Other forms of chemical treatment include those listed in Box 6.5.

Box 6.5   Types of chemical treatment.

Reduction – the addition of chemical reducing agents, such as aluminium, sodium and zinc metals, alkaline polyethylene and glycol, which are then oxidised.

Chemical dechlorination – uses reduction reagents to cleave chlorine atoms from hazardous chlorinated molecules to leave less hazardous compounds, the process can be applied to liquid wastes, sludges and soils.

Extraction – includes techniques such as the use of organic solvents, supercritical extraction and metal extraction with acids.

Supercritical fluid extraction – a form of solvent extraction which uses highly compressed gases as the solvent, this requires the temperature and pressure of the solvent to be maintained close to its critical point so that the gas is in its liquid phase and able to dissolve the contaminant.

Electrochemical – has been used for the destruction of PCBs in contaminated fluids and involves mixing the contaminated liquid with a conducting solution in an electrochemical operating at low temperature and low voltage, in the presence of a reagent.

Neutralisation – refers to the adjustment of soil or groundwater pH to an acceptable level (usually in the range pH 6 to 9) using dilute or weak acids or bases (Armishaw et al, 1992).

Precipitation – used to render contaminants insoluble and thus facilitate their removal from liquids, such as groundwater, by physical processes, for example flocculation, sedimentation or filtration.

Physical systems

> 'Physical processes do not destroy contaminants and can therefore be considered as first-stage treatment techniques in a multi-stage process; the final step being the destruction or stabilisation of the contaminant'
>
> (Armishaw et al, 1992, p. 45)

The objective of physical processing is to separate or isolate the contaminants from the uncontaminated host material, or to concentrate the contaminants, thereby reducing their bulk.

Perhaps the best known physical process is soil washing, which is one of the few rapid and relatively cheap contaminated soil treatment systems. The principle of a soil washing system is to:

- separate from the soil those particles containing the contaminants and so produce a concentrate, or
- transfer the contamination into an aqueous medium that can subsequently be treated using a sorbent or by precipitation.

(Pearl and Wood, 1994)

Much of the equipment used for soils washing originated in the minerals processing and metals extraction industries and is therefore widely available and has been well tested, albeit for other purposes. In view of its historical applications, soils washing does not fall into the category of developing or unproven technologies. Whether or not soils washing will be suitable to treat a particular contaminated soil will depend upon the extent to which it can reduce the bulk of the contaminated residues, leaving a smaller volume of material, with a more concentrated level of contamination, for further treatment or disposal.

> 'As a generalization, if soils washing is to prove cost effective on a given site, it should be possible to recover 70–90% of the mass of the feed material as cleaned, leaving 10–30% as contaminated residue.'
>
> (Boyle, 1993, p. 158)

The cleaned material can then be disposed of as uncontaminated, or can be returned to the development site for re-use. As a general rule, coarse, sandy soils or fill materials with a high proportion of gravel, ash or clinker are best suited to soils washing, as the contaminants tend to adhere to the finer particles of the soil (Figure 6.6). Therefore the process of washing the finer particles out of the coarser medium should result in maximisation of the recovery of cleaned material. 'If the recovery of cleaned product drops much below 70%, it is unlikely that the application of soils washing will be justified' (Boyle, 1993, p. 158). Other physical processes include those listed in Box 6.6.

Fig. 6.6   Soils washing plant in operation, best suited to sandy or coarse granular soils.

Box 6.6   Physical treatment methods.

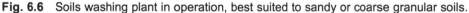

Ex-situ Steam Stripping – the compounds are evaporated by the steam and the vapours produced are treated by a number of downstream processes which separate the volatile contaminants from water, such as, steam condensation, water-immiscible oil separation and activated carbon adsorption.

Soil Vapour Extraction or Air Venting Techniques – may be used for the *in-situ* treatment of volatile or semi-volatile organic compounds (VOCs or SVCs). A series of pipes or wells is sunk into the contaminated ground. These are either connected to vacuum pumps, in which case the negative pressure gradients induce sub-surface air flows which volatise the contaminants, or hot air and steam are injected into the ground so as to volatise not only the VOCs but also many SVCs.

Electroremediation – can be applied to the clean-up of soils with a relatively high moisture content. A direct current (DC) is passed through an array of electrodes embedded in the soil and this induces contaminant flow in the pore water to the electrodes by a number of processes; electrolysis, electro-osmosis, and electrophoresis.

Solidification systems

In the context of waste management,

> 'the term "solidification" means the conversion of a liquid or a sludge into a solid with good physical characteristics (such as high compressive strength, low permeability etc.) so that the physical handling involved in disposal is made easy. However, solidification does not guarantee stabilization of the hazardous waste'.
>
> (Soundararajan, 1992, p. 160)

In order to effect treatment through the use of solidification it may be necessary to either accept that the material will still retain its hazardous properties, or to undertake some form of treatment or stabilisation as part of the solidification process. The entire phenomenon of organic stabilisation may be explained in the following two phases:

Phase 1: a binder is used with an organic compound (or compounds) in its matrix. The compound(s) would have a similar polarity to the contaminant, so that the organic waste is selectively dissolved in itself. Since the organic compound is part of the binder this may be called the stationary phase.

Phase 2: once the organic molecule has been retained in the stationary phase several chemical reactions, producing different kinds of chemical bonds, can be created between the binder and the waste molecule. A strong interaction between the binder and the waste molecule reduces the availability of the contaminant to the environment by leach processes.

Solidification systems are usually classified according to the binder system employed, as either inorganic or organic. The most important aspects of each system include the following techniques:

- Inorganic: cement based, pozzolan based, lime based, or based on liquid silicate or on vitrification. (A pozzolan is a substance that contains silicates or aluminosilicates that can react with lime and water to form stable, insoluble compounds which possess cementing properties.)

- Organic: thermoplastic microencapsulation, thermosetting and macroencapsulation.

(Armishaw et al, 1992)

The most commonly used binder systems are those which are cement based, often with cement being used in conjunction with pulverised fly ash (PFA) and sodium silicate solution. According to Armishaw et al (1992) lime based systems must always be used in conjunction with a pozzolan material and most contaminated soils could be expected to contain a significant proportion of pozzolan.

Vitrification involves heating the contaminated soil to temperatures exceeding 1000°C, at which point the inorganic toxic components are incorporated into a hard glass or ceramic-like substance, with any organic pollutants being incinerated. An effective emission control system is required to remove volatile toxic metals and any organic products formed during the process. At the time of the Armishaw report in 1992, both *in-situ* and *ex-situ* vitrification systems were being investigated. The same report also stated that 'organic binder systems have not been used for the remediation of contaminated soil as the process is very expensive, although a bench-scale test has been described' (Armishaw et al, 1992, p. 199).

Thermal systems

According to Smith (1987), there are two principal ways of using heat treatment to remove contaminants:

- removal of the contaminant by evaporation – either by direct heat transfer (convection or radiation) from heated air (or other gases), or an open flame, or by direct heat transfer,
- destruction of the contaminants by direct or indirect heating of the soil to an appropriate temperature.

(Smith, 1987, p. 130)

Thermal treatment methods are based upon the fact that all organic and inorganic contaminants have a definite vapour point (Bohm, 1992, p. 199). At this point the compound transforms from the solid to the gaseous state and, depending upon the energy input, chemical reactions take place. Oxidation will occur if oxygen is present but if it is not then vaporisation of the compounds will result. The residual compounds can be collected and either condensed out or incinerated.

Most thermal systems are applicable to a wide range of soil types, the main limitation being their associated handling systems, and installations for the thermal treatment of soil basically contains three process stages, as follows:

- **preliminary treatment** – to sort the soil so as to remove unsuitable material, such as metal parts, following which the soil is pulverised and any unsuitable soil portions removed,
- **thermal treatment** – when the soil is dried, the contaminants driven off and partially destroyed, following which the soil is cooled, with care being taken to recover heat for recycling,
- **exhaust air treatment and cleaning** – which guarantees that the pollutants are fully destroyed or removed and that emission control regulations are complied with.

Extensive treatments

For the most part, the treatment methods described in the previous section are intended to remediate the contaminated land in a relatively short period of time, so as to prepare the land for redevelopment, to prevent harm to potential targets or to mitigate harm which is actually occurring. Some of the treatments are still at the experimental stage, whilst others may involve such high levels of cost as to render them commercially unacceptable, especially if immediate redevelopment is not contemplated, only a restricted type of development is to be permitted, or when the 'do-nothing' option has been selected. In such circumstances it may be appropriate to select a long term or extensive form of treatment, in order to ameliorate the contaminative state of the site over a period of several years. The opportunities for using extensive technologies have been identified as including:

- the final cleaning up or 'polishing' of partially remediated sites whilst under redevelopment, so as to ensure continued reme- diation of the site during the lifetime of the project and hence increase its value,

- *in-situ* treatment of active industrial sites, so that they are remediated by the end of their expected useful life and before disposal of the site is envisaged,
- remediation of sites which have been dealt with by isolation or containment of contaminants and their monitoring, so that the possibility of harm from the site is reduced within the design lifetime of the containment measures,
- the treatment of sites that are too large to be cleaned economically using 'intensive' technologies, possibly because of low 'end values',
- managing or controlling contamination downstream from persistent and inaccessible sources, for example on land in other ownerships;
- the treatment of excavated material removed from contaminated sites.

(based on Bardos and van Veen, 1995, p. 1)

Research is being undertaken into the use of hyperaccumulator plants, active as opposed to passive containment barriers, the stimulation of natural on-site processes of attenuation and decay, and the promotion of biological activity through the use of plant roots. Extensive methods under consideration for use include composting or digestion for soil and waste co-treatment, *in-situ* precipitation of metal sulphides under anaerobic conditions and *in-situ* treatments contained in emplacements across aquifers or other drainage pathways. Technologies with the potential for use in extensive treatments include bioventing and various containment methods coupled with *in-situ* treatments.

Risk management should be the basis of any remediation strategy, but perhaps the key issue in the selection of an extensive treatment approach is that the lifetime of the contaminant will be extended, a factor that must be taken into account in the risk assessment exercise. It may therefore be necessary to contain the contaminated soil within a secure area, which may for example require its excavation and re-deposition within a bunded area formed with an impervious material such as clay or a geomembrane. A treatment technology which is gradual and exploits the natural processes occurring within the ground can then be employed to break down the contaminants. Monitoring of the containment area will be required, in order to ensure its security and to assess the effectiveness of the process.

Although extensive treatments may not be relevant in situations where immediate, or short term, redevelopment is desired, there may be a place for them within the development process, especially when sufficient land is available within the overall site for a containment area to be established. For example if it is intended that only part of a site will be redeveloped, with the remainder being allocated to public open space, it may be appropriate to remove contaminated soil from within the development site and establish a secure containment in the public open space area. Whether or not it will be possible to put the open space area to its intended use within the short to medium term will depend upon the nature of the contaminants and the type of treatment selected, but deferring the availability of the public open space may be preferable to disposing of the contaminated soil into landfill.

Combining treatment methods

Consideration of treatment methods in this chapter has tended to look at individual methods in isolation from each other, or in their generic groupings. In practice, however, it may be desirable, or even essential, to combine two or more treatment methods in order to secure adequate and cost effective site remediation.

For example, a soils washing technique may be preceded by a screening process, so as to reduce the quantity of material to be washed, and may be followed by a biological, thermal or chemical process, so as to either destroy the contaminants or change their characteristics. The remediation criteria may require that a 'clean-site' solution be provided under any new buildings but with the possibility of land being made available within the site area for the long term treatment of contaminated material. Similarly, a barrier system may be installed to protect a proposed development site from an adjoining landfill, with the landfill itself being treated with *in situ*, biological and venting methods, to prepare it for future development.

Combinations of technologies may also enable difficult or inac-cessible sites to be treated with minimal disturbance at ground level. Horizontal drilling techniques, developed for the oil industry, for example, can be used for monitoring landfill gas emissions and leachate dispersion (Figure 6.7a). The same method may be effective in treating contamination underneath buildings or process plants Figure 6.7b shows horizontal drilling being used to treat contamination underneath buildings through the use of either soil vapour extraction or bio-remediation. In suitable circumstances the same system can be used to provide containment of contaminants, through the installation of a slurry wall or pressure curtain (Figure 6.7c). The system can also be used, as shown in Figures 6.7 b&d, to pump and treat sub-surface contaminants, such as free phase product recovery of non-aqueous phase liquids (NAPLs) and dense non-aqueous phase liquids (DNAPLs) for ex-situ treatment.

The cost and effectiveness of treatments

The cost and effectiveness of available treatment options will have a direct impact on most, if not all, of the nine categories of factors which influence the choice of remedial strategy and design listed in Box 6.1 at the beginning of this chapter. Certainly, effectiveness of the treatment will be important when considering the legal implications, as the authorities responsible for ensuring compliance with the legislation will need to be convinced that satisfactory standards of remediation are achieved. Cost would, at first sight, seem to be less important from the legal viewpoint. However, the general principle laid down in the Environmental Protection Act 1990 is one of Best Available Techniques Not Entailing Excessive Cost (BATNEEC); therefore it would seem that cost is a relevant issue when considering treatment options. Similarly cost and effectiveness are important issues in the political context, as government and even international policies may rule out certain types of treatment.

Cost is perhaps the most important commercial issue but the effectiveness of the treatment should be of equal concern to the intending developer because unless the effectiveness of the selected option can be satisfactorily proven, the likelihood is that it will be unacceptable to future users of the site and funding institutions. Geographic conditions, especially where excessive noise, dust and transport movements might cause annoyance to nearby residents, may rule out certain types of treatment, even though they might be

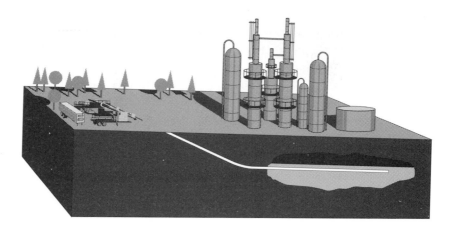

Fig. 6.7 (a) Sampling conduit. Evaluation and monitoring of present or future contamination conditions: soil gas monitoring; leachate sampling.

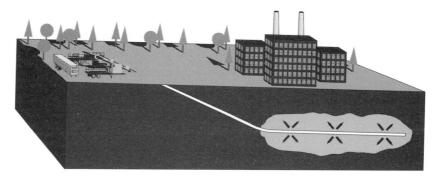

(b) *In situ* remediation. In-place (subsurface) treatment of contaminated soil or groundwater: soil vapour extraction; bioremediation.

well proven and cost effective. Environmental considerations may similarly mitigate against certain types of treatment if there are risks of air, water or noise pollution.

Some treatment options may be unsuited to the site ground conditions, or to the type of future development proposed. The potential adverse health effects and associated handling problems of the contaminants may exclude other forms of treatment. Finally, managerial and technical capabilities may remove other alternatives, regardless of their effectiveness or cost benefits, thereby reducing even further the number of treatment options remaining available for consideration.

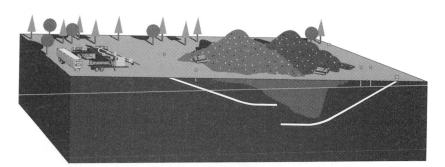

(c) Transport/pressure barrier. Prevention of contaminant migration: slurry walls; pressure curtain.

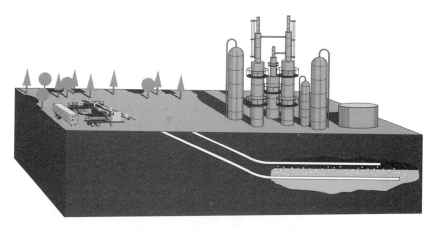

(d) Pump and treat. Subsurface contaminants brought to the surface for treatment: contaminated groundwater recovery; free-product recovery; NAPL and DNAPL recovery.
(Source: Drilex Inc., Houston, TX.)

The types of contaminants amenable to treatment by the various methods described in this chapter, and the most suitable soils for treatment are set out in Box 6.7. The chapter concludes with a discussion on the effectiveness and applicability for use in the United Kingdom of the different methods.

The costs associated with the excavation of contaminated material and its disposal to landfill in 1991 were in excess of £30/m³ for tipping costs alone but by 1996 the charges for tipping controlled wastes in, for example, north west England, had risen to between £40/m³ and £50/m³. These figures are based on information from landfill operators in November 1995. Significantly higher sums were

Box 6.7 Suitability of treatment methods according to media and contaminant types.

Treatment method	Media types	Contaminant types
Excavate and dispose of to landfill	All soil types	Most contaminants, with the exception of PCBs and perhaps cyanides. Care should be taken to prevent exceeding loading rates, especially for cyanides, phenolics, heavy metals, arsenic, mercury, selenium and antimony.
Clean cover and containment	All soil types, but liners and/or barriers required in permeable soils and rock.	Most contaminants, but subject to the same qualifications as for landfill. Some liners may also be prone to acid attack from contaminants and systems will need to be installed for the collection and disposal of leachate.
Bioremediation	Most soil types but a high content of natural organic material may assist the process.	Spent halogenated and non-halogenated solvents, compounds from the manufacture of chlorinated aliphatic hydrocarbons, wastes from the use and manufacture of phenols and benzenes, wastes from metal plating and cleaning industries, petro-chemical products and wastes.
Oxidation	Liquids only	Volatile Organic Compounds, organic pesticides, heavy metals, metalloids and cyanides.
Ultra-violet oxidation	Liquids only	Organic compounds.
Chemical reduction	Liquids and slurried soils	Organics including paraquat and PCBs, metals including chromium, selenium, lead, silver.
Chemical dechlorination	Liquids, sand, silt, clay, in sludges and soils.	Volatile halogenated hydrocarbons, PCBs, and organochlorine pesticides.
Chemical extraction	Liquids, sand, silt, clay	Organic and metal contaminants.
Supercritical fluid extraction	Sand, silt, clay, in soils and sludges	Polynuclear Aromatic Hydrocarbons, PCBs, DDT and VOCs.
Electrochemical	Liquids only	PCBs and metals.
Neutralisation	Liquids, sand, silt, clay	Organic, inorganic and metallic contaminants.

Box 6.7 *Continued.*

Treatment method	Media types	Contaminant types
Precipitation	Liquids, sand, silt, clay	Organic, inorganic and metallic contaminants.
Soils washing	Most soil types but more successful on coarse, sandy soils.	Heavy metals, PAHs, PCBs, cyanides, non-ferrous metals.
Steam stripping	All soils but best suited to water-unsaturated soils.	VOCs and some SVCs, volatile inorganics including hydrogen sulphide and ammonia.
Soil vapour extraction/air venting	Sand, silt and peat, best suited to water-unsaturated soils.	VOCs and SVCs, hydrocarbon mixtures including petrol, jet fuel, diesel, kerosene and heavy napthas.
Electro-remediation	Clays, peat and fine sand, can be used for soils with a relatively high water content.	Heavy metals, including arsenic, cadmium, cobalt, chromium, mercury, manganese, molybdenum, nickel, lead, antimony and zinc.
Solidification	Silt and clay, some methods may be effective on other soil types.	Organic and inorganic contaminants.
Thermal	Sand, silt, peat, clays present handling problems.	Organic and inorganic compounds.

Sources: Armishaw et al (1992), ENSR (1992); Pearl and Wood (1994)

being charged for some 'special wastes', which are wastes as defined in Section 62 of the Environmental Protection Act 1990. The total waste produced in the UK in 1995 was estimated to be about 402 million tonnes a year, of which about 140 million tonnes was 'controlled waste from domestic, industrial and commercial sources' (Murley, 1995, p. 206). Of the total amount of controlled waste, approximately 86% (120.4 million tonnes in 1995) was disposed of to landfill.

Excavation and transport costs have to be added to the tipping charges, together with the costs associated with both importing clean fill material, when this is required to replace the contaminated soil, and consolidation works needed to prepare the site for redevelopment. The total cost of site reclamation in 1996, by excavation and disposal, can amount to between £60/m^3 and £80/m^3 or, looked at another way, assuming that the depth of contamination is no more than one metre, £600 000 to £800 000 per hectare (£242 800 to £323 750 per acre).

Significant regional variations may be experienced in respect of this option, according to the availability, or otherwise, of suitable landfill sites. The cost of this option will also be greatly influenced by the distance between the site to be treated and the point of disposal, as this will determine the cost of transport.

The cost of a clean cover and containment solution will be subject to the influence of a number of factors, such as the extent to which barriers have to be constructed to the sides and underneath the containment area, and the availability of suitable material for cover, either on or in close vicinity to the site. The possible loss of developable site area has to be taken into account with this option and it would seem reasonable to assume that, at least for the time being, clean cover and containment will only be used in situations where it is more cost effective than disposal to landfill.

The effectiveness of bioremediation will depend upon the biodegradability of the contaminants, as well as the ability to stimulate and maintain microbial activity. The persistence of organic compounds in contaminated sites is an indication that site conditions do not support microbial activity and the inoculation of the site with bacteria will need careful research to ensure that the contaminants are fully degraded.

The estimated costs for biological remediation in the USA have been reported as being £17–£100/m^3 in 1994, using landfarming and in Germany, £70–£120/m^3 for the same process. 'Treatment duration is significantly affected by site-specific parameters. It has been reported that a typical treatment period is 2–5 years' (Martin and Bardos, 1996) but treatment periods may be much shorter, for example three months in the case of a hydrocarbon contaminated site in South Carolina, USA. *In-situ* bioremediation, using bioventing, in the USA has been found to cost between £31–£153/m^3, with a typical treatment duration being around 12 months.

The cost of chemical treatments would appear to be highly variable, depending upon the nature of the contaminants and the treatment method to be employed. For example, Armishaw et al (1992, p. 99) quoted process costs for the Ultrox (ultra-violet oxidation) process of between £0.04/m³, for slightly contaminated groundwater to £5–£14/m³, for highly contaminated industrial wastewaters; whereas the 1990 treatment costs for the KPEG (chemical dechlorination) process were estimated to range from £295/m³ to £763/m³ of soil, depending upon facility size.

The United States Environmental Protection Agency has supported a number of Demonstration Projects, intended to assess the suitability of proprietary treatment processes, some of which have been completed whilst others are ongoing. The current state of these programmes was summarised in a report *Superfund Innovative Technology Evaluation Program: Technology Profiles, Seventh Edition* (USEPA, 1994). One of the completed chemical process projects was CF Systems Corporation's *'Liquified Gas Solvent Extraction [LG-SX] Technology'*, which was found to be 90–98% efficient in the removal of PCBs from sediments at a cost of $150 to $450 per ton [£106 to £319 per tonne] (USEPA, 1994, pp. 48–49).

Boyle (1993) cited two examples where soils washing had been used to reduce the volumes of contaminated materials. In the first case, the cost of treating 300 000 m³ of contaminated soil was put at £11/m³ and in the second case the cost of treating 32 500 m³ was estimated at £14–50/m³. In both cases the treatment costs excluded on-site handling and the disposal of the contaminated residues. Boyle calculated that, in respect of the first example, unless the site could be treated by disposal to landfill or some other method for less than £15/m³ 'then soils washing will reduce overall costs. Once disposal or other treatment costs rise to £25/m³, the savings are considerable' [approximately 29% in respect of the quoted example] (Boyle, 1993, pp. 161–2). The 'break-even' figure in respect of the second example, comparing soils washing with disposal was between £10 and £13/m³.

The cost of *ex situ* treating 22 937 cubic metres (30 000 cubic yards) of waste material highly contaminated with hexavalent chromium by stabilization and solidification, was found to be '$73 per ton (£51–80 per tonne), including mobilization, labor, reagents and demobilization, but not disposal' (USEPA, 1994, pp. 22–23). By comparison, the destruction of PCBs using thermal desorption was estimated at $400 to $2000 per ton (£283 to £1419 per tonne) (USEPA, 1994, pp. 62–63).

The technologies available for the treatment of contaminated soil, and their associated costs, are changing on a daily basis. For several years the United States Environmental Protection Agency has operated a programme to evaluate soil treatments and is currently monitoring more than 200 methods at various stages of development. So far as the United Kingdom is concerned, it would seem that methods such as soils washing and bioremediation offer viable alternatives to landfill and containment options. Chemical and sta- bilisation/solidification methods may still be some way from acceptability, in terms of both cost and technological advancement, before they receive wide scale acceptance as part of the redevelop- ment process. Thermal processing costs would seem to be unac- ceptably high, except for very small volumes of highly toxic material, and public fears about emissions from mobile plants may well rule out the use of these methods for on-site clean-up purposes.

The selection of an appropriate methodology for the treatment of a contaminated site will depend upon both the cost and effectiveness of the treatment methods under consideration. Also of importance will be the impact of the remediation work on the post-treatment value of the site. Inappropriate site treatment, regardless of cost, may not produce any improvement in site value. Similarly, the environ- mental optimum may be so expensive as to significantly exceed any resultant improvement in value. In both of these situations there is no incentive for a developer to acquire and redevelop a contaminated site. It would also seem to be of little benefit to require a landowner to 'clean up' a contaminated site, regardless of legal requirements, if the cost is so onerous as to cause the financial collapse of that firm or individual.

Therefore both economic (value) and environmental considera- tions need to be taken into consideration in the selection of a treatment methodology, as part of the overall process of redeveloping a contaminated site. It is suggested that the decision making process be performed in accordance with Figure 6.8.

In the example in Figure 6.8, the cost of treatment is shown as being the same as the increase in site value but the change in site risk assessment only shows an improvement from 'very high hazard' to 'medium hazard.' This degree of improvement may well be accep- table if the site is to continue in some form of industrial use and the residual contamination is securely contained within the site. If, on the

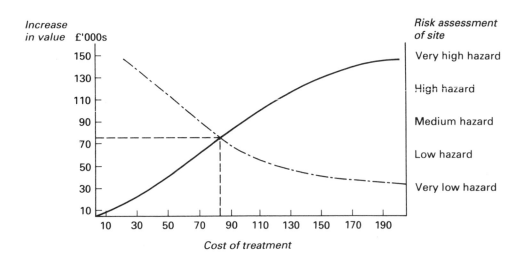

Fig. 6.8   The relationship between value, treatment costs and environmental improvement in the selection of soil treatment methods.

other hand, it is required that the risk associated with the site be further reduced to 'low hazard' or even 'very low hazard', then the increased cost involved will not produce a corresponding increase in value. It is argued that situations such as this will frequently occur in practice, leading to demands for planning consents for uses which permit higher values, or for the input of public sector funds in order to assist the process of site remediation and redevelopment.

Checklist

Excavation and containment checklist

- Can the contaminated material be treated on site, to reduce bulk or to render it less harmful?
- Check whether there is a suitable licensed landfill within reasonable travelling distance of the site.
- What licences and/or permits will be required for the proposed work?
- Ascertain whether any special site working conditions will be imposed or required, especially in relation to health and safety.

- Will the landowner be indemnified against any future liabilities, in respect of both the treated site and the landfill, once the contaminated material has been removed from the site?
- Consider whether the site can be made suitable for use through the installation of a suitably designed cover layer.
- If covering is an option, check whether any vertical or horizontal barriers (beneath the contaminated material) will be required to ensure containment.

Treatment methods checklist

- Check whether the site investigation revealed any signs of microbial activity in the contaminated material.
- Consider whether or not the contaminants on the site are amenable to treatment, as opposed to removal, either *in situ* or *ex situ*, and if suitable methods can be found, whether contractors and plant are available.
- Ascertain whether the treatment methods under consideration will destroy the contaminants, or render them inert, or whether they will simply either change their characteristics or reduce their bulk, leaving a residue for off-site disposal or tertiary treatment.
- Will the treatment methods under consideration be acceptable to end users, investors and potential mortgagees?

Chapter 7
Perceptions of Risk

The market for any class of property is made up of different actors, some of whom may interact. These actors may be performing a role of principal, as in the case of property developers, investors or owner occupiers (whether of residential, commercial, industrial or leisure premises); alternatively they may be market makers, such as surveyors, valuers and estate agents, advising on the value, or potential value, of real estate and acting in respect of its acquisition and disposal. So far as development projects are concerned, the providers of development finance, such as banks, building societies and insurance companies can have a major impact upon the market, as they control the supply of both short and long term finance. The market will also be influenced by actors such as architects, quantity surveyors and engineers in respect of the design and costing of buildings and civil engineering projects. Building contractors, sub-contractors and building material suppliers may have an indirect but important impact upon property markets, through the supply and demand of labour and materials.

The preferences of the various actors, in respect of matters such as location, age of property, building specification and many other variables, will influence an individual when considering the acquisition of a specific property, regardless of whether the proposed purchase is for occupation or investment. The same, or similar, variables will also influence the property developer, the estate agent and the property valuer. It is therefore essential to gain an understanding of the perceptions of property market actors in respect of land contamination and the treatment methods which might be used in order to overcome the problems associated with contamination.

Such an understanding facilitates the construction of a valuation model, to determine the extent to which the values of contaminated, or previously contaminated, properties may be affected under various circumstances. The purpose of the model is to assist in quantifying the cost of treating the contamination and the assessment of any stigma which may be attributable to the industrial activities performed on the site. This information is required both for asset valuation purposes and as part of the appraisal process, when the redevelopment of a contaminated site is under consideration.

Whilst it may be possible to produce a reasonable estimate of treatment costs, in the absence of transaction data in respect of industrial properties affected by similar types of contamination, the valuer will have to use his or her professional judgement in order to assess the extent to which a property has been affected by stigma. The valuer's professional judgement will be influenced by such factors as the past use or uses of the property and the degree of hazard associated with the contaminated soil at the date of valuation. If redevelopment is envisaged, the valuer's judgement will also be influenced by the proposed use of the site, the method or methods by which the contamination is to be treated and the anticipated degree of risk which will exist following treatment.

The studies described later in this chapter were designed and undertaken for the purpose of constructing the valuation model and gaining an understanding of the extent to which a valuer's perception of contaminated land may differ from that of other professionals involved in the redevelopment of such sites and from the perception of the population at large.

Perceptions of risk and uncertainty

Perceived risk is that risk which is experienced by the public in everyday life; it does not exist as an entity, independent of minds and cultures, waiting to be measured. Instead, risk is inherently subjective, invented by human beings to help us understand and cope with the dangers and uncertainties of life. There is no such thing as 'real risk' or 'objective risk' and the word 'hazard' has no meaning except in terms of human perceptions.

People form their own assessments of risk and it is possible that an individual's perception of risk, or even the wider public's perception, may be at variance with the objective assessments made of those same risks by scientists. A study by Thomas in 1981

'showed that the public does conceive risk issues in differentiated terms, taking into account several substantive dimensions of both risk and probable benefits. While such dimensions might well be specific to the risk issue in question, it does seem likely that both risks and probable benefits will form part of belief systems in most instances where risk acceptance, or otherwise, is an issue.'

(Thomas, 1981, p. 35)

The higher the perceived risk of a hazard, the more people will want to see its current risks reduced. The risk perceptions of 'experts', on the other hand, are not closely related to any of the various risk characteristics but are instead seen as being synonymous with expected annual mortality rates. Such differences in perception between 'experts' and the 'general public' may result in many conflicts about risk and when this occurs recitations of 'risk statistics', by so called 'experts', will do little to overcome people's fears.

Perceptions of risk will directly influence decision making processes, as individuals, organisations and governments all make decisions based on the perceived consequences of their actions. Some seemingly inevitable consequences may not be recognised by the decision maker. In addition, there may be gross misconceptions about the likelihood or magnitude of those consequences that are recognised, whilst other perceived consequences may be more imagined than real. In practice therefore, there may not be much overlap between the actual and the perceived potential outcomes.

The property development process is an activity which will be affected by the perceptions of individuals, organisations, and governments about the likely consequences of their actions, and the outcome of those perceptions will directly influence the financial viability of a development project. Redevelopment of land which has been affected by contamination is likely to be extremely sensitive to variations in perception of risk, and perceived risk will be influenced by a disinclination on the part of an individual to believe that a source of contamination is safe. The individual's perception of risk also varies with the nature of the cause of the contamination and whether or not the source might result in a catastrophic accident.

It is sometimes claimed that people perceive a risk to be less serious if they accept it voluntarily. Thus the discovery of a previously unknown landfill found to be generating landfill gas close to a housing development is likely to be perceived as a serious risk. If, however, the same development is situated in a low lying flood plain, the perception of risk from flooding is likely to be much lower than the risk from potentially explosive landfill gas. This is because the risks associated with flooding are voluntary whereas those associated with the landfill gas are involuntary.

The degree of familiarity with a hazard is another factor that is often thought to influence perceptions of risk and the level of 'perceived risk' associated with contamination will vary according to the level of familiarity with the particular contaminants. Given this assumption, it may be that residents living in an area dominated by an aluminium smelter which had been in operation for almost one hundred years would be unlikely to have a very high perception of the risks associated with contamination caused by the smelter. Research by Kinnard et al (1995) found that this had in fact been the case, until such time as the existence of contaminated soil in the neighbourhood of the smelter became publicly known. This was followed by closure of the smelter, the commencement of legal action by the owners of the affected properties and commencement of the soil treatment operations.

The smelter was situated in Tacoma County, Washington, USA and in a study of property transactions covering an eighteen year period spanning the closure of the smelter, Kinnard et al (1995) compared property values within the area immediately adjacent to the smelter (one and a half mile radius) with those in a control area more than two miles from the smelter. They found that there was no significant difference in values between the two areas, except following periods of high publicity, for example after initial discovery of the contamination, commencement of the legal action and the 'clean-up' operation, following each of which 'down-turns' in value were observed. This was in spite of the fact that there was no change in the actual hazards or contamination over the study period, leading the researchers to conclude that, at least in the United States, 'perceptions of potential buyers of residential properties about the character, extent and meaning of on–site soil contamination may not necessarily be informed and rational, but they are very real' (Kinnard et al, 1995, p. 11).

Slovic (1992, p. 118) reviewed several studies which had used questionnaires 'to ask people directly about their perceptions of risks and benefits and their expressed preferences for various kinds of risk/ benefit tradeoffs'. This approach appealed to Slovic and his fellow researchers for several reasons, including the ability to elicit current preferences and to consider many aspects of risk besides financial considerations and/or the numbers of persons to whom actual harm had been occasioned. A questionnaire approach also enabled data to be gathered for large numbers of activities and technologies, thus allowing the use of statistical methods to analyse the results.

A distinguishing feature of the work reviewed by Slovic (1992) was the use of a variety of psychometric scaling methods 'to produce quantitative measures of perceived risk, perceived benefit, and the other aspects of perceptions' (Slovic, 1992, p. 119). A number of generalisations were drawn by Petts and Eduljee (1994) in respect of risk, from the psychometric literature:

'● Perceived risk is greater for hazards whose adverse effects are considered to be involuntary, uncontrollable, unfamiliar, catastrophic, fatal, delayed and therefore present a threat to future generations, generated by man, and not offset by direct (to the individual) compensating benefits.
● These characteristics of risks are highly correlated with one another. For example, risks that are regarded as voluntary are also regarded as controllable and understandable (e.g. driving a car). Conversely, risks regarded as involuntary are often also regarded as potentially catastrophic and a threat to future generations. . . .
● Experts tend to apply equal weight to consequences and probabilities, whereas the public tend to put more weight on consequences.'

(Petts and Eduljee, 1994, p. 390)

In discussing the psychometric paradigm, Slovic stated that the results are dependent upon the hazards studied, the questions asked about those hazards, the types of persons questioned and the data analysis methods. He acknowledged that the use of psychometric studies does have limitations but studies using this approach have produced coherent and interesting results.

One aspect of the psychometric work undertaken by Slovic and his co-workers was to examine the role of perceptions in respect of environmental hazards and to compare the responses of laypeople with those of experts. They observed that:

'many of the qualitative risk characteristics that made up a hazard's profile were highly correlated with each other, across a wide range of hazards. For example, hazards rated as 'voluntary' tended also to be rated as 'controllable' and 'well-known'; hazards that appeared to threaten future generations tended also to be seen as having catastrophic potential, and so on.'

(Slovic, 1992, p. 121)

As a result of this research they classified the risks into two groups of factors; *known* or *dread risks* and *unknown risks* which they represented spatially to show the respective influences of the two groups of risks, see Figure 7.1. Most important is the *dread risk factor* (Factor 1), shown on the horizontal scale, with the result that the higher the hazard's score on this factor, the further to the right it will appear reflecting the higher level of perceived risk. The *unknown risks* (Factor 2), those perceived to be less catastrophic and unlikely to threaten future generations, are represented on the vertical scale and the nearer to the top a hazard's score appears, the higher the perceived level of risk attaching to that hazard.

Figure 7.2 presents in a spatial form the results of a psychometric study into the perceived unknown risks and dread risks of a number of every day activities and environmental issues. The risk effects of some of the activities and issues considered are only likely to manifest themselves on a personal basis, affecting only the individual and his or her immediate family. Other activities and issues are known, or may be perceived, to have much wider reaching impacts, with the ability to affect whole communities and the wider environment. A similar approach has been adopted in this book to assess the importance of land contamination when compared to other environmental issues.

The psychometric approach has direct relevance to the redevelopment of contaminated land as it enables comparisons to be made

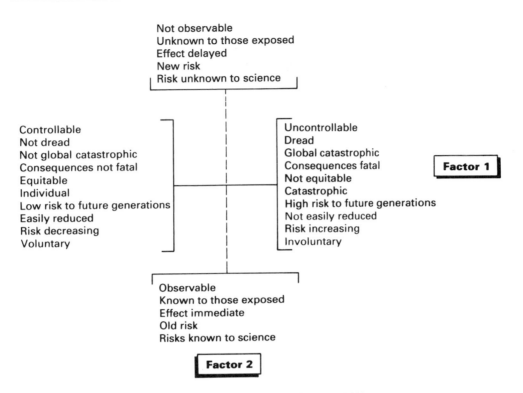

Fig. 7.1   Factors of known and unknown risks (after Slovic, 1992).

between the perceptions of members of the general public (the end users of development projects), valuation professionals and other professionals involved in the redevelopment process. If the psycho-metric approach is to be used in studying perceptions of risk associated with the redevelopment of contaminated land, then it is reasonable to assume that perceptions will vary according to factors such as the nature of the contaminants, their exposure route to potential targets, the nature of the targets (e.g. adults, children, animals, plants or buildings) and the proposed use of the site.

The results of any study will also depend upon the questions asked, for example if they relate only to land contamination or if they are framed in a wider environmental context, and whether they are directed to 'experts', representatives of government, or the 'general public', providing scope for varying degrees of uncertainty. One of the concerns, in respect of the research described in this book, was to avoid focusing too closely upon contaminated land issues and thus

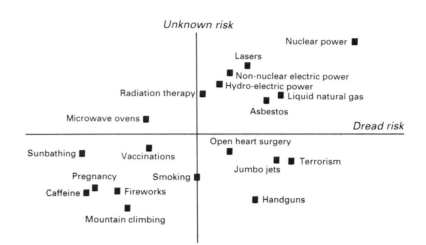

Fig. 7.2 Hazard locations on *unknown* and *dread risk* risk factors (after Slovic *et al.*, 1992).

'hype up' the responses. Care was therefore taken to place land contamination in a wider environmental context, so as not to distort the research findings.

Statisticians tend to see issues of risk and uncertainty in terms of probabilities, and assess expected outcomes accordingly. An alternative view, however, may be to define 'risk' events as being those whose probabilities are 'knowable' and to define events of 'uncertainty' as those that are 'unknowable'. Morgan and Henrion (1992) found this distinction unhelpful as 'it renders the theory of probability virtually inapplicable to real world decision making'.

Whilst such a distinction may be seen as unhelpful to the statistician, there is a link which will be found in the reality of property markets, where, as identified by both Mundy (1992a) and Kinnard et al (1995), seemingly irrational decisions are commonplace. Property market decisions may not, however, appear in any way irrational to the purchaser or occupier of the property in question. The decision to purchase a certain house at a price which exceeds that paid for a nearby property of similar type, may be determined by its orientation to the afternoon sun or the view from the living room window. Similarly the decision in respect of a commercial property may be influenced by proximity to a specific customer or supplier.

In the redevelopment of contaminated land, a developer's perception of risk may be based upon the best available technical and professional advice but it will be tempered by the uncertainties imposed as a result of the differing perceptions of other individuals, organisations or governments. The perceptions of those individuals, organisations and governments may be less well informed about the specific risks than the developer, who is promoting the project. Alternatively, they may have placed a different interpretation upon the same information and thus have arrived at a different conclusion. If the perceptions of any of the actors in the property market, such as future tenants, institutional investors or the local authority, differ from those of the developer, then a high degree of uncertainty is introduced into the project. The developer may find that development finance is not available or that, if finance can be obtained, the project is stigmatised by the previous use of the site and is unattractive to potential occupiers.

In order to reflect the influence of those actors beyond the control of the developer, the term 'risk' has been used in the book to represent those factors which are perceived by property market actors to affect directly the redevelopment of contaminated land and which are identifiable, although not necessarily quantifiable, such as the adequacy of site investigations or alternative forms of soil treatment. The term 'uncertainty' has been used in respect of factors which are not readily identifiable, and are invariably almost incapable of economic quantification, such as perceptions of possible future changes in environmental legislation and changes in the attitudes of end users.

Associated with risk perception is the concept of 'stigma' which is defined in the Oxford English Dictionary as a 'mark of disgrace or infamy, stain on one's good name' and as a 'definite characteristic of some disease'.

> 'The term stigma is taking on new uses, particularly with regard to real estate and its valuation. When a property has been contaminated with wastes or hazardous materials, it is becoming fashionable to suggest that such a property acquires a stigma.'
>
> (Elliot-Jones, 1995, p. 1)

This may manifest itself as having an impact on the individual's perception of the desirability or utility of a particular property, for its present or intended purpose, and hence affecting its value.

> 'In the world of "fair market value", what knowledgeable and prudent buyers and sellers do free from duress and compulsion is of

paramount importance. However, why they do the things they do can be of equal significance. Some reasons for behavior can be purely subjective. They may be based in half-truth or even fiction. Sometimes, as with the concern over asbestos, a legitimate issue can be raised to unreasonable proportions or, as in the case of environmentally blighted land or leaking landfills, the subjective fear may be well-grounded in scientifically measurable and objective fact. Even where an adverse effect on property value is apparent, it may be extremely difficult to describe, measure, and quantify.

... Public fear can and will affect market transactions so long as market participants actually share those fears.'

(Jaconetty, 1996, p. 63)

Where land is contaminated as a result of industrial activities, whether through the disposal of waste materials or as a result of accidental spillages, the effect of stigma in terms of public fear and reduced property values may extend beyond the boundaries of the site in which the contaminants are located.

'The stigmatization of environments has several important implications for hazardous waste management in general. First, it implies that, whatever the health risks associated with waste products, there are likely to be significant social and economic impacts on regions perceived as polluted, or as dumps. Second, it also gives additional importance to managing wastes so that stigmatizing incidents (even ones without significant health consequences) will not occur.'

(Slovic, 1992, p. 145)

To some extent, the impact of stigma may be heightened or reduced by the way in which the nature of the hazard and the risks involved are communicated to those individuals, or firms, who are most directly involved and to the wider public. This is especially relevant to the way in which the British government handled the proposed registers of potentially contaminated sites. Whilst the government and its advisers may have genuinely believed that 'it is better for everyone concerned to be aware of possible contamination' (DoE, 1991a, p. 11), the manner in which it was expressed in the consultation paper engendered widespread apprehension amongst those most directly concerned, including valuers, developers, financiers and investors. Media attention then ensured that the proposed registers were presented to the wider public in a way which was not intended by government.

According to Dr Judith Petts,

> 'The communication of information is an inherent and critical component of the contaminated land risk management system. The communication pathways are not just from authority to affected public, but form a complex web of pathways with information flowing within and between multiple parties and interests (authorities, consultants, advisory agencies, landowners/ site users, financial institutions, local communities, the media and doctors). As complexity increases in any communication system so does the inherent potential for distortion, inaccuracies, over-simplification and disagreement.'

(Petts, 1994, p178)

'Thinking clearly about risk is difficult. Unfortunately, it is also necessary.' (Slovic et al, 1992, p. 478) Where the health and lives of individuals and their families are concerned, the communication of information about risks associated with land contamination is fraught with problems. A statement to the effect that the likelihood of contracting cancer from the hazardous materials contained on a site is less than 10^{-6} is unlikely to be given much credence if a child living near to the site is dying of leukaemia. Local perceptions are more likely to outweigh the opinions of experts and will probably be given far greater prominence in the local press.

Communicating about risk in an adequate manner means finding cogent ways of presenting complex, technical material. This task is made especially difficult as the material to be communicated is often shrouded in uncertainty but, it has to be admitted, in the emotive situations which often surround land contamination, the most carefully thought out and sympathetically worded presentation may still not succeed in calming the fears of local residents.

Information provided on contaminated sites must be as comprehensive as possible. The providers of information must be sensitive to the hazards which are likely to be of concern and where information could, as a result, be misinterpreted. They should not attempt to conceal important facts and these should be presented to those people and organisations most directly concerned as early as possible. This can cause problems, for example, presenting information on potential contamination in advance of a site investigation will undoubtedly result in the public being provided with an incomplete picture, but to delay until after the site investigation has been completed is likely to result in inaccurate rumours being generated once neighbours observe investigative activity on the site. It may therefore be appropriate to communicate information through a series of public meetings, as work progresses, and to encourage the involvement of local residents by taking heed of information which they may have to offer in respect of the site.

Professional perceptions of risk

The values ascribed to contaminated properties and their development potential will be influenced by the valuer's individual perception of land contamination issues. That perception will be affected by a number of factors, including personal experience, education, training and press reports. Government policies in respect of liabilities for the registration and treatment of contaminated sites will also influence the perceptions of valuers and of their clients, the property developers and investors. Conversely, as was demonstrated by the response to the registration proposals contained in Section 143 of the Environment Act 1990, the perceptions and reactions of property market actors concerning adverse impacts may be so strong as to result in a complete re-evaluation of Government policies. Perceptions and policies are therefore linked and have the potential to impact upon each other, with resultant implications for valuation and the redevelopment of contaminated land.

Faced with a lack of certainty over Government legislation and only limited professional guidance, valuers and developers have approached the task of preparing contaminated land valuations with a great deal of caution and have tended to adopt one of three approaches:

- to prepare valuations of affected land only when supplied with reports prepared by environmental and engineering consultants detailing the nature of the contamination and the estimated cost to treat,

- to value on the stated assumption that no contamination is present on the site (even if contamination is known to exist),
- to decline the instruction, usually on the basis that the valuer concerned does not hold professional indemnity insurance for environmental work.

The first approach is not always practical, although possibly desirable, especially if the existing use is to continue and the valuation is required for security or asset purposes, whilst the second approach does not reflect actual circumstances and the final course of action deprives the valuer of possible income.

The perceptions of professionals involved in the valuation and redevelopment of contaminated land were studied between January 1994 and March 1996, as part of a wider research project (Syms 1996). The purpose of the research was to assess the extent to which values may be affected by perceived risks. The research into professional perceptions involved 130 members of different professions and 50 individuals in non–property related occupations.

The research was conducted in three phases, as follows:

Phase 1   A questionnaire survey of professionals involved in valuation, property development, engineering and architectural design, town planning, development finance and other related professions. This survey was undertaken at the beginning of 1994, after the Section 143 registers proposal had been withdrawn and the first valuation guidance had been published.

Phase 2   An interview survey of experienced real estate valuers representing national and regional surveying firms practising in north west England. The interviews were conducted in September 1994, following publication of the consultation paper *Paying for our Past* but before publication of the outcome and conclusions from the Government's review.

Phase 3   A questionnaire survey undertaken at the beginning of 1996, more than six months after the Environment Act received Royal Assent but before any of its provisions relating to contaminated land were implemented. As with the Phase 1 questionnaire, this survey involved a wide range of property professionals. Members of the general public were also involved for part of the survey.

The first phase of the research comprised a questionnaire survey, in which the respondents were asked to indicate their perceptions as to the extent to which different classes of actors would expect post-development values/desirability to be affected, if at all, in respect of a hypothetical former industrial site. The site was to be redeveloped for one of five alternative uses, under four different remediation scenarios. Post-remediation options for use of the site included residential estate development, business park development, industrial estate development, a retail park and an undefined leisure use. Remediation options included excavation and total removal of contaminated material (a 'low' technology approach, referred to as Scenario 1), removal of contaminated 'hot-spots' and the retention of remaining contamination on site using 'clean cover and containment' ('low' to 'medium' technology, Scenario 2), physical processing of the contaminated material using a 'soils washing process' ('medium' technology, Scenario 3) and 'high technology processes' (Scenario 4), such as chemical and biological treatments. The results for all of the end-use and treatment scenarios is summarised in Box 7.1.

The second phase of the perceptions study took the form of an interview survey of valuation surveyors, who all occupied senior positions in national or regional firms, or were sole principals with many years valuation experience. The interviews dealt with a number of aspects concerning contaminated land, including individual approaches to the task of valuation, the extent to which Government and the professional bodies should take the lead in both redevelopment and valuation, and the adjustment which they would make for the 'stigma' effect of contamination, both before and after remediation.

Part of the interview survey addressed the interviewees' perceptions of impact on values, but unlike the earlier phase of the research, no treatment methods or future uses were suggested for the contaminated site. The valuers were asked only to assess the impact on value according to five levels of hazard classification. The results are summarised in Box 7.2.

Several of the interviewees questioned the appropriateness of treating a site with a 'very high hazard' classification if, after treatment the hazard classification was unchanged. In an ideal situation the objective of treatment should be to reduce the hazard level of the site by at least one or two classes, resulting in 'very low' and 'low hazard'

Box 7.1   Perceived acceptability of alternative treatment scenarios in respect of different end-use options.

Treatment methods under consideration	Perceived acceptability and expected impact on value, according to proposed end use
Scenario 1 Excavation of contaminated material, so far as this can be determined, removal to landfill and backfilling with clean material, consolidated in layers.	Considered to be acceptable to all actors for the full range of future uses under consideration. Less than 5% perceived impact on value. Up to one third of respondents considered that this method could produce a value more than 5% greater than for a comparable 'greenfield' site, due to the fact that any naturally occurring abnormalities would have been removed as part of the treatment process.
Scenario 2 The removal of contaminated hotspots and regrading of remaining contaminated material to an agreed sub-base level and the import of clean cover material.	Considered to be acceptable to most actors for all the end uses, with less than 5% impact on value. Some concern in respect of investor and occupier reactions for residential use, with a perceived 6–10% impact on value/desirability. A similar perception of impact in respect of investors in business park developments.
Scenario 3 The on-site screening of contaminated material and subsequent treatment in a soils wash so as to reduce contamination below ICRCL[1] trigger levels.	Considered to be acceptable in respect of all uses, with only a 6–10% reduction in value perceived for developers, investors, tenants and residential occupiers. A change of less than 5% in value/desirability expected for workers, shoppers and other users.
Scenario 4 The on site treatment of containments, using bio-remediation or chemical methods as appropriate, so as to reduce residual contamination below ICRCL trigger levels.	Less acceptable for residential developments than the other three methods, with a 6–10% reduction in value expected for developers and building societies, and a reduction of 11–25% for housing associations and occupiers. A perceived reduction in value/desirability of 11–25% in respect of business park, retail park and leisure investors. For all other actors in respect of the non-residential uses, a perceived impact of less than 10% of value.

[1] ICRCL, the Interdepartmental Committee on the Redevelopment of Contaminated Land, a government body with secretariat provided by the Department of the Environment.

Box 7.2 Perceived impact before and after treatment.

Hazard classification	Before remediation	After remediation
Very low hazard Contamination below ICRCL trigger levels, unlikely to be harmful to humans, animals, plants, structures or the environment.	Reduction of 3.71%	Reduction of 1.90%
Low hazard Some contamination, possibly phytotoxic[1] but unlikely to be harmful if contained below a cover layer.	Reduction of 8.51%	Reduction of 5.75%
Medium hazard Contamination well in excess of trigger levels, possibly harmful to structures or services but unlikely to cause harm to human or animals, except through prolonged exposure. Treatment necessary.	Reduction of 22.43%	Reduction of 9.90%
High hazard Contamination levels likely to cause harm to persons and/or property, with high levels of toxicity or other harmful substances. Comprehensive remediation required.	Reduction of 58.19%	Reduction of 15.10%
Very high hazard Sites requiring decontamination under stringent controls, contaminants likely to cause harm even from short term exposure. Must be removed or treated before development or occupation.	Reduction of 90.38%	Reduction of 53.90%

[1] Phytotoxic, harmful to plant life.

classified sites being suitable for residential end use, with 'low' and possibly 'medium hazard' sites being suitable for commercial and industrial uses. For some 'very high hazard' sites it may not be possible to achieve such an outcome if, for example, the contaminants are to be retained on site in a secure containment. In cases such as this the purpose of the soil treatment may be to render the site safe for continuation of the existing use.

The final phase of the perceptions research, undertaken in early 1996, adopted a psychometric approach to environmental perceptions. This was intended to place contaminated land in context with other environmental issues and to facilitate a comparison between the perceptions of the two expert groups and a non-expert population. The respondents and interviewees involved in this part of the study were divided into three groups: the 'valuers' group, valuers and development surveyors; the 'non-valuers' group, non-valuation experts, including engineers, environmental scientists, architects and property lawyers; and a 'general population' group of individuals not having professional connections with property valuation or development.

A total of twenty environmental issues were selected for this study, comprising a mix of property and non-property related issues. These were carefully chosen to represent ordinary, everyday concerns and avoided 'catastrophic' type concerns, such as earthquakes and nuclear accidents. The respondents were asked to indicate their perception of risk in respect of the *known* risks, those that are well researched or publicised, in respect of each of the issues, together with their perceptions of the *unknown* risks, or *uncertainties*, using the five levels of hazard classification, 'very low' to 'very high' as used in the interview survey described above.

The research method was derived from the earlier work by Paul Slovic (see for example Slovic 1992, Petts & Eduljee 1994) and the results from the three sample populations, valuers, non-valuers and general, are presented spatially in Figures 7.3 to 7.5, in the same style as that work. The highest perceptions of risk are located in the top

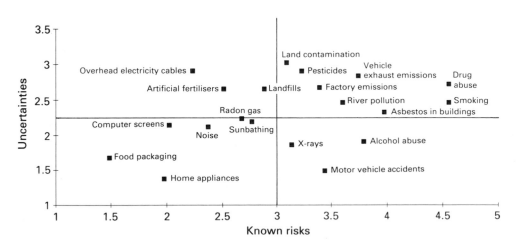

Fig. 7.3   Perceptions of environmental risk – the 'valuers' group.

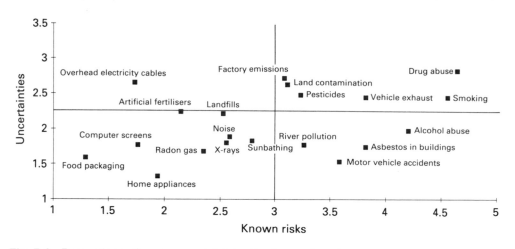

Fig. 7.4 Perceptions of environmental risk – the 'non-valuers' group.

right quadrant and the lowest perceived risks are in the bottom left quadrant.

Of the non-property related risks, drug abuse and smoking are seen as being of most concern to all three groups, with very similar levels of concern in respect of the 'uncertainties,' but with the 'general population' seeing a higher level of 'known risk.' The 'general population' considered three of the property related issues, river pollution, land contamination and landfills to have very similar levels of perceived risk, all just within the top right quadrant.

Both the 'valuers' group and the 'general population' group had similar perceptions in respect of the 'known risks' attaching to land

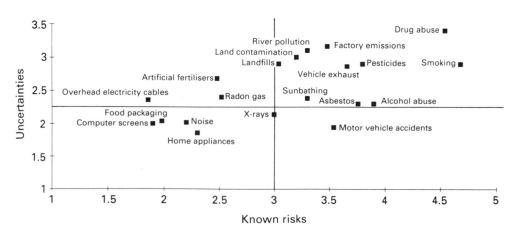

Fig. 7.5 Perceptions of environmental risk – the 'general population'.

contamination but the 'non-valuers' perception of risk was somewhat lower. All three groups indicated similar degrees of 'uncertainty' perception for land contamination. The 'non-valuers' perception of risk for landfills and radon gas was significantly lower than for either of the other two groups, possibly due to the technical background of many members in this group.

For all three groups the issues of least concern were home appliances, food packaging and computer screens. Surprisingly, all three groups indicated a low level of risk perception in respect of overhead electricity cables, especially in terms of 'known' risks. Co-incidentally however, a few weeks after the survey was conducted, this issue received considerable exposure in the British press and a different result may be produced if the study was to be repeated.

The study then focused upon contaminated land as an environmental issue and sought to compare the views of the expert groups in terms of a number of harmful effects which might be associated with land contamination. It was not considered appropriate to involve the 'general public' group in this part of the study as the responses required a degree of 'expert' knowledge. The results from this part of the study are presented spatially in Figures 7.6 and 7.7, from which it will be noted that the perception of land contamination associated risks held by the valuers and development surveyors was considerably higher, for both known risks and uncertainties, than for the 'non-valuers' group of experts.

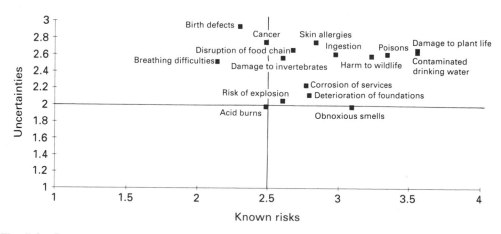

Fig. 7.6 Perceptions of contaminated land risks – the 'valuers group'.

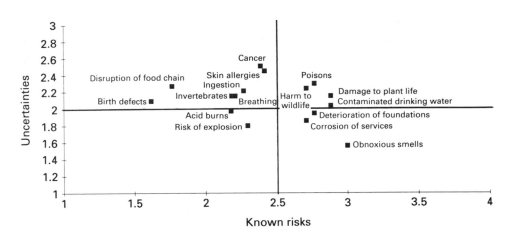

Fig. 7.7 Perceptions of contaminated land risks – the 'non-valuers' group.

As may be seen from a comparison of Figures 7.6 and 7.7, the 'valuers' perception of risk relating to the hazards associated with contaminated land was very considerably greater than for the 'non-valuers' group. It is suggested that this may be due to the fact that the technical professions in particular started to respond to the problems of land contamination at an earlier date than the valuers. Their 'perception of risk' may therefore have peaked some time ago and those professions may now be coming to terms with land contamination as a routine problem which needs to be properly managed.

Valuers, on the other hand, will inevitably experience problems in providing clients with advice on the subject of contaminated land, a situation which will exist until such time as the appropriate guidance is provided by both government and professional organisations. In the absence of such guidance, valuers will continue to adopt a cautious attitude to the valuation of contaminated land, both before and after treatment, and this will be reflected in the advice provided to their developer clients. The valuers' perception risk may therefore not reach a peak until such time as the implications of the statutory guidance to local authorities, issued by the government, are fully understood.

Another objective of this part of the study was to compile a ranking, in respect of the perceived environmental risk attaching to a number of 'potentially contaminative' industrial uses. The 26 industrial uses had been identified from earlier research, described in

Syms (1996b), as having 'the greatest potential to cause serious contamination'. The two 'expert' groups were asked to indicate their perception of risk for each industry, using the five degrees of hazard from 'very high' to 'very low'. Once again the intention was to compare and contrast the perceptions of the two expert groups. The outcome of this part of the study is in Table 7.1.

Table 7.1   Rank order of perceived industrial lists.

Industry type	Valuers sample	Non-valuers sample	Combined rank
Asbestos manufacture and use	1	1	1
Chemicals manufacture and store	3	2	2
Radioactive materials process	2	7	3
Gas works	7	3	4
Waste disposal sites	4	4	4
Oil refining and storage	5	6	6
Dyestuffs manufacturing	8	4	7
Paint manufacture	6	10	8
Tanning and leather works	10	8	9
Metal treatment and finishing	9	11	10
Metal smelting and refining	12	9	11
Explosives industry	13	12	12
Iron and steelworks	11	13	13
Scrapyards	14	16	14
Heavy engineering	15	17	15
Mining and extractive inds.	17	15	16
Electricity generating	16	19	17
Pharmaceutical industries	19	14	18
Paper and printing works	18	20	19
Glass manufacture	21	18	20
Timber treatment works	20	21	21
Sewage treatment works	22	22	22
Railway land	23	23	23
Semi-conductor man. plants	24	26	24
Textiles manufacture	26	24	25
Dockyards and wharves	25	25	26

In the final part of the study the 'valuers' group was asked to indicate to what extent they considered that contamination would have an impact, in terms of a) timescale and b) land value, when compared to a similar but 'greenfield' site, on the assumption that site remediation work had been completed on the 'suitable for use' basis. The results from this question are set out in Table 7.2.

Table 7.2 Perceived impacts on value and duration of effect immediately following site 'suitable for use' remediation – average time and percentage impact at each level of hazard.

Severity of previous hazard	Timescale duration of impact on value (years)	Impact on value reduction in value (%)
Very low hazard	1.85	4.47
Low hazard	3.63	7.05
Medium hazard	6.80	19.07
High hazard	12.79	25.77
Very high hazard	14.53	39.53

As with the interview survey, a number of the respondents were of the opinion that even after treatment those sites regarded as having had a 'very high hazard' classification would suffer a valuation impact in excess of 100% of the value of a comparable greenfield site. The respondents holding this opinion however only represented 7% of the 'valuers' group sample, compared to 38% of the interview sample. One member of the 'valuers' group indicated that even after treatment, the impact on the value of a site previously classified as 'High Hazard' would still exceed 100% of greenfield site value, whereas none of the interview sample expected values of these sites to be affected by more than 60% of value.

Conclusion

The interview and questionnaire surveys confirmed that valuers, in general, have a poorly developed perception of the problems associated with contaminated land. Many would prefer not to become involved with its valuation and would only consider offering advice to clients on its redevelopment if the assessment and remediation aspects were dealt with by other professionals. Approaches to valuation are ill-formed and valuers tend to adopt those methods which they, as individuals, consider to be appropriate. Guidance is expected from the professional institutions but government should not intervene in valuation issues.

Government should, however, take the lead in encouraging the redevelopment of contaminated land through the use of grants and other incentives. There would also appear to be general support for the establishment of environment agencies, although concern was expressed regarding their ability to undertake the task and the degree of bureaucracy involved.

The valuation profession appears to have a fairly poor understanding in respect of site remediation methods and a distrust of innovative technologies. In spite of this, valuers tend to place a relatively low valuation significance on the selection of remediation methods, compared to pre- and post-treatment risk assessments. This may be the result of valuers placing reliance on other professions to select the 'right treatment' and thus ensure that the site is made 'suitable for use'.

A multi-disciplinary approach is undoubtedly required to tackle the problems of contaminated land but this should not mean that valuers should hesitate in performing their normal functions. Contaminated land can be valued and its development potential appraised, provided that valuers learn to make reasoned assumptions, as part of a risk assessment approach, and state those assumptions in their reports.

Checklist

- Check whether the contaminants on site are harmful to human and/or animal life, or phytotoxins which are harmful to plant life; or if more than one type of contamination is present.
- Check whether the materials are likely to be aggressive to building structures and/or services.
- Check whether the materials are producing explosive or flammable gases or noxious fumes.

- Has the site been the subject of any adverse publicity, or is 'known' to the locals as a 'dangerous place'?
- Are any possible risks from the site relevant to the proposed use(s)? For example contaminated soil which may present a hazard for small children through ingestion, 'pica' syndrome, could be acceptable on an industrial estate which is to be largely covered by buildings and yards.

Chapter 8
Determination of Risk

Suitability for use

> 'Greenfield sites are the natural first choice for developers; but in such a small and crowded island as this, they are a finite, and steadily disappearing resource. There is no doubt that, as we move into the next century, the supply of greenfield sites will become more scarce, the conditions attached to developing them will become stricter and their cost will rise.'
>
> (Richards, I. 1995)

Town planning policies, such as the retention of green belts (PPG2, 1988), are intended to restrict the outward growth of many towns and should encourage developers to consider the option of redeveloping previously used sites. However, policies do not always operate as intended and many developers will resist redeveloping former industrial sites, unless they can be assured that they will not be incurring future liabilities in respect of contamination.

The lack of an adequate supply of 'greenfield' sites, the accessible, but not necessarily attractive, location of many old industrial sites and the widespread nature of contamination have resulted in the redevelopment of many contaminated sites. This development-driven market is becoming more and more influenced by environmental legislation, arising out of increased public awareness and political pressures to protect human health and the wider environment. As discussed in Chapter 4, the policy adopted by the British government with regard to the treatment of contaminated sites, is that they should be remediated only to such an extent as to make them suitable for the actual use undertaken on the site, or the use which is proposed if the site is to be redeveloped. Inherent in such a policy is the likelihood that some contaminants will remain on the site, either untreated but covered and contained, or reduced in toxicity following some *in-situ* treatment. The potential may thus remain for future users of the site and neighbouring properties to be exposed to a higher degree of risk, however remote, than if the contamination had been removed in its entirety.

Dr Judith Petts identified a number of key questions in respect of the risks attaching to contaminated land:

- Who is to bear what level of risk?
- Who is to pay for risk taking?
- Where is the line to be drawn between risks which should be managed by Central Government and risks that are to be managed by individuals, groups, organisations?
- Where is the balance to be drawn between corrective measures to reduce the effects of contamination, preventative measures to reduce the potential for contamination to arise, and acceptance of certain impacts but with the costs or risks appropriately shared?
- What information is needed for rational and defensible risk management and how should it be evaluated?
- Who evaluates success or failure in risk management and how?
- Who decides on what should be the desired trade-off between different risks?

(Petts, 1994)

Consideration of these questions needs to be undertaken in two broad contexts; firstly the environmental risk, in terms of hazards to human health and to the wider environment, and secondly the economic risk attaching to the ownership of an interest in an affected property. The word 'risk' needs to be defined and the relationship between environmental and financial contexts has to be examined.

So far as a definition is concerned, the following is considered appropriate in the context of contaminated land:

'... a combination of the probability or frequency of an occurrence of a defined hazard and the magnitude of the consequences of the hazard. In the context of land contamination a hazard could relate to a situation which has potential for human injury, damage to property, damage to the environment or economic loss

(Source: Petts, 1994)

The question of risk in the context of contaminated land may also be divided into those risks which can be measured or predicted and those which are not readily capable of measurement or prediction. As discussed in the previous chapter, the latter group may be specifically related to the uncertainty which surrounds public and professional perceptions, changing government policies and changing attitudes to remediation methodologies. This chapter considers only the measurable or predictable risks, whilst uncertainty is addressed when considering valuation and redevelopment issues in Chapters 9–11.

It can be argued that any residual risk is unacceptable and that land contamination should be remediated to a uniformly 'clean' state, regardless of current or proposed use. It must be questioned, however, whether the expense of such treatment is really justified. If such a policy was to be applied it would be necessary to decide upon a uniformly 'clean' standard to be applied to the treatment of contamination. No doubt developers, environmentalists, government agencies, valuers, investors and occupiers would all have differing views in respect of any such standard.

Achieving the highest possible standard of remediation necessary to fully remove any potential health hazard or other environmental impairment may not be financially viable, for example in situations where the cost of treatment exceeds the economic potential of the site. In such situations contaminated sites may remain untreated, especially if the polluter is no longer in existence or there is no legal liability requiring any party to undertake remediation work.

This chapter describes situations which may lead to land contamination, suggests procedures which should be adopted in determining the nature and extent of such contamination and considers how appropriate risk management techniques would have assisted the companies involved in respect of the examples under consideration.

The Government's consultation paper *Paying for our Past* (DoE, 1994a) proposed, in paragraph 4A.5, that contaminated sites should be improved in line with the 'suitable for use' approach as and when hazards are tackled. This approach was subsequently confirmed as policy in the paper *Framework for Contaminated Land* (DoE, 1994b) and in *Planning Policy Guidance Note 23* (DoE, 1994e). Government policy on the subject of contaminated land is therefore quite clear. Sites need not be remediated to a uniformly 'clean' state regardless of proposed end use. From this it may be deduced that the remediation method used in respect of a site which is to continue in industrial use may be less stringent than that applied to a site which is to be redeveloped for residential purposes.

Similarly, it may be acceptable not to undertake any remediation work in respect of factory premises which are currently used for industrial purposes and are likely to remain in such use for the foreseeable future, provided of course that there are no health and safety risks and the contaminants are not leaching or migrating from the site. There may, however, be financial implications in terms of impact on the existing value of the asset in its contaminated state. The property owner's policy decision may be influenced by commercial factors, rather than property issues, but this policy decision is of significant importance to the valuers of all types of premises, whether valuations are required for asset, mortgage, insurance, sale or acquisition purposes.

'Suitable for use' case studies

As discussed in Chapter 4, government policy in respect of the treatment of contaminated land is based upon 'suitability for use', but in view of the professional guidance issued by the Royal Institution of Chartered Surveyors, coupled with the attitudes of lenders and occupiers, it may not be sufficient for developers simply to adhere to government policy when considering redevelopment options. The following case studies, all of which are based on the personal experience of the author, provide examples of situations where it may not be appropriate merely to take account of suitability for existing use when deciding whether or not to reflect contamination when preparing a valuation or considering the possibility of redevelopment.

Case study 8.1: Proposed purchase of a manufacturing business

At the Clayton Environmental Seminar held in London in October 1994, the author was asked to comment on the following problem, posed by a solicitor:

'I act for a client who owns a manufacturing business which he is in the process of selling to a public company. Included in the sale is the freehold interest in the manufacturing premises used for the purpose of the business. A site investigation has been undertaken on behalf of the acquiring company and it has been found that the ground is contaminated as a direct result of the manufacturing operations. Both parties and their consultants agree that there is no health and safety risk and that the contaminants are not migrating, nevertheless the purchaser is insisting on a reduction in the purchase price so as to reflect the future cost of having to clean up the site. When the vendor refused to reduce the price because the premises were 'suitable for use', the purchaser responded that it was its policy to provide for environmental liabilities in the company's accounts.'

It might appear that the acquiring company is being unreasonable in its demands in attempting to purchase the premises for less than what might be regarded as their open market value. Both parties accept that they are suitable for continued use for their existing purpose and there is no need for the acquiring company to incur any expenditure in improving the ground conditions. If the company decides at some future date to extend the existing buildings or to change the nature of the manufacturing process, then it may be necessary to undertake decontamination work. There is also the possibility that, at some future date, legislation may be introduced which requires the owner of the property to undertake works of a remedial nature.

It is suggested, therefore, that, in taking account of contamination when preparing valuations or development appraisals, the valuer should have regard to the suitability of the premises for their existing (or previous) use and any foreseeable future use which is in reasonable conformity with the existing planning consent. Such an approach should have the result of recognising the potential impact of the contamination in the event of a disposal in the short to medium term. The possibility of legislative changes is however far more difficult to take into account and the likelihood of properties being so affected can only be judged on individual circumstances.

In the event that such use, or uses, would require some improvement of the ground conditions in order to render the premises suitable for use, then the valuation should take account of the procedures set out in Guidance Note 2 of the *RICS Appraisal and Valuation Manual* (RICS, 1995d). A suggested method of valuation is described in Chapter 9 but, in brief, the guidance note requires the valuer to take account of the costs of remediation, including necessary changes to production processes, civil and criminal penalties, professional fees, insurance and future monitoring costs.

Case study 8.2: Former dye works

The occupier of a modern industrial building with a successful manufacturing business needed to expand but was unable to do so on his existing site. A building immediately adjacent to his factory had been used for the previous one hundred years as a dyeworks and seemed to offer a much cheaper expansion solution than relocating the entire business to new premises. He therefore bought the building, on the basis of a valuation prepared for his bank. Plans were drawn up for the redevelopment of the site which was entirely covered by the dye works building. Tenders were received and a contractor was duly appointed. The contractor moved on to the site, demolished the building and started to break up the floor slab. Beneath the slab was a mixture of earth and black slime.

Following enquiries it was found that for the previous one hundred years, waste dyes had been poured through a drainage hole in the floor of the building, into the drain which connected to the public stormwater sewer. The public sewer eventually discharged into a river, approximately half a mile from the premises (see Figure 8.1), which was one of the most heavily polluted rivers in the United Kingdom due to the large number of industrial concerns discharging liquid and solid wastes into the river and its tributaries.

It appeared that at some time, probably many years earlier, the drainage system had broken and for a considerable period of time most, if not all, of the waste dyes had been getting no further than the ground under the building itself. The entire area was contaminated and had to be excavated to a depth of more than four metres, using special precautions to protect the workforce and in hauling the contaminated material away to a licensed tip. The total cost of the remediation works, including fees and an additional payment to the contractor for delay whilst re-design work was undertaken, added 40% to the cost of the new building. Whilst work on site was stopped for the re-design, an application was made to the Department of the Environment for a Derelict Land Grant which covered a substantial part of the additional expenditure.

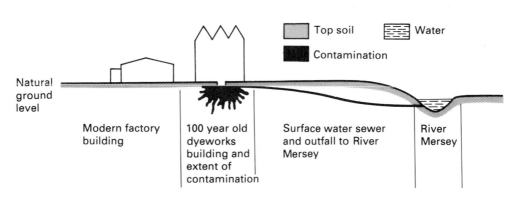

Fig. 8.1   Section through factory and former dye works sites, showing discharge through public sewer to the river.

The valuer who acted for the company's bank was not expected (in 1988) to know about the problem lying under the floor of the building, but bearing in mind the previous use, the question must be asked as to whether or not he should have recommended that a site investigation be undertaken prior to issue of his valuation. There is no doubt that the dye works building was suitable for continued use for its original purpose, or for any other purpose which did not require demolition of the building, and many years could have passed before the problem was discovered. Indeed, the problem may have lain undetected until such time as the contamination was found to be leaching into adjoining land or a potable water source, at which point the current owner could have been faced with an action for nuisance.

Case study 8.3: Ceramics factory

The original factory buildings had been constructed over the course of three decades, commencing in the 1930s, on a gently sloping site. The rear boundary of the site is formed by a watercourse feeding the reservoir which served adjoining textile mills, now redundant. Clay wastes and broken or sub-standard ceramic products had been disposed of on the site throughout the entire period that the factory was in production. These waste products had been used to raise the site levels between the rear of the buildings and the watercourse, so as to form a level area (see Figure 8.2). The levelled site was used for open storage of completed products awaiting despatch and for the parking of vehicles.

The waste products themselves did not constitute an environmental hazard as the amount of heavy metals contained within the glazes was minimal. However, drums of waste glazes had also been buried in the

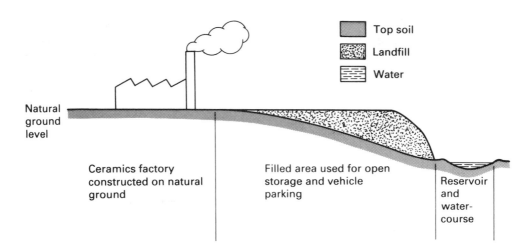

Fig. 8.2   Section through ceramics factory site.

ground and the company had allowed a local building contractor to deposit demolition materials on the site to complete the hardstanding. When, in 1990, the company wished to expand its production facilities, the open storage and parking area was considered to be the ideal location for a factory extension, but a site investigation revealed extensive contamination by heavy metals and friable asbestos. The additional development costs were considered to be prohibitive and the site was not eligible for Derelict Land Grant as it was in current use. The project was therefore abandoned.

The fact that contamination remains on the site does not in any way affect the use of the factory complex for its existing use, but it must be recognised that there is a substantial contingent liability which may need to be met when the buildings reach the end of their useful life. There may also be an earlier liability if any of the contaminants migrate into the adjoining water areas. The valuer, when preparing the company's asset valuation, should therefore take account of the fact that contamination exists on site, regardless of the fact that no disposal or redevelopment is envisaged within the foreseeable future. However, unless the valuer asks specific questions of the client relating to the possibility of contamination, it is quite likely that the potential liability will remain undetected, thus resulting in an erroneous valuation.

Case study 8.4: Former bus depot

A major, publicly quoted property development company purchased the former depot at the peak of the property market in the late 1980s for a sum of approximately £2 500 000 per hectare. The company subsequently entered into a Section 52 Agreement under the Town and Country Planning Act 1971 (superseded by Section 106 Agreement, Town and Country Planning Act 1990) to provide extensive off-site infrastructure works which added almost £1 000 000 per hectare to the site costs. The intention was to develop the site as a business park and, at that time, the expenditure level could be justified.

Instructions were given prior to purchase to a leading firm of consulting engineers to advise on any ground problems, but as the site was still in full operational use, it was not possible to undertake a full site investigation. The site was also being offered in the open market for sale to the highest bidder and the company was reluctant to commit itself to a considerable amount of potentially abortive expenditure. Invasive site investigation was therefore limited to the excavation of a small number of trial pits in areas of hard-standing where filling was known to have taken place. A 'walk over' of the site showed that spillage of fuel oils and other hydrocarbon based materials had occurred in the maintenance garages and in the areas around above-ground oil storage tanks. Taken altogether the contamination was judged not to be a serious problem, and a provision of around £150 000 per hectare was made in preparing the development appraisal.

No research was undertaken into the past uses of the site and working practices; in other words, a desk study was not carried out. When work started on site it was found that there were a number of leaking under-ground storage tanks and it was also discovered that it had been the practice of vehicle mechanics working on the site to dispose of waste oils into the redundant underground air raid shelters; leaching had taken place which allowed the waste oil to penetrate the substrata of the site (see Figure 8.3). It is believed that the cost of treating this site eventually escalated to a figure in excess of £500 000 per hectare, at a time when the property market had entered a period of recession. Grant aid could only have been made available if work had stopped on the site, allowing it to become technically

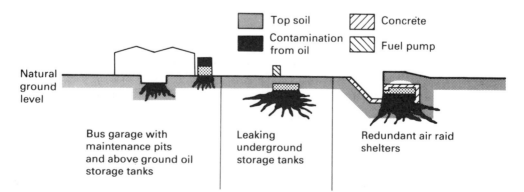

Fig. 8.3 Section through part of bus garage site.

derelict, but it was considered that this would have a detrimental effect on shareholder confidence and the work therefore went ahead without public sector support.

In this case the development surveyor would have been perfectly justified in producing a valuation based on the consulting engineers' assessment of the contamination risk, notwithstanding the fact that this was erroneous. It demonstrates the need for accurate information to be obtained in respect of ground conditions and for this to be reflected in valuations and also for the lack of such information to be notified to clients, through the use of contingencies or written warnings.

In all of the case studies the sites were suitable for their existing or previous uses and so far as the owners and their advisors were concerned there were no health and safety risks. So far as could be determined at the time of the relevant site inspections, there were no identifiable hazards likely to affect the wider environment. None of the case studies involved a change to a sensitive use, such as housing, and it could be argued that site investigations were unnecessary, although the case studies demonstrate that the lack of information may result in the land owner being faced with a considerable amount of unexpected additional cost. When considered for intensification of use, or a reasonably substitutable alternative use, it is apparent from the case studies that contamination was a significant issue, requiring costly remediation, and that there was likely to be an adverse impact on value or the price that could be offered.

A more detailed consideration of the valuation issues is contained in Chapter 9, together with a discussion as to the questions which valuers should address to their clients or the landowners when preparing valuations on sites where contamination may be an issue.

Risk management

The execution of a well planned site investigation should provide the client, and members of the professional team, with a good insight into any physical problems which may have to be overcome and their associated risks, in order to render the property 'suitable for use', or for it to be redeveloped. It should not be necessary for the valuer or the development surveyor to be closely involved throughout the various stages of the investigation, but it may be desirable for him or her to be present at certain times. This may especially be the case during the site reconnaissance where both the surveyor and the site investigator may be able to combine their knowledge and draw each other's attention to matters of significance. It may also be appropriate for the surveyor to be on site during part of the invasive investigation, so as to gain an understanding of the ground conditions which will need to be ameliorated before any development takes place. Before any treatment is undertaken however, it will be necessary to assess the risks associated with the site and decide how they can be managed.

'Risk assessment and risk reduction together comprise the overall process of risk management. There is an overlap between risk assessment (comprising hazard identification and assessment, risk estimation and risk evaluation) and risk reduction (comprising risk evaluation and risk control). In the context of contaminated land, the need to assess the risks associated with contaminants and to decide appropriate levels of control, is the primary consideration in the development of the investigation strategy. In developing the remediation strategy the aim is to explicitly remove or control risks in a transparent and justifiable way.'

(Smith and Harris, 1994)

The results obtained from the site investigation will need to be analysed and their relevance determined in accordance with the development alternatives proposed for the site, so as to assess the degree of risk involved and the targets likely to be affected. It should, however, be borne in mind that 'absolute truths are always beyond the scope of risk analysis in the complexities of land contamination' (Cairney, 1995, p. 25) There may also be a need to consider other matters, not strictly relating to the development proposals, which may constitute a risk to the landowner, for example the possibility that the site may at the present time be the cause of a statutory or private nuisance. The objective of risk analysis is to relate events, such as emissions of toxic substances, to their effect at some sensitive point, or 'target' in the environment. For many redevelopment projects on contaminated land, a hazard assessment and qualitative risk assessment of the site may be sufficient to decide upon the most appropriate course of action. The outcome of the risk assessment process may be the realisation that the preferred development option is not viable but that other options work.

Where a qualitative, or generic, assessment of the risk is deemed to be sufficient, both *dedicated* values (relating specifically to land contamination) and *non-dedicated* values may be used. Dedicated reference values, i.e. those that relate to soil contamination, would include those produced by the Interdepartmental Committee on the Redevelopment of Contaminated Land (ICRCL, 1987) which, it must be stressed, are guidelines not standards, as well as those published by the governments of other countries, such as the Netherlands, Canada, and Australia/New Zealand. Other dedicated reference criteria may be contained in publications from Her Majesty's Inspectorate of Pollution (now part of the Environment Agency), the Building Research Establishment and the Construction Industry Research and Information Association. Non-dedicated reference values, so far as soils are concerned, might include the criteria applicable to drinking water standards, the standards of bathing beaches and the permitted levels of particulate emissions applicable to specific industries.

Care should be taken to note the legal status of the reference values used and to consider their validity to both the site itself and to the country in which it is located. For example, Dutch reference values (Dutch Ministry of Housing, 1987) have been compiled with regard to the official Netherlands policy of soil multi-functionality, or suitability for any use. This contrasts with the UK Government's official policy of suitability for the actual or proposed use. Differences in geography between the two countries need to be taken into account in order to understand the different policies. The Netherlands is a predominantly low lying country, with much of its land area below sea level, and in consequence it draws much of its drinking water from shallow groundwater, whereas the United Kingdom obtains a much larger percentage of its drinking water from deeper aquifers and surface reservoirs in hilly, mostly rural, regions.

A suggested procedure to be followed in determining the level of risk presented by each individual hazard found on the site is shown in Figure 8.4.

Risk assessment of a contaminated site will usually result in a decision that either:

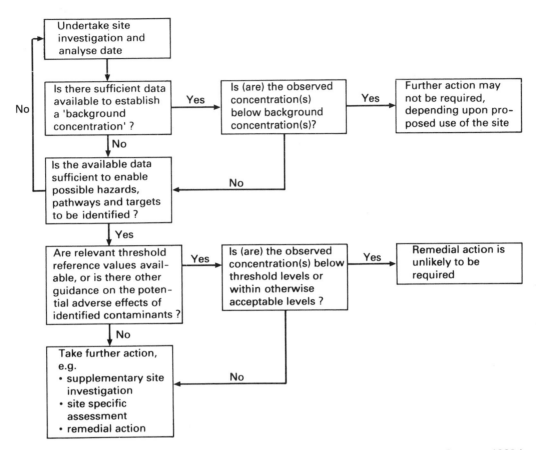

Fig. 8.4   Hazard identification and assessment. (based on Welsh Development Agency, 1993.)

- nothing needs to be done, or
- that measures are required to eliminate or reduce the risks.

Once the decision has been made that risk control measures are required, a remediation strategy must be developed. In situations where the site is to be re-used following treatment, this must take into account not only contamination related risks but also engineering requirements (e.g. minimum load bearing capacities) and management objectives, such as the need to make a profit and the likely perceptions of future occupiers or investors.

In situations where generic criteria are not available for the contaminants being assessed, or in circumstances where the available criteria are deemed to be inappropriate for the individual site or proposed end use, site specific values may have to be determined.

Even in the wider context, the use of generic criteria, or 'trigger concentrations' has been questioned, for example by Beckett (1993b pp. 67-70) who considered the use of trigger values in respect of arsenic contamination in both the ICRCL guidelines (ICRCL, 1987) and the Greater London Council (GLC) 'guidelines' (Kelly, 1979). Beckett concluded that the ICRCL threshold trigger value for arsenic, of 40 mg/kg for non-residential uses of land, 'could safely be deleted from future guidance on trigger concentrations' and that 'there are likely to be other values included in the current ICRCL guidance on trigger concentrations of which the same can be said'. He also expressed the view that the 'inclusion of additional contaminants in future guidance may impair, rather than improve, the usefulness of the concept of trigger concentrations' (Beckett, 1993b, p. 70).

In at least one of the case studies in Chapter 10 the published 'guidelines' were considered to be inappropriate for the proposed use. In such situations, site specific standards will need to be established and agreed with the regulatory authorities. This may involve a quantitative risk assessment being prepared for the specific contaminant relative to the specific target of concern.

In view of the concerns expressed over the use of generic criteria, and the fact that these are only available for a relatively small number of contaminants, it may be argued that generic criteria should only be used for the purpose of 'bench marking' standards to be achieved in soil treatments and that remediation values should be calculated on an individual site basis according to the degree of risk to potential targets. The authors of the *WDA Manual on the Remediation of Contaminated Land* expressed the view, however, that,

'full site-specific risk assessment leading to quantified estimates of risk to defined targets is unlikely to be justified or economic except when dealing with complex problems'
(Welsh Development Agency, 1993),

which might include situations where:

- the frequency and level of exposure are likely to be high and the effects significant,
- sites in existing use present, or are likely to present, significant health and/or environmental risks,

- public perceptions of risk are such that, despite the evidence of a generic assessment, quantified estimates of risk have to be produced,
- local background concentrations of contaminants are high relative to generic threshold concentrations, prompting a consideration of the contribution of the site to local environmental burdens.

(Welsh Development Agency, 1993)

The WDA Manual was written before the Environment Act 1995 came into force and it is important to note the use of the word 'significant' in both the definition of contaminated land contained in the Act and the situations described above as possibly requiring 'quantified estimates of risk'. It may, therefore, be reasonable to assume that in situations where the local authority and/or the Environment Agency determine that there is a risk of significant harm being caused, or the pollution of controlled waters, then a quantified estimate of risk may be required in order to determine what action, if any, needs to be taken in order to overcome the problem.

In the opinion of Cairney (1995)

'current inadequacies in national guidelines and standards ... and the scientific uncertainties over the fates and interactions of contaminants as they move through the complexities of air-soil-water environments are such that a fully quantified environment risk assessment approach cannot yet be advocated'.

He has therefore proposed that a 'Semi-Quantified Risk Assessment Approach' be adopted. In using such an approach seven environmental risk situations would be considered:

Group I   (1)   Risks of polluting surface waters
            (2)   Risks of polluting groundwaters
            (3)   Risks of producing area-wide air pollution

Group II   (4)   Risks of gases and vapours entering dwellings and structures
            (5)   Risks of attack on construction materials
            (6)   Risks to plant populations

> (7) Risks to human health by contaminant contact, ingestion or inhalation.
>
> (Cairney, 1995, p. 58)

The Group I risks are those of interest to the bodies responsible for ensuring compliance with environmental legislation, whilst the Group II risks are those of more concern to individuals and organisations occupying or investing in land which was formerly contaminated. These seven risk categories 'adequately cover the risks of concern to the various parties interested in the re-use of a formerly contaminated site' (Cairney, 1995, p. 58), although Cairney did acknowledge that some workers, (for example Ferguson and Denner, 1993) considered that the human health risks arising from the ingestion and/or inhalation of contaminants should be considered in more detail.

According to Cairney (1995), the semi-quantified approach is capable of assisting the decision making process and meeting the usual practical requirements which tend to fall into one or other of the following categories:

- Pre-purchase decisions when an un-reclaimed and contaminated site is offered for sale.
- Deciding which remediation method best fits the remediation budget, the planned land use, and the liabilities which are of most concern.
- Proving that a reclamation has fully satisfied its aims and that the site is acceptably safe for its projected re-use.

The relationship of these three stages, the essential links between the various stages and types of site investigation are set out in the risk assessment analysis in Box 8.1.

Most of the guidance given in literature is directed primarily at the technical aspects of site investigation and remediation, with little or no consideration being given to the economic and valuation aspects, although Cairney does state in the preface to his book that it has 'been written specifically to assist developers who reclaim contaminated land for productive re-use'. If the economic and valuation aspects are taken into account, risk assessment and estimation may be justified on a site specific basis in order to satisfy investors, occupiers,

Box 8.1   Risk assessment analysis.

Part [A]	**Desk study. Establishing relative potentials of liabilities. Buy/reject option.**
	Necessary form of site investigations to establish if potential liabilities are real (Chapter 5)
	Selection of that chemical analytical strategy best suited to establish the likely risks (Chapter 5)
Part [B]	**Evaluation of site investigation/analytical data to establish the magnitude of future environmental liabilities. Confirmation that site investigation/analytical coverage has been adequate. Identification of where additional undefined detail may be required.**
	Choice of the form of contaminated land remediation which best addresses the liabilities of most concern to the planned re-use of the site.
	Identification of any additional investigation/reclamation method proving which may be required. (Chapter 6)
Part [C]	**Proving that the reclaimed site is acceptably safe for its planned re-use. Identification of any additional proof needed to reach a decision.**
	Relative final weightings of environmental liabilities may be given standardised cost values. This will be necessary in order to assess the impact on value attributable to the contamination and any residual effect on value following treatment, as well as to establish whether or not insurance cover can be arranged and the premiums which should be charged. (Chapters 7, 9, 10, 11 and 12)

Source, after Cairney, 1995

purchasers and other parties having an interest in the future use of formerly contaminated sites. In other words a particularly complex situation may not have to exist in order for a quantified, or semi-quantified, estimate of risk to be required, possibly in order to satisfy non-technical criteria.

Conclusion

No two sets of circumstances affecting contaminated sites are ever likely to be identical. However, given sufficient thought and planning, it should be possible to undertake sufficient investigative work to enable a reasoned assessment to be made of both the environmental and the economic risks. Whether or not the 'Semi-Quantified Risk Assessment Approach' advocated by Cairney is adopted will depend upon individual choice and the circumstances relating to specific sites. But if for any reason whatsoever it is not possible to produce such a risk assessment, then the owner, surveyor or developer should err on the side of caution and regard the property as a potential liability.

Returning to the examples of land contamination described earlier in this chapter, the following lessons may be learned:

- **The proposed purchase of a manufacturing business**; the prospective purchaser of the business had adopted the correct approach in undertaking a site investigation and was justified in seeking a reduction in the purchase price of the business property to reflect the future cost of having to treat the site. The example quoted involved a freehold property, but it is argued the same approach is valid in respect of leasehold properties. It may be particularly relevant in respect of leases with a relatively short unexpired term, where the tenant may become responsible for the cost of any treatment at the end of the lease and long before the buildings reach the end of their economic life. In such circumstances the tenant may be faced with the cost of demolition and rebuilding, in order to deal with the contamination. A suggested method for tackling asset valuations of damaged properties, whether freehold or leasehold, is described in Chapter 9.

- **The former dye works**; no site investigation was undertaken in respect of this property, only a valuation for bank purposes. At the time when the property was acquired for redevelopment, contamination was not perceived within the surveying profession generally to be an issue, and its impact was not regarded as being a factor to be taken into account when preparing valuations. The total coverage of the building to the site area represented a major constraint in undertaking an invasive investigation and it is doubted that the vendor would have been willing to permit holes to be drilled through the floor of the building. Nevertheless, a preliminary investigation should have been carried out, including a review of the former occupier's working practices, which would have assisted in the preparation of a risk assessment and possibly enabled the purchaser to negotiate a conditional contract, providing for a reduction in price if contamination was found to exist. The purchaser in this case suffered a substantial financial loss, which was only partly offset by grant aid. It is argued that, in similar circumstances, today the valuer could be held to have been negligent.

- **The ceramics factory**; the problem had been caused by the occupier of the site who had also allowed dumping of hazardous materials. At this time land contamination was not an issue of any significance, and no third party was involved. A site investigation had been undertaken and the risks, in valuation terms, were assessed as being unacceptable. The company in question had other land available on which to construct the factory extension and it was not therefore necessary for the site to be developed. No remedial work was proposed, but the existence of the contamination should be reflected in future asset valuations, provided of course that the company brings it to the attention of the valuer.

- **The former bus depot**; quite clearly the site investigation work undertaken by the consulting engineers was inadequate for the purpose of identifying the type and extent of any contamination existing on the site. Whether they were negligent or not is a debatable point, but perhaps they should have advised their client that it was not possible to undertake an adequate site investigation given the operational constraints and the available budget. They would almost certainly have been better employed in carrying out a preliminary investigation, with particular reference to a study of working practices, than in the limited invasive investigation which was performed.

Checklist

- Always obtain as much information as possible regarding working practices of the site occupier, past and present, when acquiring, valuing or redeveloping an industrial property.
- Ascertain whether or not the working practices carried out on the

site were in accordance with regulations pertaining to the industry, and in compliance with any town planning conditions or discharge licences.

- Ask if any enforcement notices have been served on the site operator.
- Enquire about on-site waste disposal practices, for example pouring liquid wastes down the drain or using solid wastes to fill hollows on the site.
- Ascertain which potentially contaminative materials have been used or stored on the site or in production processes.
- Ask if any fill materials have been imported onto the site at any stage in its development, and ascertain their nature.

Section 3
Valuation and Redevelopment Issues

Chapter 9
The Valuation of Contaminated Assets

In Chapter 2 it was suggested that economic value in the context of contaminated land may be defined in terms of the price which would be paid by a willing buyer to a willing seller, in an open market, subject to town planning controls, after deduction of the lowest cost attributable to overcoming the damage to the land. It may not be necessary for any immediate work to be undertaken to remove or reduce the level of contamination, but some allowance should be made in the valuation, so as to reflect the cost of correcting the situation. In addition to the 'cost to correct', the economic value of contaminated land may be impacted by a fear of the unknown, or 'stigma' effect. This chapter seeks to identify the way, or ways, in which that value might be determined in accordance with current professional guidance in the UK.

Guidance for valuers

Simm (1992) stated his hypothesis that 'the capital comparison based approach to valuation of contaminated land is no longer tenable and is, in fact, dangerous'. In his opinion, the only way in which valuers can effectively approach the problem, whether in terms of valuing existing portfolios or appraising land for development, is to adopt residual valuation techniques. Laing (1992) suggested that 'the market perception of contaminated land ... will in reality vary considerably depending on location, strength of the market and the type of development to be carried out'. He too advocated a residual approach to the valuation of contaminated land and proposed that contamination be looked at in relation to four key variables:

- **time** a disposal may be delayed as a result of the need to deal with contamination, resulting in increased interest charges,
- **cost** the direct costs associated with overcoming the problems of contamination,
- **value** the value of the property may diminish because of the previous contamination,
- **risk** the existence of contamination may mean that potential purchasers of land will no longer be interested and that the land is therefore likely to be sold to a more restricted market.

(Based on Laing, 1992)

Both of these authors acknowledged the possibility that the existence of contamination may result in negative property values. When such properties comprise part of the assets of a company, the valuer is under a duty to ensure that the negative values are reported separately in the valuation certificate and not set off against positive values on other properties (see Practice Statements PS 3.4 and 7.4.12 of the *RICS Appraisal and Valuation Manual*, 1995d). This means that, in valuing company assets, the problems of land contamination should be recorded. To simply place a nil value on such land is inappropriate, because it will not reflect the true position in terms of asset value. Quite clearly, a requirement to identify potential liabilities, in the form of negative values, brings with it a need to formulate a method by which properties suffering from contamination may be valued. The valuer therefore needs to be able to reflect in the valuation the adverse effects which may be attributable to different industrial uses and their associated contaminants (Figure 9.1).

In October 1993 the Royal Institution of Chartered Surveyors published Valuation Guidance Note 11 (VGN 11), as an addition to its *Manual of Valuation* (the 'White Book') (RICS, 1993). The publication of the guidance note, 'Environmental factors, contamination and valuation', essentially adopted the recommendations of The International Assets Valuation Standards Committee in its draft guidance note 'The effect of environmental factors or pollution on the valuation of fixed assets for financial statements' published in September 1990 (TIAVSC, 1990a).

Fig. 9.1   Many different industrial uses can result in contamination which may not always be apparent during the course of a normal valuation inspection.

This guidance note and its associated background paper 'The Consideration of Environmental Factors and Pollution in the Valuation Process' (TIAVSC, 1990b), attempted to set out the procedures to be followed by valuers when confronted by the existence of contamination on properties being valued for company accounts purposes. It provided a brief description of the ways in which contamination and/or pollution might occur. A background paper published by The European Group of Valuers of Fixed Assets 'Valuation of Land Subject to Soil Pollution' and its accompanying technical note on the restoration of contaminated land (TEGO-VOFA,1988) also provided useful guidance. Prior to the publication of Valuation Guidance Note 11 none of the recommendations made by the European and International Asset Valuation bodies had been adopted for use in connection with valuations undertaken in the United Kingdom.

Valuation Guidance Note 11 provided a brief history of the legislation applicable to contaminated land and this has been retained in the subsequent Guidance Note 2 (RICS, 1995c) in *RICS Appraisal and Valuation Manual* (RICS, 1995d) which states that the importance of contamination to surveyors, and valuers in particular, depends upon the factors shown in Box 9.1.

Box 9.1 Factors of concern to valuers.

(a) the state of knowledge at any time of the existence and effect of the particular form of contamination;
(b) the current interpretation of the law;
(c) the effect of possible changes in legislation;
(d) current technology and expected changes in technology;
(e) the previous uses of the subject land/buildings and property nearby;
(f) the existing uses of the subject land/buildings and property nearby;
(g) the proposed use of the subject land/buildings and property nearby;
(h) the financial effect of the above

Source: RICS (1993)

This manual came into effect in January 1996, but the list of factors affecting the valuation of contaminated land remains unchanged. To take account of all the factors described above would undoubtedly involve valuers in considerably more detailed research than they would normally undertake in preparing reports and valuations. This is especially the case where valuers have to take into consideration the previous, existing and proposed uses of both the subject property and nearby properties. It would also appear to involve them in areas of knowledge not usually included in the training of surveyors and valuers.

Guidance Note 2 is only a 'stop-gap' measure, reflecting the legislative changes arising out of the Environment Act 1995. The Guidance Note was to have been revised during 1996 so as to take account of Parliamentary Guidance issued under the Act but, as detailed in Chapter 4, the delays associated with the introduction of regulations mean that this revision has been deferred.

When receiving an invitation to carry out a valuation on a property which may suffer from some form of environmental impairment, valuers must decide whether they wish to accept or decline the instruction. Before indicating acceptance to the client, the valuer must determine whether the type of property, disregarding the impairment, is within his or her sphere of competence and whether or not he or she is covered by professional indemnity insurance.

As a starting point, it is suggested that valuers and intending developers, should assume that there is a strong likelihood of con-taminants being present on sites which are identified in Guidance Note 2 (paras. GN 2.2.3 and GN 2.2.5), as being most prevalent in producing contamination (see Box 9.2). Whether or not such sites are also 'contaminated' in the legal sense of the word will also depend upon whether or not relevant receptors are present, and the potential for 'significant harm' to be caused. It should be stressed, however, that the legal definitions are only intended to apply to existing uses and targets, and not to any possible change of use and/or future targets.

Box 9.2   Potentially contaminated sites.

• waste tips	• electricity generating stations
• iron and steel works	• explosives industry
• gas works and similar sites	• glass manufacturing
• oil refinery and storage	• heavy engineering works
• petrol storage sites	• metal smelting and refining
• chemical manufacture and storage	• metal treatment and finishing
• animal product works	• paint manufacture
• dockyards and wharves, particularly inland waterways	• paper and printing works
• defence and research establishments	• pharmaceutical industries
• sewage works	• radioactive material and processing
• pipelines	• scrapyards
• tanneries	• semi-conductor manufacturing plants
• railway land	• electricity substations
• asbestos manufacturing and use	• timber treatment works
• dye-stuffs manufacturing	• waste disposal to landfill

Source: Syms (1995) & RICS (1995d)

If the type of property, and the locality in which it is situated, is such that the valuer feels competent to undertake the instruction, then as much information as possible should be obtained in order to assess the extent, if any, to which the value of the property is affected by contamination. The nature of any contaminants arising out of the industrial activities in Box 9.2 and their possible harmful effects are discussed in Chapter 3. The dispersion and concentrations of contaminants within the site may be disclosed to the valuer as part of the instruction, possibly in the form of a site investigation, or may be ascertainable from enquiry or research.

With the need for fullest possible information in mind, a list of questions is given in Box 9.3, to assist the valuer in determining whether or not contamination may be present and its impact on value.

Box 9.3 Questions which need to be answered.

- What is the present, or last known use of the property?
- Is there documentary evidence of the past uses and development of the site?
- Are the present or past uses likely to be potentially contaminative in nature?
- What is the land use history in the immediate vicinity? say, within one kilometre.
- What is the geographical and geological setting of the site?
- Are there any known, or suspected, mineshafts or landfill sites in the vicinity?
- Has there been asbestos product manufacture or iron and steel smelting in the area?
- Is there a waterway near the property?
- Is the site underlain by a producing aquifer?
- Has any fly tipping taken place?
- Has there ever been a programme of asbestos removal from the property (Figure 9.2)?
- Does documentary evidence exist of any tanks or pipeworks having been emptied or flushed?
- Has there been any on-site disposal of manufacturing wastes or other residues and, if so, is adequate documentation available?
- Do plans of the buildings or works exist and are they complete?
- Has the present and any previous, occupier complied with all statutory regulations relating to the nature of the business and, if so, is there documentary evidence of such compliance?
- Has a decommissioning audit been carried out and/or has any past contamination been dealt with?

Source: based on Syms (1992)

In addition to the questions set out in Box 9.2, there will undoubtedly be other questions, of a site specific nature, which need to be answered. The valuer will also need to ascertain whether or not the land is classed as 'contaminated' or as a 'special site', in accordance with the legal definitions of contaminated land and significant harm, or if it is merely affected by the presence of contaminants. This may involve the valuer in making his or her own judgement as to whether the nature of the contaminants present on the site, relative to the actual or proposed use, is likely to result in the land being designated as contaminated by the local authority. Land value may also be affected by contamination on adjacent or nearby sites and valuers should be prepared to take account of industrial activities within, say, a one kilometre radius of the site being valued.

Case study 9.1: Contamination caused by airborne emissions

A local authority housing committee, undertaking a review of its housing stock, commissioned a report on one of its low-rise housing estates which

Fig. 9.2   Whilst this old industrial building remains in use there is little risk of contamination from the asbestos cladding, but careless demolition may result in asbestos fragments causing contamination of the site.

had been constructed during the 1960s. The purpose of the report was to determine whether the houses were suitable for refurbishment or if they should be demolished and the site redeveloped. The report was therefore to consider both the structural condition of the houses and also the ground conditions with regard to the redevelopment option. As part of the ground investigation, soil samples were taken and subjected to chemical analysis.

The ground investigation revealed a small amount of landfill gas in one corner of the estate, and elevated levels of sulphates together with some heavy metals generally across the estate in the top half metre of soil. Although the estate had been constructed on natural ground it adjoined a former brickworks. The clay pits had been filled and levelled to create playing fields, hence the landfill gas. Remedial action was not required, only future monitoring.

The sulphates and metals contamination was more of a problem, until an historical study revealed that the estate was situated to the north-east of a number of different industrial activities including gas works, foundry and railway wagon works, all of which had ceased to exist. The contamination was therefore attributed to airborne emissions from these industries, carried by the prevailing south-westerly wind (Figure 9.3).

Assuming that adequate answers are received to the questions, the valuer should be in a position to decide whether or not it is possible to prepare a valuation on the basis of the information available. If adequate answers are not received, or if they reveal inconsistencies, or

Fig. 9.3   On this abandoned site, airborne emissions may have ceased many years earlier, but can still have caused ground contamination, especially high sulphate levels in the vicinity of coal burning industries.

simply lead to the conclusion that insufficient records have been maintained, then it may be appropriate to advise the client to commission a comprehensive site investigation, in accordance with the procedures set out in the British Standards Institution's *Draft for Development Code of Practice for the Identification of Potentially Contaminated Land and its Investigation* (BSI:DD175, 1988), with a view to the preparation of a full Land Quality Statement.

On the other hand if the information obtained, albeit confirming that contamination exists, is sufficient to proceed with a valuation in accordance with Guidance Note 2, the valuer then needs to decide how the valuation should be produced. Paragraph GN 2.9.2, shown in Box 9.4, details eight categories of costs, net of grants or other financial incentives, which should be taken into account in the valuation:

In spite of having clearly identified the heads of costs to be taken into account, Guidance Note 2 does not provide the valuer with any guidance as to how the information should be treated in preparing the valuation. The valuation method described later in this chapter is suggested as one way in which these heads of costs may be taken into account in the valuation.

Box 9.4   Site remediation and other costs.

(a)   clean-up of on-site contamination and associated requirements, liability therefore and the ability to pay of the person liable;

(b)   effective contamination control and management measures;

(c)   re-design of production facilities;

(d)   penalties and civil liabilities for non-compliance;

(e)   indemnity insurance for the future;

(f)   compliance with legal obligations relating to migration of the contamination to adjacent sites and its future prevention;

(g)   the control of migration from other sites;

(h)   the regular monitoring of the site.

Source: RICS (1995c)

The stigma effect

Taking account of the items described in the previous section should be sufficient to enable valuations to reflect adequately the quantifiable costs of tackling contamination. There is, however, an unquantifiable aspect to land contamination; described as 'stigma' and referred to in paragraph GN 2.9.7 of Guidance Note 2.

The existence of stigma has been considered by a number of researchers, most notably Patchin (1988, 1991a, 1991b, 1994) and Mundy (1992a, b and c). Patchin used the term 'stigma' to represent a variety of intangible factors from possible public liability and fear of additional health hazards to the simple fear of the unknown (Patchin, 1991a). In the United Kingdom context, and for the purpose of this book, stigma is defined as:

> 'That part of any diminution in value attributable to the existence of land contamination, whether treated or not, which exceeds the costs attributable to a) the remediation of the subject property, b) the prevention of future contamination, c) any known penalties or civil liabilities, d) insurance and e) future monitoring.'
>
> (Syms, 1995a)

In other words, stigma includes all those matters likely to have an influence on value, other than those which are readily quantifiable or for which reasonable estimates can be produced. Stigma may arise due to:

- inability to effect a total 'cure',
- prejudice arising out of the past use (referred to as stigma in Valuation Guidance Note 11),
- the risk of failure of treatment,
- compensation payable or receivable, under Section 78G of the Environmental Protection Act 1990, or otherwise,
- risk of legislation/remedial standards changing,
- a reduced range of alternative uses of the site,
- uncertainty.

This approach is embodied in Guidance Note 2 (para 2.9.7), which states that these 'other influences affecting market value ... may be referred to collectively as stigma'.

The issue of property values possibly being adversely affected by contamination was first considered by Patchin in 1988, when he suggested that the costs involved in cleaning up toxic contamination, together with liability to the public, and stigma, often eliminated or significantly reduced a property's value. Many industries had simply disposed of hazardous wastes on site, with 'little, if any, concern for the fact that ecologic and economic time bombs were being created' (Patchin, 1988).

Responsibility for treatment costs

In 1988, awareness of the potential problem had only recently come to be recognised in the United States. Patchin attributed this to the enactment of the Comprehensive Environmental Response, Compensation and Liability Act of 1980 (CERCLA), otherwise known as 'superfund'. This legislation and other similar legislation passed by various state governments, was to affect significantly the use and valuation of properties which were in some way affected by contamination. He summarised the basic provisions of the legislation as:

(1) The party who placed the contamination in the ground must bear the costs of clean-up as directed by either the federal or state agency having jurisdiction.

(2) If the parties originally responsible for the contamination are no

longer financially solvent or no longer exist, the responsibility falls on successors in the chain of title; most likely the existing or present property owner.

(3) Other parties associated with the title to a contaminated property may also be held responsible for the costs of clean-up.

(Patchin, 1988)

Patchin referred to two court cases where successors in title and 'associated parties' had been held responsible for the cost of dealing with contamination. One of these involved the *State of New York* v. *Shore Realty Corp.*, 759 F.2d 1032 (2d. Cir. 1985) and the other dealt with the *United States* v. *Maryland Bank and Trust Co.*, 16 E.L.R. 20557 (D. Md. April 9, 1986). The second of these concerned a bank which had foreclosed in respect of a property loan amounting to $335 000 but was additionally liable to meet clean-up costs of $460 000 because the previous owners were insolvent or no longer in existence. This introduced the notion of 'deep pockets', whereby the most financially secure party in the chain of title, or associated with the ownership, might be held responsible for costs far in excess of any interest they might have in the property itself. This concept caused considerable concern in banking circles in the United States.

In the United Kingdom, similar concerns were expressed by banking organisations in respect of the registers of potentially contaminated land uses proposed under Section 143 of the EPA 1990; see for example the statements made by the British Bankers Association in September 1993 and April 1994 (British Bankers Association, 1993 and 1994). These concerns were recognised by the government in a policy statement and were subsequently addressed in the Environment Act 1995.

'... regulatory authorities should not be able to treat financial institutions as "deep pockets", being made liable for the costs of any remedial works regardless of any responsibility.'

(DoE, 1994b)

Under the 1995 legislation the person (individual or organisation) responsible for remediation is termed an 'appropriate person' and a new clause 78F(2), to be included in Part IIA of the Environmental Protection Act 1990, provides that

'... any person, or any of the persons, who caused or knowingly permitted the substances or any of the substances, by reason of which the contaminated land in question is such land to be in, on or under that land is an appropriate person'.

However, by virtue of section 78F(3), such a person will be the 'appropriate person' only in respect of those substances which he 'caused or knowingly permitted' to be in, on or under the ground in question.

Section 78F(6) and (7) provides that where two or more 'appropriate persons' may be identified, the local authority shall determine the extent to which each of them shall be held responsible for the cost of remediation. Thus it would appear that joint and several liability is not intended to apply in respect of soil clean-up but that responsibility is to be limited by the extent to which each person caused the contamination or allowed it to be caused.

Under normal circumstances, it would appear that the definition of 'appropriate person' does not include a mortgagee and the legislation specifically excludes mortgagees 'not in possession' from the definition of 'owner' and it would seem possible that, in some situations, the providers of finance could be left with the responsibility for remediation. This could occur, for example, if a bank endeavoured to assist a company through its trading difficulties by providing management advice, or if it had a representative on the board of a valued customer in good standing who could be deemed to have 'knowingly permitted' the contamination. The Royal Institution of Chartered Surveyors, in its evidence to the House of Commons Select Committee on the Environment, has strongly criticised the draft statutory guidance to local authorities for its 'lack of plain English' and it would appear that the question of responsibility attaching to financial institutions is far from being resolved.

The valuer's approach to stigma

Patchin (1988) stated that 'the tendency of most appraisers in valuing contaminated property is to approach the problem on the basis of discounting the value before contamination'. Such a method was, he suggested, 'difficult, if not impossible to support with market data' and instead, 'market research will disclose that contaminated properties suffer from varying degrees of reduced marketability or total unmarketability'.

The likelihood of reduced marketability was very much in keeping with the views expressed by many property groupings in the United Kingdom in response to the registers proposed under Section 143 of the Environmental Protection Act 1990. In Patchin's opinion, based entirely upon United States property markets, the presence of contamination would have implications extending beyond the costs of simply remediating the land and could be expected to impact upon the yield rate, the mortgage terms available and the future anticipated appreciation or depreciation of the property concerned. In other words, the value of the property would be stigmatised as a result of the contamination, even if the contaminants themselves had been removed or otherwise treated.

Over the course of the next two years Patchin was repeatedly questioned and it was suggested that perhaps the 'concept of stigma' was a figment of his imagination (Patchin, 1991a). In 1991, therefore, he revisited the issue of stigma and concluded that the market had become 'significantly more aware of the issue of toxic contamination on real estate values'. He also formed the opinion that, in attempting to determine the extent of stigma, extensive research would be necessary to disclose the relevant information, including previous uses of the site and contamination related price reductions. In this context, information relating to sales which did not go through could be more important than those sales that actually did occur.

One problem which Patchin identified was the expectation on the part of many appraisers 'that there should be a rational or logical cause for any loss in value' and he went on to stress that appraisers 'must recognise that there are many irrational factors in the marketplace' (Patchin, 1991a). No matter how well a site remediation programme has been undertaken, and regardless of the quality of the supervision and reporting procedures, it must be accepted that there will always be those individuals or corporations in the purchasing marketplace, who will refuse to consider a former contaminated site for their own use or development. If a treatment option is selected which leaves some residual contamination in the ground, either safely contained or at a reduced level of toxicity, then the market for such a site is potentially reduced even further. The different impact which alternative treatment methods may have on value is discussed later in this chapter and in Chapters 10 and 11. Such limiting factors as a reduction in the size of the potential market, also referred to by Laing (1992) as part of the 'risk' variable, will have an impact on the sale price achievable for a particular property and hence upon its 'open market value', the extent of such impact being determined by the number of remaining bidders and the degree to which they are prepared to disregard the past history of the property – the stigma effect.

Patchin (1991a) suggested that 'it may be helpful to think of stigma as a negative intangible' and stated that it is likely to be caused by one or a combination of the following factors:

- Fear of hidden cleanup costs; including the uncertainty of cost over-runs if the remediation work has not yet been undertaken, continuing market resistance after treatment and the possibility of further, unforeseen, contamination,
- The trouble factor; the monetary compensation required by a potential purchaser [over and above the straight treatment costs] for the trouble involved in dealing with the problem,
- Fear of public liability; the possibility of any future liability to third parties would mitigate against a formerly contaminated property in favour of one which was perceived as being more problem free,
- Lack of mortgageability; the inability to obtain financing, either for the sale of a property or its future development, which Patchin regarded as being 'one of the most frequent causes of stigma related loss'.

(after Patchin, 1991a, p. 168–9)

In the conclusion to his 1988 paper Patchin had stated that:

'There is no quick fix to appraising contaminated property. The results are very dependent on individual circumstances. The extent and nature of the contamination are the crucial factors in estimating the after-value of a contaminated property.'

(Patchin, 1988, p. 16)

This view was confirmed by his later empirical work (Patchin, 1991b) based on four case studies, from which he found that the diminution in value attributable to stigma, taking account of the four factors described above, varied from 25% to 65%. From these studies he concluded that 'the nature, extent and circumstances of environmental contamination have the greatest influence upon the final value of a property'.

In a further development of his research, in 1994, Patchin described seven case studies where agreed transactions had failed to be completed, or had been completed at reduced sales figures, as a result of contamination. From these, he postulated that the impact on property values, attributable to the stigma of contamination, was between 21% and 69% of the unimpaired value of the properties. In his paper Patchin also described an eighth case study, which indicated a stigma effect of 94%, but subsequently agreed in correspondence with the author that not all of the reduction in value could be attributed to stigma. This case study has therefore been omitted from consideration. In all cases remediation work had been undertaken, so as to render the site 'fit for use', or the site itself was not contaminated, but merely suffered from the effect of being adjacent to a contaminated property. The wide variation in impacts was, he suggested, due to differences in the severity of contamination and whether the site itself was contaminated, or merely adjoining contamination.

Patchin's method was to use case study examples and compare them with properties for which values had to be determined. The basis of comparison was not, however, the usual valuer's method of comparing the similarities and dis-similarities of properties, in terms of location, site, size and specification. Instead, comparisons were made as to the nature and extent of contamination in order to assess the percentage stigma effect to be applied to the property being valued. The percentage stigma effect could then be applied to the unimpaired value to arrive at a value for the property as impaired by contamination.

Patchin recognised the problems involved in obtaining data on transactions, failed or completed, concerning contaminated property. This is an even greater problem in the United Kingdom where there is very little public or professional access to information regarding property transactions. It must be stressed that, in using any case study or sales comparables methods to identify the extent of stigma on real estate values, values and prices paid may be impacted by a number of factors other than contamination. Therefore, it is important to identify those factors which relate most directly to the contamination issue.

Valuation methods

The way in which Guidance Note 2 is applied will differ according to the nature of the property and the purpose for which the valuation is required. If the property is to be valued on the basis of immediate redevelopment, then account should be taken of all of the costs listed in paragraph GN 2.9.2 and shown in Box 9.4. However, if redevelopment is not expected within the foreseeable future, it may be appropriate to defer at least some of the costs.

A number of alternative valuation methods have been considered for use, both in the United Kingdom and the United States. These include the sales comparison approach (Patchin 1994); the cost approach (Wilson, 1994); and the cash flow approach (Wilson, 1996). Richards, T. (1995) has considered the yield adjustment approach and the discounted cash flow approach, in respect of investment properties affected by contamination.

The focus of this book is not, however, on investment properties but on those types of property which more usually form part of the assets of manufacturing companies and infrequently change hands in the open market, except as part of the assets of a business. This includes those properties used for the purposes identified in RICS Guidance Note 2 as having the greatest potential to cause contamination (Box 9.2). Such properties are rarely found in investment portfolios and, in consequence, it may not be possible to determine appropriate rents and yields to facilitate an investment type valuation approach.

The valuation method adopted is therefore a traditional method, essentially a residual valuation as suggested by Simm (1992) and Laing (1992), and is based on the sales comparison approach described by Peter Patchin in 1994. Box 9.5 sets out a suggested method by which property assets may be valued when the existing use is expected to continue for the foreseeable future.

The first step in using the method is to prepare a valuation for the whole property which assumes that the site is uncontaminated. A number of different methods may be used, including comparison of site values, cash flow or depreciated replacement cost, as may be appropriate for the type of property involved. This gives an unimpaired value for the property as a whole. The suggested method then requires the unimpaired land value to be calculated, as a base value from which the effects of contamination can be deducted in the second step in the valuation.

Worked example: Asset valuation of industrial premises

A valuation is required in respect of a five hectare site which is currently used for the manufacture of chemicals. Previous uses include a foundry and metal plating works. The old foundry buildings were demolished thirty years ago and much of the demolition material was retained on site as hardcore. The three existing buildings were constructed and extended in several phases between 20 and 30 years ago.

A site investigation has found that the soil is extensively contaminated with metal residues from the previous uses, especially copper, nickel and zinc, which are phytotoxins (substances harmful to plant life) and with a variety of chemical wastes, including hydrocarbons and organic compounds from the chemical works. The chemical wastes are in two identifiable areas of the site and appear to originate from drums of waste chemicals which were buried on the site, a practice which was discontinued by the chemical company more than ten years ago. None of the contamination appears to be migrating from the site and there is no immediate risk of controlled waters becoming polluted. There are no health and safety risks, provided that the contaminants remain undisturbed. The freeholder also owns the chemical company and is therefore responsible for the contamination.

A valuation of this property on the assumption that there is no contamination present on site, produces an unimpaired asset valuation of £2.5 million. The uncontaminated land value is £1.5 million, £300 000 per hectare, leaving a residue of £1 million for the buildings. The site is of course contaminated and the costs of dealing with the contamination are taken into account using the method shown in Box 9.5.

It will be noted from the example that no costs have been included for items (c) process re-design and (d) penalties/civil liabilities. This is because these should be regarded as immediate costs, not capable of

Box 9.5 Asset valuation of contaminated property.

Unimpaired value of land and buildings	£2 500 000
(calculated by an appropriate method, such as open market value or depreciated replacement cost, disregarding the existence of any contamination) – of which	
Value of buildings	£1 000 000
Unimpaired value of land element	£1 500 000
-say 5 hectares @ £300 000 per hectare of serviced site	

Remediation costs in accordance with GN 2.9.2 (Box 9.4)
(applicable if the site is to be redeveloped at the date of valuation)

(a)	clean-up of on-site contamination;	£250 000
(b)	effective contamination control and management measures;	£ 75 000
(c)	re-design of production facilities;	N/A
(d)	penalties and civil liabilities for non-compliance;	N/A
(e)	indemnity insurance for the future;	£ 10 000
(f)	the avoidance of migration of the contamination to adjacent sites;	£100 000
(g)	the control of migration from other sites; and	£ 15 000
(h)	the regular monitoring of the site.	£ 10 000
	Estimated total cost of treatment	£460 000

Anticipated **economic life** of buildings – 20 years

Present value of £1 for 20 years @ 7.5%	£0.235413
Present value of treatment costs	£ 108 290
Adjusted value, **impaired value**	
– excluding any allowance for stigma	£1 391 710

Percentage reduction in value attributable to anticipated future remediation	7.22%

Source: Syms (1995a)

deferment to the end of the economic life of the buildings. There may also be a case, depending upon site specific circumstances, for treating all or part of item (b) contamination control and management measures, in the same way. All such non–deferrable costs should be treated as current liabilities in the valuation and specifically reported upon. The valuer may also consider it appropriate to consult with the company's auditor, so as to determine which, if any, of the liabilities should be treated as general liabilities of the business, rather than related to the specific property.

In the example set out in Box 9.5 most of the remediation cost has been deferred to the end of the economic life of the buildings on the site, on the assumption that, at that time, the buildings will be demolished in order to facilitate 'clean-up' of the site. In practice it may be appropriate to undertake the site remediation in phases, whilst the manufacturing activities remain in operation. The valuation method would remain the same, except that the cost deferment, using the present value of £1, would be replaced by a discounted cash flow related to the expenditure programme, in order to arrive at the present value of the treatment costs.

Consideration was given to the need, or otherwise, to reflect inflation in the valuation method. Whilst it is possible that soil treatment costs may rise during the remaining life of the buildings, it was considered that any increase in costs should be countered by an inflation related increase in the value of the reclaimed development site. It is also possible that, as new treatment methods are developed, the cost of remediation may fall and, on balance, it was considered that the impact of inflation was likely to have little, if any, material effect.

The same valuation method may be applied to the valuation of leasehold interests, with the proviso that the period of deferment in respect of remedial works will be limited by the duration of the lease and not the economic life of the buildings. It may also be appropriate, when using this method to value leasehold interests, to make allowance for the landlord's costs and loss of income during the treatment period. The need for this will depend on the terms of the lease and whether the ultimate liability for the cost of treatment rests with the tenant or the landlord.

The principal problem in adopting an approach such as that described above, where detailed costs are not available, is in producing reasonable estimates of the costs involved. There is an obvious concern that any figures which are used may be wildly inaccurate, but the situation is not so very different from reflecting the likely cost of dilapidations when preparing a valuation of a building. In both cases the valuer will almost certainly need to consult with other professionals, such as engineers and quantity surveyors, and both valuations

Box 9.6   A method of assessing stigma.

Unimpaired value of land	£1 500 000
(a medium hazard risk property as used in the example in Box 9.5)	
Present value of remediation costs (from Box 9.5)	£ 108 290
Impaired value 1 – not allowing for stigma	£1 391 710

Comparable case studies

Case Study Number	Indicated percentage of impaired value 1 lost to Stigma	Comparison to the property to be Valued
1	25.9%	Treatment completed, stigma caused by fear of additional contamination, less severe than subject property.
2	29.2%	No treatment proposed at present, continued industrial use, similar risk level to subject property.
3	20.9%	Site not contaminated but is situated adjacent to a contaminated site.
4	32.7%	Similar type of contamination to subject property but slightly more severe.
5	45.4%	Heavily contaminated site, derelict land, more severe than the subject property.

Range of stigma effects indicated by comparables 20.9% to 45.4%
Comparables closest to subject property; numbers 2 and 4, 29.2% to 32.7%
Therefore percentage stigma applicable to the subject property is 31%

Amount of stigma @ 31% of impaired value 1	£ 431 430
Impaired value 2	£ 960 280
(taking account of treatment and associated costs and stigma)	
Add value of buildings from Box 9.5	£1 000 000
Total value of asset say	£1 960 000
Percentage reduction in value attributable to contamination	21.60%

Source: Developed from Patchin (1994) and Syms (1995)

inevitably require a degree of expert judgement on the part of the valuer. Two different aspects of dealing with land contamination are:

(1)   that much of the liability may be hidden from sight
(2)   the lack of information in respect of site remediation costs.

These will require reasoned assumptions to be made and demonstrate the need for a readily available source of costs information.

The method set out in Box 9.5 takes account of the 'cost to correct' aspects of the contamination but does not address the subject of stigma. Using the same case study, an approach to the assessment of stigma, adapted for use in the United Kingdom from Patchin's method, is shown in Box 9.6.

The total fall in value, reflecting both the physical and non-physical aspects of the contamination impact, is therefore £540 000 or 21.60% of the open market value of the property disregarding the existence of the contamination. Whilst it is appropriate, in circumstances such as the example described above, to defer most of the physical costs of remediation, the stigma effect is a current liability. This is because the calculation of stigma reflects present day attitudes to the former use of the premises, the type of contaminants and the associated hazard level. These attitudes may vary in the future.

Valuation for redevelopment

The example set out above produces an asset valuation for an industrial site which is expected to continue in production for the foreseeable future, reflecting both the estimated costs of treatment and stigma. The same method can be used when the buildings have reached the end of their economic life, or are otherwise redundant, and the site is to be redeveloped, as shown in the following example using the same property details.

In addition to preparing an asset valuation, the valuer has been asked to advise on its possible redevelopment as a residential estate. The planning authority is prepared to consider either option and a developer is willing to purchase the site for redevelopment, provided that he can be satisfied on the contamination issue.

Box 9.7 sets out a suggested method by which the property may be valued when the existing use is to cease and the site is to be redeveloped for an alternative, more sensitive, use. The first step in using the method is to value the site for redevelopment purposes on the assumption that the land is uncontaminated, but after deducting any demolition costs. This gives an unimpaired development value for the property and a base value for the site, from which the effects of contamination can be deducted, as the second step in the valuation.

Box 9.7   Redevelopment valuation of contaminated property.

Unimpaired value of land as a residential development site	
– say five hectares @ £800 000 per hectare	£4 000 000
Remediation costs in accordance with GN 2.9.2 (Box 9.4)	
(applicable if the site is to be redeveloped at the date of valuation)	
(a) clean-up of on-site contamination;	£400 000
(b) effective contamination control and management	
measures;	N/A
(c) re-design of production facilities;	N/A
(d) penalties and civil liabilities for non-compliance;	N/A
(e) indemnity insurance for the future;	£ 10 000
(f) the avoidance of migration of the contamination	
to adjacent sites;	£ 0
(g) the control of migration from other sites; and	£ 50 000
(h) the regular monitoring of the site.	£ 10 000
Estimated total cost of treatment	£485 000
Anticipated **Economic life** of buildings – 0 years	
Present Value of £1 for 0 years @ 7.5%	1.00
Present value of treatment costs	£ 485 000
Adjusted land value – impaired value 1	
– excluding any allowance for stigma	£3 515 000
Amount of stigma @ 31% of impaired value 1.	£1 089 650
– as calculated in Figure 9.6	
Impaired value 2 – as a residential development site	£2 425 350
Percentage reduction in development value due to contamination	39.36%

The total fall in the development value of the land, reflecting both the physical and non-physical aspects of the contamination impact, is therefore £1 574 650 or 39.36% of the open market value of the land if it had not been contaminated.

It will be noted that in the redevelopment scenario, no costs have been included for items (b), (c) and (d), contamination control, process re-design and penalties/civil liabilities. This is because production will have ceased prior to redevelopment and these items are therefore not applicable. Although no cost has been included under item (f), the avoidance of contamination migration to other sites, valuers should be aware of the need to avoid such migration both before and during the site reclamation, so as to limit the likelihood of any action being taken against the client for criminal or civil nuisance.

As shown in the example valuations, different costs criteria may be adopted, depending on whether the site is to continue in use or be redeveloped. The redevelopment option is for a more sensitive use, possibly requiring a higher standard of treatment, whereas the 'continued use' valuation assumes that upon expiry of the economic life of the existing buildings the land will continue to be used for industrial purposes, with greater emphasis therefore being placed on controlling the migration of contaminants.

Reporting contaminated land valuations

In view of changes to both government policy and professional guidance, valuers of industrial land and buildings have been faced with a dilemma when preparing valuations, or when advising on redevelopment, in respect of properties used for potentially contaminative purposes. Statements to the effect that valuations be issued, or revised, in the light of adequate environmental data concerning a property may be acceptable in circumstances where the site is vacant, or redevelopment is proposed and there is no competition from other potential purchasers. But, in almost all other circumstances, such an approach is unlikely to be acceptable to clients and does not provide the standard of service which should be expected of a responsible profession.

A report which relies upon caveats to avoid any liability may be of little use to a client interested in acquiring a manufacturing business and wishing to satisfy himself as to the value of the premises. The same argument may also apply in situations where the valuation is required for accounts purposes, or for bank security purposes where lending is to be secured against the business as a whole, rather than simply against the property assets. A recommendation that a Land Quality Statement be produced (see RICS, 1995a) is not very helpful in circumstances where continued operational use of the premises rules out the possibility of an invasive site investigation, and a report which reserves the right of the valuer to reconsider the valuation may be totally unacceptable to the bank.

The valuation of contaminated land may be distinguished from the valuation of other classes of property, including those damaged by fire, flood or decay, by virtue of its 'newness' in terms of being recognised as a valuation problem. The perceptions studies, described in Chapter 7, have confirmed that valuers have a fairly poor understanding of contamination and environmental issues in general. Contamination problems are often hidden from sight, under floor-slabs, concrete yards or hardstandings and are therefore less likely to be obvious to valuers than other types of property damage. The enquiries and observations, described in Chapter 5 in relation to preliminary site investigations, are little different from those which a prudent valuer should make as part of the valuation process.

Valuers may be concerned that if they produce valuations which attempt to take account of the existence of land contamination or other environmental impairment, without full knowledge of the potential liabilities, they may leave themselves open to allegations of professional negligence. This is a most important issue as 'any professional indemnity insurance cover for giving advice about the effects of contamination [for a valuer], is unlikely to be available as part of the normal PII [Professional Indemnity Insurance] policy or is likely to be strictly limited in scope.' (Wilbourn, 1995) It can be argued, however, that if valuers follow a common practice in respect of such properties, thoroughly researching available data and ensuring that clients are made fully aware of the limitations in respect of information concerning the property to be valued, then negligence should not be an issue.

The 'sales comparison' method of assessing stigma, described in this chapter, has been criticised by other commentators. For example,

Dixon (1995) expressed the view that such an approach is possible only when unimpaired and impaired transaction data are available, and that 'using contaminated comparables is fraught with difficulty: every contaminated case is different and often has circumstances which are unique'. (Dixon and Richards, 1995). Comments such as these are not fully substantiated. Certainly it is not necessary to have access to unimpaired transaction data in order to use the sales comparison method, as the uncontaminated value is arrived at using whatever valuation method is appropriate to the property and its current circumstances, disregarding contamination.

Whilst it is accepted that every contaminated case is different, the sales comparison approach requires transaction data to be carefully analysed so that comparisons can be made between sites, even when they are affected by different contaminants. In other words, the 'sales comparisons' should be used as a means to compare the level of risk associated with each site.

In the opinion of Richards (1996), use of the sales comparison approach 'in the case of income-producing properties, could produce absurd results.' This is correct if, as Richards suggests, the method is used to assess the post-treatment value of investment properties. He demonstrated this anomaly by applying the same percentage 'stigma' effect to the post-treatment investment value of a property and produced a far greater discount in value. Such an application would be a totally inappropriate use of the sales comparison method and has not been suggested in this book and the associated research.

The sales comparison method is most suited for use in respect of properties, such as those listed in paragraph 2.2.3, of Guidance Note 2 (RICS, 1995c). As mentioned earlier, these types of property are rarely found in investment portfolios and are infrequently sold in the open market. The method may also be suitable for use in respect of investment properties which are to remain in industrial use, provided that due regard is paid to any impact which the covenant strength of the tenant may have on the value.

Research by Turner et al (1994) has considered the effect of tenants' environmental policies on investment portfolios and concluded that assessing the risk,

'associated with the tenant's wider commercial activities ... involves a number of different stages utilizing new sources of information which the property investment market is unfamiliar with.'

It would seem likely however that the environmental record of an individual tenant, or even a whole industry, may have an impact on property investment values.

The impact of contamination on the value of investment properties was considered by Lizieri et al (1995) who stated that 'there are a number of technical difficulties associated with using an all risks yield approach to deal with potential environmental hazard'. The research included a survey of property investors and advisors, from which it was concluded that the,

'standard approach ... takes the local initial yield for the type of property under consideration then adjusts the value either by deducting estimated clean up costs or by adding a risk premium for the additional risk of environmental liability.'

(Lizieri et al, 1995)

In some cases, the researchers found that costs were being deducted and yields adjusted upwards, with a potential risk of double counting the impact of contamination on value.

The research undertaken at the College of Estate Management, by Dixon and Richards, has focused primarily on investment properties and, in the example scenarios, reflected the impact of stigma by way of adjustments to the All Risks Yield (Richards, T. 1995). The All Risks Yield (market yield) is the remunerate rate of interest used in the valuation of freehold and leasehold interests, reflecting all the prospects and risks attached to the particular investment. The amount of adjustment was derived from the result of an interview/questionnaire survey of valuation professionals but was based on a very small sample of valuation scenario responses. The general nature of contamination was reflected in the scenarios, for example 'non-migratory heavy metals' and 'groundwater contamination' but no attempt was made to reflect the degree of hazard associated with the contaminants. The survey responses produced ranges of suggested adjustments to the 'all risks yield' which, in some cases, were quite wide, for example an upwards yield adjustment in respect of non-migratory metals varied between 0.5% and 5.0%. It is suggested, therefore, that adjusting the 'all risks yield' in order to reflect stigma is at best arbitrary and may result in a misleading result, unless the yield adjustment is made with the benefit of a thorough understanding of the degree of risk associated with the property.

Recognising the problems associated with both the 'sales comparison' and 'yield adjustment' methods of valuing contaminated properties, the present author has examined the impact of contamination on the value of the land itself, rather than the investment value of land and buildings. One objective has been to develop a model which takes account of a wider range of factors, is less reliant upon comparable evidence or arbitrary yield adjustments, and more accurately reflects the true level of risk associated with the property to be valued. The development of this model is considered in the following section.

A 'risk assessment' model for the assessment of stigma

The following model has been developed out of research undertaken between 1991 and 1996. It has a theoretical basis and has been empirically tested. The purpose of the model is to assist in the valuation of properties affected by industrial contamination, where the industrial use is to continue for the foreseeable future, or when the site is to be redeveloped. It is intended that the model should be used to deduce land values only and it is not intended for use in respect of investment valuations, although it may be used to assess the value of the land element in those valuations. Also the model is not intended for use in respect of 'post-remediation' valuations.

To be of benefit the model needs to reflect practical considerations and to withstand testing against case study scenarios of actual transactions. Any proposed model needs to conform, so far as is possible, to the procedures recommended by the surveying profession, otherwise it is unlikely to be accepted by practitioners.

Commentators such as Simm (1992) and Laing (1992) have expressed opinions that the normal capital approach to valuation is not appropriate for the purpose of valuing contaminated land and, instead, have advocated use of the residual valuation method. This method can allow for the quantifiable costs of treating contamination but it fails when stigma has to be assessed. Patchin (1994) proposed the use of the 'sales comparison' approach but, unless good comparables are available, this too has limitations. The basis for the proposed model is a three step valuation process, similar to that described by Patchin, but with the final 'sales comparison' step being replaced by a 'risk assessment' technique. This change overcomes the problems associated with obtaining reliable comparable evidence. The three steps of the valuation process are as follows:

- **Step 1** – the preparation of a valuation of the property on the assumption that contamination does not exist, in order to deduce a base or 'Unimpaired Value'.
- **Step 2** – calculation of the expenditure required to treat the contaminated site, together with any associated costs, deferred as appropriate in order to arrive at 'Impaired Value 1'.
- **Step 3** – the assessment of any stigma attaching to the past or present industrial use(s) of the site, using a risk assessment based model, in order to arrive at 'Impaired Value 2.'

The first two steps of the valuation process have been described earlier in this chapter. The third step in the valuation process, as set out in Box 9.6, relied upon the use of comparables so as to adjust the valuation in order to reflect the stigma effect; this is replaced by the risk assessment part of the model.

The model draws upon the earlier work, in accepting both the residual approach and the sales comparison method. It also applies the 'professional perceptions' which influence the judgements the valuer will have to make in order to arrive at his or her opinion of value. In order to construct the model, five sets of data were required, as follows:

(1) observed stigma effects as reported in the literature;
(2) perceptions as to the relative levels of risk associated with different industrial activities, using a list of 26 uses adopted for research purposes;
(3) the assessed risk, in respect of the site to be valued, before any remediation work is undertaken;
(4) the perceived impact on value attributable to alternative methods of remediation and the expected end use of the site following treatment;

(5)   the estimated assessment of risk, following treatment and redevelopment of the site.

The relationship between the five sets of data is shown in Figure 9.4.

For the initial model development, the extent of stigma impact has been taken from the results of Patchin's 1994 study, which indicated a range of reduction in value of 21% to 69%. There are problems in adopting these results for the purpose of the model, not least of which is the fact that they are based on United States transactions but, to date, the UK literature does not provide a theoretical basis for determining a range of stigma effect. As an alternative to using an observed range of stigma effects obtained from the literature, valuers could produce a range based on their own experience. However, one valuer of contaminated properties has stated that, in his experience 'it is not possible to define a level of stigma discount allied to the level of contamination' (Wilbourn, 1996). It may be necessary for valuers to pool information in order to obtain data on a sufficiently large number of transactions to construct a base range of stigma impact.

The third phase of the perceptions studies enabled the 26 industrial activities used for the research to be ranked according to the risk perceptions of professionals involved in the valuation and redevelopment of contaminated properties. This produced the second set of data for the model and the ranking used is that obtained from the combined sample of valuation and non-valuation experts. The combined sample was selected in order to reflect the full range of professional opinions which may be available to an intending purchaser or developer, but there was in fact very little difference of opinion between the two expert groups. For use in the model, the perceived highest risk use 'asbestos manufacture and use' was given the value of the highest observed stigma effect of 69%, whilst the perceived lowest risk use 'dockyards and wharves' was ascribed the value of the lowest observed stigma effect of 21%. The other industrial uses were given intermediate values from the study, as in Table 9.1.

The purpose of the first two sets of data was to provide a framework to be applied to the valuation of specific properties. Information regarding the property to be valued is not required for either of the two data sets. The remaining three sets of data all required the input of property related information.

Fig. 9.4 The risk assessment model for the assessment of stigma. RET = retail park; RES = residential estate; BP = business park; IND = industrial estate; LEI = leisure use.

Table 9.1   Industrial activity and perceived stigma effect.

Industry type	Rank	Stigma
Asbestos manu. and use	1	69.00%
Chemicals manu. and store	2	63.23%
Radioactive mats. process	3	57.72%
Gas works	4	55.36%
Waste disposal sites	4	55.36%
Oil refining and storage	6	54.05%
Dyestuffs manufacturing	7	52.48%
Paint manufacture	8	50.11%
Tanning and leather works	9	47.75%
Metal treatment and finishing	10	46.97%
Metal smelting and refining	11	45.39%
Explosives industry	12	44.08%
Iron and steelworks	13	43.03%
Scrapyards	14	39.89%
Heavy engineering	15	37.79%
Mining and extractive inds.	16	37.26%
Electricity generating	17	36.21%
Pharmaceutical industries	18	33.85%
Paper and printing works	19	32.02%
Glass manufacture	20	30.44%
Timber treatment works	21	30.18%
Sewage treatment works	22	27.30%
Railway land	23	25.98%
Semi-conductor man. plants	24	21.79%
Textiles manufacture	25	21.52%
Dockyards and wharves	26	21.00%

The third set of data is the perceived impact on value, from phase two of the perceptions study, according to a risk assessment for the site in its untreated state (Box 7.2). A formal risk assessment may be available; alternatively it is suggested that a valuer with appropriate experience should be able to allocate the site into one of the five hazard categories used for the research. Whether or not the valuer is able to make such an allocation will depend upon the answers received in response to the questions set out in Box 9.3, together with any further enquiries which may be considered necessary.

The fourth set of data is intended to reflect the site treatment and future use aspects of the valuation. This uses the results from the first phase of the perceptions study and, as with the industrial activities in set two, reflects the views of both valuation and non-valuation professionals (see Box 7.1).

In situations where immediate redevelopment of the site is not anticipated and the site is to remain in its present use for the foreseeable future, the valuer will have to make assumptions at the date of valuation as to the method of treatment and the future use(s) which might be considered appropriate, and set out the basis of those assumptions in his or her report. The same assumptions will also be required to assess the costs of possible treatment to complete the second step of the valuation method.

The final set of data comprises the impact on value attributable to the degree of hazard which is expected to exist on the site following redevelopment (see Box 7.1). This issue was addressed in both phases two and three of the perceptions study, but the results from the phase two study have been disregarded for the purpose of this model.

A value has been included in the model for the possibility of severe contamination, 'very high hazard,' remaining on site after treatment. Although it would appear, at first sight, to be pointless to undertake any form of treatment if the resultant hazard classification is not reduced, this category has been retained in respect of the post-treatment state of the site, to deal with situations such as the excavation of radioactive material or toxic chemicals and their re-interment in a secure containment within the curtilage of the building. Other situations where the 'very high hazard' classification would apply after treatment might include industrial properties where the contaminants are covered by existing buildings or impervious yard areas and treatment works are undertaken to prevent migration of the contamination to adjoining properties or groundwater. In such cases the sites would be suitable for continued industrial use but would present a very high degree of risk if the containments were to fail or be breached.

Application of the model

The range of stigma effect, referred to as the first set of data, sets a baseline for the impact of stigma on property values, whilst the second set of industry specific data enables stigma values to be determined for a range of activities, based upon the research. Data sets three to five link the empirical research to actual properties which are to be valued, using risk related data for the present and expected conditions of the land.

In this way 'value adjusters' are obtainable in respect of strands two to five and, in order to apply the model, these 'value adjusters' should be aggregated then divided by four to give a mean value. The mean value thus arrived at is the stigma effect to be applied as a percentage reduction against 'Impaired Value 1' to give 'Impaired Value 2'. Use of this method enables the valuer to take account of the present and/ or past uses of the site, the present level of risk attaching to the contaminants in the ground, the valuation impact of the selected method of treatment and the expected 'post-treatment' level of risk. The method brings together actual site conditions and the perceptions of professional valuers.

A number of actual redevelopment case studies are described in Chapters 10 and 11 and these are used to test the validity of the valuation model. A formal risk assessment was prepared for only one of the case study sites and, in all other cases, the 'risk assessments' used for the purpose of testing the model have been derived from analysis of the site investigations and consultants' reports.

Checklist

Valuation instructions

- Is the valuation within your sphere of competence, or is there sufficient expertise within the firm to enable you to undertake the valuation?
- Has sufficient information been supplied by the client?
- Check whether or not you will be able to obtain access to the operational records of the site.
- Ask the questions in Box 9.3 and consider whether any additional information is required.
- Ascertain whether the valuation is required for asset purposes, loan security, redevelopment or any other purpose.

Preparing the valuation

- Does the information obtained indicate that contamination is not likely to be present on the site, or does it confirm that contamination is an issue which will need to be taken into account in the valuation?

- Take care to observe and note any visible signs of contamination, such as staining on the ground or unsatisfactory working practices, when making the site inspection.
- Consider the need for a site investigation.
- Can you obtain sufficient information about soil treatment costs and other possible expenditure from within the firm, or will specialist advice be required?
- Has a formal risk assessment been prepared for the site in its present condition, or is one proposed? If not, is there sufficient information available to enable you, or colleagues, to form your own assessment or will specialist help be required?
- Is the proposed treatment method the most suitable for the present or expected end use?

Chapter 10
Redevelopment of Contaminated Sites: for Industrial or Commercial Use

One aspect which would appear to be quite clear from the previous chapter, is that quantification of the impact of contamination on value is extremely difficult. It may be possible to ascribe a range of value impacts to a particular type or severity of contamination, as in Patchin's work, but these may be liable to significant variations according to market conditions. Generalisation of the effects of contamination on value is virtually impossible, hence the suggested 'risk assessment' approach to valuation, which seeks to reflect the actual hazard of attaching to an individual site in its present use and through the process of redevelopment, into its future end use. Whilst it is important to reflect the presence of contamination when preparing valuations, it is during redevelopment that the possible effects of contamination come to the forefront.

In a valuation the full cost of remediating a contaminated site may be deferred many years into the future, for example, until such time as the existing buildings have become economically or functionally obsolete. When considering the redevelopment of a contaminated site, the need to tackle contamination assumes an immediacy which cannot be ignored. If an intending developer decides simply to disregard the existence of contamination, he is likely to encounter problems in obtaining development finance and may be unable to sell or let the completed development.

Therefore a prudent developer will take full account of any contamination existing on the site and use an appropriate treatment method, or methods, in order to overcome the problem (Figure 10.1). The valuation methods discussed in the previous chapter demonstrate how valuers may take account of possible, or actual,

Fig. 10.1 The intending developer needs the fullest information possible, including whether or not these pipes have been flushed out and if they are lagged with asbestos.

contamination when preparing their valuations. The implications of contamination for the redevelopment process are considered in the next two chapters, together with the effects on value before and after treatment. This chapter considers the redevelopment of contaminated sites for continued industrial use, or for alternative uses of a commercial nature, such as business and retail parks. Chapter 11 deals with the change of use from industrial to perhaps the most sensitive of all end uses, residential development, both for sale and to rent.

'The success of any development relies on close co-operation between the developer, the architect, the engineer and the quantity surveyor – success being the fulfilment of the developer's requirements at an economical cost'.

(Lord 1991, p. 145)

The role of the valuer is not mentioned. However, the valuer has a pivotal role to play in the development process – especially where contaminated land is concerned. For if the valuer is not satisfied with the remediation methods selected for the treatment of a particular site, he or she may not be prepared to produce a valuation at a figure needed to provide the developer with a profit.

Choice of remediation methods

The remediation method, or methods, recommended by the engineer as satisfying present day requirements, and identified by the quantity surveyor as being the most cost effective, may be unacceptable to a valuer advising a client contemplating a long term commitment to the completed development. Indeed, the site may not be classed as contaminated in the true legal sense, using the definitions of 'contaminated land' and 'significant harm' proposed by the government, but may be merely derelict or redundant. The valuer acting for a prospective purchaser, investor or mortgage provider may, however, perceive the site to be affected by contamination, notwithstanding the legal definition, and advise against the purchase, investment or loan. Valuation issues therefore need to be taken into account with regard to proposed redevelopment projects, on derelict or contaminated sites, from their inception.

The two methods of site remediation most commonly used in the United Kingdom have been the excavation of contaminated material and its disposal to landfill, and on-site containment of the contaminated material, although biological and soil venting methods have been widely used for the treatment of hydrocarbon contamination. As discussed in Chapter 6, any treatment which leaves behind residual contamination, whether securely contained or at reduced toxicity levels, is likely to result in values below those which may be attributable to a greenfield, but otherwise similar, property. On the other hand, a site which has undergone the most thorough cleansing may still suffer from stigma due to its past use or uses. Therefore the costs and benefits attaching to all possible treatment options need to be carefully evaluated before a final decision is taken.

Environmental objections to the transfer of contaminants from one location to another, more stringent controls arising out of the Environmental Protection Act 1990 and the Environment Act 1995, and the reduced availability of suitable landfill sites have significantly increased the cost of the option of excavation and off-site disposal. Alternative forms of treatment can therefore be expected to become more attractive in both cost and environmental terms, but it remains to be seen to what extent the alternatives will be acceptable to actors involved in the development process. It is argued that, in the short term at least, developers, funders, occupiers and other property users will approach untried or unconventional treatment methods with considerable wariness, especially if the methods are designed to reduce, rather than remove, contamination.

Case study 10.1: Consideration of alternative remediation methods

A chemical manufacturing company wished to construct a new warehouse for its own use on part of its site which had previously been used for open storage. The site was larger than required by the company for its own use and the company also wished to rent, rather than own, its new building. An approach was made to a local developer who would build two identical units, one pre-let to the company and the other to be let in the open market. The site was severely contaminated with heavy metals, which were immobile, and discussion ensued as to the method of treating the site prior to redevelopment.

The manufacturer was familiar with the nature of the contaminants, which had originated from its own manufacturing processes, and was happy for these to remain in the ground under the new industrial units. A clean cover, consisting of concrete yards and vehicle parking areas was therefore proposed. The developer, on the other hand, was less than happy about the contaminants remaining on site and wanted them to be removed at significantly increased cost. A stalemate ensued and the development did not proceed.

The case study may be used to examine the issues relating to remediation options at three levels; firstly in respect of the land itself, as a site already owned or to be bought for use by an owner occupier; secondly from the viewpoint of the potential tenant of a new development, intending to sign a lease for a term of 25 years on a full repairing and insuring basis with upwards only rent reviews; and finally as perceived by the ultimate investor in the completed development. Reflecting current approaches to dealing with contamination, the two remediation options under consideration were the removal of the contaminated material and its disposal off site, to be replaced with clean fill, and the containment on site of the contamination under a layer of clean cover.

Box 10.1 compares how the viability of site reclamation may be calculated when using the two selected methods of treatment. The first method involves excavating contaminated material and replacing it with clean fill. It can be argued that the value of a site treated in this way with good engineering design, carefully supervised and well documented, is no different from the value of a previously undeveloped

Box 10.1 Impact on development land values: comparison of treatment methods.

Treatment method (a one hectare site)	Excavate and replace per hectare	Contain and cover per hectare
• **Existing site value** say for open storage or lorry parking	£60 000	£60 000
• **Cost of site remediation** Excavate contaminated material, cart away to landfill and backfill with 'clean' material, inclusive of fees but excluding finance costs — say	£210 000	
OR –		
Containment of contamination within the site and covering with 'clean' material, inclusive of fees but excluding finance costs — say		£120 000
• Total cost of reclaimed site	£270 000	£180 000
• Value of reclaimed site, reflecting perceived risk — say	£330 000	£240 000
• Deduct existing value and treatment cost	£270 000	£180 000
• Residue for finance and profit	£ 60 000	£ 60 000
• Residue as a percentage of existing site value plus remediation costs	22.22%	33.33%

Source: Based on Syms (1994b)

'greenfield' site. The residue of £60 000 per hectare for finance and profit is, by normal development criteria, a reasonable return (22.22%) for the capital and risk involved in reclaiming the site. The viability of the alternative method, using containment, is shown in Box 10.1. It will be noted that in spite of a lower realisable value, the residue for finance and profit is the same as that for the removal option because of the lower level of expenditure on site treatment. The post remediation value of the site is below that obtained using excavation and clean fill because contamination remains on site, but the containment option produces a better return, at 33.33%, on capital employed (see Box 10.1). The risk factor may be significantly reduced as the remediation becomes less susceptible to outside influences, such as increases in haulage and landfill disposal charges.

Either of the remediation methods used in Box 10.1 may be perfectly acceptable to an individual or organisation wishing to construct a building for owner occupation, as in the case of the chemical company referred to in the case study, especially if the occupier can adequately assess the risks involved. Indeed, for a continuation of industrial use the less costly treatment method, with its resultant lower site value, may be preferred and it may be inappropriate to attempt to achieve a higher standard of remediation. Problems may, however, arise in the event of a sale at some future date, or if the owner wishes to use the premises as security for a bank loan. It is therefore necessary to consider how another occupier, in this case a potential tenant, and a funding institution might perceive the two alternative treatment methods.

Box 10.2 illustrates a simple residual valuation for the development of an industrial building of 4250 square metres on the same one hectare site as considered in Box 10.1. The owner occupier would be satisfied with the containment and cover option but a potential tenant and an investor may have a different perception. In other words, the speculative unit development in the case study example.

So far as the removal and replacement option is concerned, it is assumed that the valuer acting for the prospective tenant is satisfied with the site treatment and so too is the valuer acting for the institutional investor; stigma in this case is considered to be of little or no significance. The rental and yield rates used in the appraisal are in keeping with those which might be applied to a development on a greenfield site in the same locality, at the time when the development was to be undertaken. The residue for finance and profit is such that the project would be an attractive development proposition for a pre-let development.

If, however, the site had been treated by the cover and containment method a very different result might emerge. The valuer, acting on behalf of the prospective tenant, might take a more cautious approach and, although satisfied with the adequacy of the remediation method for continued industrial use of the site, might be justified in having some concerns with regard to the long term nature of his client's responsibilities under a 25 year lease. He would therefore seek to exclude any liability from attaching to his client in respect of the contamination containment and also demand a reduction in the rent to be paid, of say £5.00 per square metre per annum.

The fact that contamination remains on site, and that the tenant refuses to accept any future liability in respect of that contamination,

Box 10.2   Impact on investment/mortgage values in the open market.

Proposed development of a light industrial/warehouse building of 4250 square metres on a site of one hectare, comparing two treatment methods

		Excavate and replace	Contain and cover
• **Treatment method**			
• Rental value 4250 square metres			
@ £45-00 per square metre	£191 250 per annum		
• Capitalisation yield 11%	9.09 Years Purchase		
• **Investment value of development (gross)**		**£1 738 600**	
OR –			
• Rental value 4250 square metres			
@ £40-00 per square metre			
reduced because of perceived risk	£170 000 per annum		
• Capitalisation yield 13%	7.69 Years Purchase		
• **Investment value of development (gross)**			**£1 307 700**
Deduct costs			
• Site cost as Box 10.1		£ 270 000	£ 180 000
• Building (design and build package), same for both options		£1 130 000	£1 130 000
• Total cost		£1 400 000	£1 310 000
• **Residue (deficit) for finance and profit**		£ 338 600	(£ 2 300)
• **Residue as a percentage of existing site value plus remediation costs**		24.19%	–0.18%

Source: Based on Syms (1994b)

will have a direct impact on the yield obtainable in the investment market. Any potential investor will require a higher return on capital employed to compensate for the possibility that the contamination may represent a future liability. In this example, the anticipated investment yield has been moved out by two percentage points to reflect the fact that the completed development may not be attractive to an institutional investor but is acceptable to a private investor. The combined result of the tenant's and the investor's perceptions of the treatment method will, therefore, be one of turning a profitable development into a loss. On the basis of this case study, a prudent developer would tend towards the treatment option which removes, rather than contains or reduces, the contamination risk. Such an approach may be totally out of keeping with the actual level of risk involved on the site and redevelopment opportunities may be lost.

The simplified example described in Box 10.2 considers only two methods of dealing with contaminated land and assumes that, once treated, the site will remain in industrial use. There are, of course, many other methods of site treatment available today, as discussed in Chapter 6, and it is also quite possible that, following remediation, the formerly contaminated site will be redeveloped for another, non-industrial use.

Redevelopment case studies – industrial or commercial use

At the present time there is no readily accessible source of information relating to property transactions in respect of contaminated land in the United Kingdom. In spite of the lack of a comprehensive database it is possible to make assessments as to the likely impact of industrial contamination on values, using case studies for which transactional data are available. The following case studies describe actual developments undertaken between 1987 and 1996 on sites which had previously been used for different purposes, were treated by different reclamation methods and were redeveloped for a variety of end uses. The case studies were chosen for their different past uses and forms of contamination and differing methods of site remediation.

A table is provided for each of the case studies, which sets out the stigma effect which may be expected in accordance with the 'risk assessment' valuation model described in Chapter 9. The expected stigma effect is also compared to the actual reduction in value, attributable to stigma, observed in each of the case study transactions. The 'model value adjusters' given in the tables are those determined by the value adjusters, derived from the 'risk assessment' valuation model in respect of: the perceived highest risk former use of the site; the pre-treatment risk assessment; the remediation method(s) selected for the site; its proposed use and expected post-treatment risk assessment. The aggregate of the 'value adjusters' is then divided by four to give the 'Expected Stigma Effect' as a percentage reduction in value.

Case study 10.2: Former colliery site

This site of 6.705 hectares (16.57 acres) was originally developed in 1984 to provide a factory of 7480 square metres (80500 square feet) for a packaging company. The project was to construct an extension of 12 077 square metres (130 000 square feet) on two sides of the original factory.

The colliery was a deep mine, with workings to 426 metres (1400 feet) below ground level. A number of previous uses are known to have existed on the site, including a Baum plant, bunkers, and tanks, two of which could possibly have been gasometers. Part of the site had been occupied by a quarry and a number of mine shafts were known to have existed on, or adjacent to, the site. The colliery was closed in 1976 and the shafts sealed up.

At the time of the 1984 development the site was covered by up to three metres of colliery waste, overlying sands and gravels from the glacial age. The bedrock was of carboniferous coal measures, consisting predominantly of siltstone, shales and coal. The calorific value of the colliery spoil was so high as to present a potential for spontaneous combustion.

The area upon which the original factory was constructed, plus a three metre wide strip around the perimeter, was excavated down to natural ground and the waste material removed from site. The excavated spoil was deposited in a nearby quarry, from which stone fill was obtained to make up

Fig. 10.2   The completed factory showing the adjoining land, used for the containment of colliery waste, mounded and landscaped. (Source: Pochin plc.)

the void. Thus the remediation undertaken for the original building covered the minimum site area required to enable construction to take place.

As the result of the method used for the site remediation, when the proposed extension was being considered in 1994, all of the available expansion land, except for the three metre perimeter strip, was covered by colliery waste. A detailed site investigation was undertaken by environmental consultants and in some places the depth of waste material was found to be at least five metres. This investigation also confirmed that the calorific values, an indication of the combustibility of the fill material, were well in excess of the safety level, with values exceeding that level by between 170% and 230%. The consultants also found that the spoil was contaminated with coal tar products, including semi-volatile organic compounds. There was no evidence of methane generation from the site, but concentrations of carbon monoxide, above the ICRCL threshold level, were found in some locations.

The original treatment method of removing the waste to a quarry and refilling with clean material from the same source was no longer available as the quarry had closed. Alternative treatment methods were therefore considered, with preference being given to on site or *in-situ* methods. Advice was taken from a specialist engineering consultant, who suggested that it would be possible to remove the risk of combustion by excavating the spoil and re-interring it in layers with limestone intermediate layers. This would have resulted in raising the level of the expansion land by up to one and a half metres, which was not feasible in the context of the proposed development.

Attention then turned to the identification of an alternative depository for the colliery spoil and an area of adjoining land was purchased, which increased the area of the site from the original area of 3.804 hectares (9.4 acres), to 6.705 hectares (16.57 acres). The additional site was landlocked and suffered a 50% reduction in value (based on the principle in *Rathgar Properties and Merrydale Motor Co.* v. *Haringay London Borough* (1978 EG vol 248 p. 693)). It was purchased for an almost nominal sum, which reflected the fact that it could only be developed at considerable expense.

The additional land was immediately adjacent to the existing site and its acquisition enabled the layout of the extension to be re-designed, using part of the additional land. The remaining area of the additional land was used as a depository for the coal waste, using the natural fall of the land and extending the embankment beside the adjoining trunk road. The newly created spoil heap contains colliery waste up to 12 metres in depth, landscaped with grass and trees.

The cost of excavating the waste material and replacing it with clean fill was estimated at £600 000, considerably in excess of any economic value attaching to the expansion land. An application was made to the Welsh Office for an Urban Investment Grant, the Welsh equivalent of City Grant. The grant subsequently awarded was the same sum as the estimated remediation cost.

At the time of the development, serviced industrial land in the vicinity of the site was available for around £148 250 per hectare (£60 000 per acre) but, if the cost of treatment and the access problem are taken into account in respect of the case study site, the price paid for the land equated to a reduction of 67% against the value of industrial development land in the area. The completed development was let to the existing tenant on a new lease, on full repairing and insuring terms. No reduction in rent was allowed to reflect stigma but future responsibility for the spoil heap was retained by the developer.

Several different industrial uses had existed on this site, all related to the coal mining industry. The highest risk uses were considered to be the use of part of the site for coal products and as a depository for highly combustible coal wastes. Therefore, a 'very high hazard' assessment was applied and the site would almost certainly be classed as contaminated in accordance with the draft guidance issued by the

Table 10.1   The risk assessment model applied to case study 10.2.

Comparable case study:	Former colliery site	Model value
Present or past industrial use(s):	Coal tar and gasification plant, coal mining, colliery spoil heap	
Highest risk present or past use:	Gas works and waste disposal site	55.36
Pre-treatment risk assessment:	Very high hazard	90.38
Proposed or probable treatment method:	Group 2 Excavate from development area, contain within site.	2.50
Post-treatment expected risk assessment:	Medium hazard	19.10
Aggregate model value:		167.34
Expected stigma effect:		41.84%
Observed stigma effect:		67.00%

Department of the Environment. The treatment method used for the site, the excavation of contaminated material and its replacement with clean fill, was a 'low technology' Group 1 method, but the excavated material was to be retained in a depository constructed within the curtilage of the site, therefore a Group 2 value has been used for the model. Because of the existence of the depository a 'medium hazard' post-treatment risk assessment has been used, although it should be stressed that responsibility for the deposited material has not been passed to the tenant or subsequent investor. The model as applied to this site is set out in Table 10.1.

Case study 10.3: Former chemical works

This case study is located within an area of mixed industrial uses and occupies 11.736 hectares (29 acres). The site was acquired for redevelopment purposes in 1989, following closure and demolition of the chemical works. All of the buildings had been demolished and the site levelled with most, if not all, of the demolition materials remaining on site. The site had been levelled to form a plateau with fill material at the rear of the site (Figure 10.3). Prior to demolition all asbestos within the buildings was removed and taken from the site for disposal.

Fig. 10.3 Rubble from the demolished factory had been used to fill and level the site but had been inadequately consolidated.

Chemical production on the site started in 1908, with the manufacture of dyestuffs, a use which continued into the late 1950s. For a period of about five years, 1914 to 1919 the site was government run, after which it was owned by several different chemical companies up to the time of its closure. In addition to dyestuffs the plant was known to have produced the chemicals described in Box 10.3.

According to the site history, provided by a former employee of the last site operator, 'as the small amounts of site contaminants were not toxic, no remediation was undertaken and hence no area of the site was sold off as

Box 10.3 History of chemical production at former chemical works.

Chemical	Period of production	Raw materials stored on site	By-products
Sulphur dioxide	Late 1920s–1983	Sulphur Sulphuric acid	none
Sodium hydrosulphite	Early 1920s to 1984/5	Zinc Sulphur dioxide Sodium hydroxide Ethyl alcohol	Zinc hydroxide Zinc sulphite/ Sulphide sludge
Zinc hydrosulphite	Mid 1960s to early 1970s	Zinc Sulphur dioxide	Zinc sulphite Sulphide sludge
Sodium formaldehyde sulphoxylate	Early 1930s to 1980	Zinc Sulphur dioxide Sodium hydroxide Formaldehyde	Zinc hydroxide Zinc sulphite/ Sulphide sludge
Potassium acetaldehyde sulphoxylate	Late 1950s to 1985	Zinc, Sulphur dioxide Potassium hydroxide Acetaldehyde	As above
Zinc formaldehyde sulphoxylate	Early 1930s to 1980	Zinc Sulphur dioxide Formaldehyde Ethyl alcohol	Zinc sulphite/sulphide sludge
Formaldehyde	Late 1930s to pre-1958	Methanol	
Sodium metabisulphite	Mid 1950s to 1983/4	Sulphur dioxide Sodium carbonate	none
Zinc oxide	1977 to 1985	Zinc hydroxide by-product	none

having been remediated'. The same source also stated that 'small amounts of liquid sulphur which could not be pumped out were probably left in the base of the sulphur pits. This would solidify once the heating was turned off. The pits were later filled in'. Also mentioned in the site history was the fact that the zinc sulphite/sulphide sludges produced as by-products were retained on site in bunded areas and that there would 'be some contamination in this area'. Reference was made to the possibility that small traces of cadmium sulphite/sulphide may remain 'as some 0.01–0.05% of cadmium was present in the zinc dusts used on site'.

In 1988 the local authority commissioned and paid for a site investigation to be undertaken by a firm of consulting engineers. This investigation consisted of the excavation of 29 trial pits, one per acre, over the entire area of the site. The extent of this investigation fell far short of the recommendations contained in BSI Development Draft 175 (BSI, 1988) which, if complied with, would have required 200 sampling points on a site of this size.

Chemical analysis on samples obtained in the site investigation revealed the presence of many of the chemicals referred to in Box 10.3, and the consultant noted that some of the chemicals 'are extremely aggressive to plants, animals and building materials'. From the limited scope site investigation it was recommended that 'the thick layers of chemical waste and other surface contamination need to be removed and taken off site. The removal of this material would involve excavating material to depths of up to 2.3 metres'. In addition to the contaminated fill material on the site, the sludge lagoons were up to 1.6 metres in depth and contained approximately 2500 metres of concentrated contaminants.

The fill material on the site was underlain by sandstone bedrock, with minimal surface cover, which out-cropped in the south-east corner of the site. The water table was at a depth of between 30 and 45 metres and was a producing aquifer used for industrial purposes. The natural topography of the site was a fall from south to north towards the River Mersey but the fill material had been used to create an almost level plateau, which was steeply banked at the northern end of the site.

On the basis of the information contained in the consultants' reports, an application was made to the Department of the Environment, in April 1990, for a City Grant to reclaim the site, provide the infrastructure for a new development and construct a business park development. After a considerable amount of discussion a revised application was approved in respect of a first phase of development, covering the front 4.05 hectares (10 acres) of the site, which was the area believed to be least affected by the contamination. The grant covered not only the estimated site remediation costs but also contained a significant commercial subsidy intended to encourage employment by creating development in a depressed area. Private sector funding was provided by the company's bank and one new factory has so far been built upon the site (Figure 10.4).

Fig. 10.4 The first new factory on the site, with the neighbouring power station in the background.

The Phase 1 grant was based on the removal of contaminated material from site and its replacement with clean fill. The amount of fill material in the front ten acres was estimated as being between 5000 and 10 000 cubic metres. After 3000 cubic metres had been removed from site the volume of material was re-estimated at 17 000 to 20 000 cubic metres. The remediation method was therefore re-examined with a view to reducing the amount of material removed from site. As the contaminants of greatest concern were primarily phytotoxic, and as most of the site was to be covered with industrial buildings, yard areas and car parks, it was decided to set a site specific standard for the remediation. The ICRCL threshold trigger concentration for zinc is 300 mg/kg for any uses where plants are to be grown. In view of the nature of the proposed end use for the site, a standard of 2500 mg/kg was adopted and agreed with the Environmental Health Department of the local authority. The remainder of the Phase 1 area was remediated to this standard.

Consideration was given to alternative methods of site remediation, including the construction of an on-site containment area in the form of a bund formed with an impervious geotextile, but this would have resulted in the sterilisation of a significant part of the site area. Soils washing was considered, and an initial appraisal was undertaken which concluded that the volume of clean material recovered for re-use on site would probably not be sufficient to make this option financially viable. Enquiries were also made regarding the possibility of recovering the metals either *in-situ* or *ex-situ* for re-processing, and again this was found to be not financially viable. One further option, under consideration at the time of writing, is that of emulsifying the contaminants within a coarse material to be used as an aggregate for road and service yard sub-bases.

The developer purchased the site on the basis of the reports prepared for the local authority and in the belief that grant aid would be sufficient to overcome the contamination problems. The price paid for the site reflected the fact that it was an old industrial site but, as shown in the site history, the vendor did not consider it to be contaminated. At the time of acquisition. industrial land in the area was available for around £123 550 per hectare (£50 000 per acre), excluding infrastructure and, after allowing for the cost of the non-contamination related abnormal costs, the price paid by the developer represented a discount for stigma of 25.91%.

This site had a long history of use for chemicals and dyestuffs

Table 10.2 The risk assessment model applied to case study 10.3.

Comparable case study:	Former chemical works	Model value adjuster
Present or past industrial use(s):	Chemicals manufacture, dyestuffs manufacture	
Highest risk present or past use:	Chemicals manufacture	63.23
Pre-treatment risk assessment:	Medium hazard	22.43
Proposed or probable treatment method:	Group 2 Excavate most severe contamination, cover and contain remainder	2.50
Post-treatment expected risk assessment:	Low hazard	7.05
Aggregate model value:		95.21
Expected stigma effect:		23.80%
Observed stigma effect:		25.91%

manufacture, with the former being considered the highest risk use for the purpose of the valuation model. The pre-treatment hazard level was considered to be 'medium', but as the contamination was phytotoxic in nature and the proposed end use was for industrial purposes, the site would probably not be considered to present a threat of 'significant harm' and therefore would not be classed as contaminated. The selected treatment method was in Group 2, cover and containment, and the post-treatment risk level was estimated as 'low hazard'. The model as applied to this site is set out in Table 10.2.

Case study 10.4: Former chemical works

This site has an area of approximately 8.9 hectares (22 acres) and had been used for the manufacture of dyestuffs, with the original factory having been constructed in the 1920s and subsequently extended in the 1930s. Following closure, the site operator made its records available for the site investigation, but for the earlier part of its existence the site had been in other ownerships, with the result that the early records were not available.

The site was purchased in 1988 by a local company with considerable development experience in the area. The buildings and plant were demolished, with the site cleared to ground level. Architects, quantity surveyors, consulting engineers, letting and investment agents and an economic consultant were appointed to advise in respect of the project. All of the appointed consultants had either worked with the developer on previous projects or had been recommended by other members of the professional team.

The topography of the site was level, and prior to the commencement of redevelopment much of the area was covered with buildings and hard surfaces. A site investigation was undertaken in 1988, comprising a desk study and an invasive investigation conducted in accordance with BSI DD 175, British Standards Institution (BSI, 1988). The geology of the site was flood gravels of glacial age, overlying a bedrock of Bunter sandstone; peat deposits were found over approximately 40% of the site.

From the information supplied to the consultants it was apparent that a number of known carcinogens had been used on site, notably beta napthylamine, and this was confirmed by analysis of samples taken from the site. The analyses also identified high levels of chromium contamination with concentrations up to 32 times the ICRCL trigger level for open space (ICRCL, 1987), and of mercury with concentrations up to four times the ICRCL trigger level.

Acidic conditions were encountered over much of the site with pH values down to 4.5 over most of the area, at depths down to 3.2 metres. High sulphate concentrations were encountered in the groundwater at depths of between 2.2 and 3.1 metres. The contamination was distributed generally throughout the site and probably originated from a combination of burying industrial wastes and the use of similar material in the substructures of factory extensions and the formation of hardstandings.

Three remediation methods were considered by the consultants;

(1) total removal of the contaminated material and its replacement with suitable fill; this would mean that services and sub-structures would not require protection from potentially aggressive contaminants;

(2) partial replacement of contaminated material from 'hot spots' and replacement with suitable fill, with the remaining contaminated material covered with suitable break layers to prevent the upwards migration of contamination, and finished with a suitable capping for the end use envisaged;

(3) leave all of the contaminants in place, finish the site with a suitable break layer and capping as in the second option.

The third option was considered to be viable only if the site was not to be redeveloped with new buildings and was used instead for a purpose such as open storage or vehicle parking. The risk of further groundwater contamination would remain. The professional team was unanimous in its recommendation to the developer that the first option should be adopted. This recommendation was made because not enough was known about the possible effect the retained contamination in option 2 would have on the future investment values of buildings constructed on the site.

The drawback to option 1 was the high cost of site reclamation, estimated at almost £5 million, excluding professional fees and finance charges for the six month period required for the engineering work. This equated to almost one and a half times the price being paid at that time for serviced and uncontaminated industrial land in the locality.

An application was made for a City Grant to meet the cost of removing the contamination from the site. During the course of the grant negotiations further consideration was given to the possibility of adopting option 2, but again the conclusion was reached that this would leave too many unknowns.

Whilst the City Grant negotiations continued, the remediation work had been put out to tender and one of the tenderers proposed that pulverised fly ash (PFA) be used to re-fill the site, instead of the granular fill specified in the tender documents. The engineering and environmental consultants were initially unwilling to accept this proposal as PFA is sometimes heavily contaminated. However, the contractor had access to a source of PFA which had been tested free from contaminants, and offered to undertake the whole of the remediation work for a price of £3.9 million, compared to the budget of almost £5 million. As a result, a grant of £3.9 million was awarded.

The remediation programme was subsequently carried out under the full-time supervision of an environmental consultant and a chemist, with materials being tested both entering and leaving the site. At the peak of the remediation contract up to 400 vehicle movements a day were taking place under stringently controlled conditions (Figure 10.5).

In spite of the detailed site survey which had been undertaken prior to commencement of the project, approximately 1000 tonnes of nitro-benzene, a carcinogen, was discovered under a concrete slab in the centre of the site. The maximum concentration of nitro-benzene in the fill material was 26% and the landfill to which the contaminated spoil was being consigned would not accept it in concentrations exceeding 10%. One of the options considered for dealing with this unexpected problem was to transport it in sealed containers to an incinerator in the Netherlands, at a total additional cost of £1.4 million. Eventually a solution was agreed with the receiving tip and the Waste Regulation Authorities for the contaminated fill to be mixed on site with a similar volume of crushed stone and then to be consigned to the landfill, at an additional cost of around 10% of the incineration alternative.

The total removal option was vindicated when the London based solicitor acting for an overseas manufacturing company which wished to lease a purpose built factory on the development, advised his client that,

Fig. 10.5 The site was excavated to an average depth of two metres over its entire area, then lined with a geotextile, covered with crushed stone to act as a capillary break layer and then refilled to its original level with pulverised fly ash.

'the site was formerly used for chemicals manufacture, is probably contaminated and will undoubtedly appear on any future register of contaminated land, therefore the property is not likely to be a good investment and the company should reconsider its decision to acquire premises on this site'.

At a meeting involving the developer and the entire professional team, the remediation method and the way in which it had been managed was explained to representatives of the overseas company. As the result of this meeting, the company proceeded with its acquisition but, if either of the other two options had been adopted, the outcome would undoubtedly have been very different.

Although the developer had acquired the site for a sum which was substantially below the price which would have been achievable had the site been capable of immediate development, it was still more than the grant appraiser was prepared to accept as base value. Some credits were deemed to accrue to the developer out of the demolition work and the existing value, for grant purposes, was adjusted downwards to a figure which was considered to be equivalent to its alternative use value for a lower level economic purpose, such as open storage or car parking, not requiring any grant aid.

After allowing for the cost of providing roads, services, infrastructure and structural landscaping for the development, the base value approved by the grant appraiser represented a discount for stigma of 42.34% against the open market value of uncontaminated land on competing developments. The de-contamination expenditure has been disregarded as this was funded entirely by grant aid.

The development was completed in October 1996 and a total of almost 44 590 square metres (480 000 square feet) of industrial floorspace had been constructed during one of the worst periods in history for industrial property development in the North West. Part of the development was constructed on a speculative basis, demonstrating the confidence of the developer in the project, but most of the buildings had been constructed to meet the specific requirements of the occupier. A newly completed bakery on the site is shown in Figure 10.6.

In addition to the overseas company referred to above, the solicitors acting for other tenants on the estate requested details of the site remediation work and, so far as is known, all were satisfied with the

Fig. 10.6   A newly completed bakery on the former chemical works site.

replies received. All leases were entered into on full repairing and insuring terms. The rents achieved and yield rates in respect of investment sales were similar to those obtained elsewhere in the

Table 10.3   The risk assessment model applied to case study 10.4.

Comparable case study:	Former chemical works	Model value adjuster
Present or past industrial use(s):	Chemicals manufacture, dyestuffs manufacture	
Highest risk present or past use:	Chemicals manufacturer	63.23
Pre-treatment risk assessment:	Very high hazard	90.38
Proposed or probable treatment method:	Group 1 Excavate and remove all contaminants	2.50
Post-treatment expected risk assessment:	Very low hazard	7.05
Aggregate model value:		163.16
Expected stigma effect:		40.79%
Observed stigma effect:		42.34%

locality, an indication that there was no post-development stigma.

The historic uses in respect of this site were in the same general classifications as case study 10.3 but the nature of the chemicals involved was very different. Many of the materials known to be buried within this site were carcinogenic or toxic and the pre-treatment risk assessment was therefore considered to be 'very high hazard', and this site would certainly have been classed as contaminated. A Group 1 treatment method was used to remediate the site, with all identifiable contaminants being removed to an average depth of two metres. Following treatment the risk level was considered to be 'very low'. The model as applied to this site is set out in Table 10.3.

Case study 10.5: Former railway goods yard

This site of approximately 3.04 hectares (7.5 acres) is located to the north of Manchester city centre, adjoining a dual carriageway link road to the motorway network. Previously owned by British Rail, the site was offered for sale by tender, in 1990, together with an adjoining site in the ownership of the local authority.

At the time of the tender sale, part of the site was derelict and the local authority land was used as a winter base for travelling showmen. The railway land had previously been used as a goods yard and a substantial portion was transected by a deep railway cutting leading from a tunnel. The cutting had been filled up to ground level by fill material of an unknown nature. The local authority site had been occupied as a town gas works, which had since been demolished down to ground level. Opposite the site were located gas holders and a depot used by British Gas.

The highest tender price offered for the land was made on the basis of a soil survey, consisting of 22 trial pits, which had been undertaken on behalf of the joint vendors in February 1990 and copies of the report had been provided to prospective bidders. The bid price reflected the fact that ground problems had been disclosed by the survey and the site was probably worth only about half to two-thirds of the price which might have been expected for a problem free site in this prominent location. There was, however, very little transaction evidence for uncontaminated sites in this part of the city.

The site investigation report provided by the vendors was considered by the developer to be insufficient for development purposes and consultants were commissioned to undertake a further site investigation, including chemical analysis. This work was undertaken in August 1991.

The site was found to be immediately underlain by glacial boulder clay overlying Permo-Triassic Bunter sandstone. A fault was found to run north-west to south-east through the south-west corner of the site, with downthrow to the north-east. The original ground level of the site, excluding the railway cutting, was predominantly an extensive layer of hardstanding material consisting of stone setts, tarmac, roadways and concrete. These hardstanding materials were underlain by fill comprising ash and cinder, railway ballast and sleepers, which were associated with the past railway sidings. Irregular thicknesses of variable fill, mainly comprising fly-tipped material, lay across most of the site area.

The railway cutting had been filled throughout its length to depths of up to eight metres. The cutting had been filled in an unsatisfactory manner with no consideration given to any future site development. The nature of the fill material was extremely variable, including very large broken sections of reinforced concrete, brickwork and mortar, metal sections, clays and organic contaminants. Little or no effort had been made to achieve compaction of the material and numerous voids existed.

Results of the chemical analysis confirmed that the site was contaminated and that the contamination pattern was extremely variable in distribution. Elevated levels of cyanide, cadmium, mercury, arsenic and toluene-extractable matter were recorded in the results, as were single incidences of mildly acidic fill material and high sulphate levels. Significant levels of methane were also recorded.

The consultants recommended that, prior to commencement of the development, all fill material, made ground and organic clay should be removed from the site (Figure 10.7). Any uncontaminated material, including concrete and brickwork crushed to a suitable size, could be used to re-fill the railway cutting. The remediation method proposed was therefore one of careful selection of contaminated material for removal from site and the re-use of as much of the fill material as possible.

Following completion of the decontamination work, it was proposed that the site should be redeveloped as an industrial estate and this proposed end use was reflected in the offer made for the site. Realisation of the full extent of contamination on the site meant that the project was no longer viable and an application was made for a City Grant. The price offered for the site, in a closed tender, was not considered to be appropriate for a grant aided scheme, indeed the grant appraiser's initial view was that the site had a nil or even negative value, and the acquisition terms had to be renegotiated.

The figure finally agreed for grant aid was almost exactly the same as the estimated cost of overcoming the site problems. Only a small amount of infrastructure work was required as the main estate road already existed, and once the site reclamation work had been completed it was possible to proceed very quickly with the development of a new industrial estate of 10 870 square metres (117 000 square feet).

The reduction in the price paid for the site may, in its entirety, be assumed as the discount attributable to the uncertainties associated

Fig. 10.7 Two tracked excavators working together to remove contaminated fill from the railway cutting.

with the land contamination. This indicates a 'stigma' effect of 55%. The additional site investigation work, grant negotiations and re-negotiation of the purchase price took almost two years during a period in which the market for industrial property was stagnant or even in decline.

By the time agreement had been reached on all points, the original developer had decided to withdraw from speculative development in order to concentrate on contracting. The project was therefore in danger of being abandoned, until Maple Grove Developments, a subsidiary of the Eric Wright Group, agreed to become involved with the development as controlling partner, leaving the original developer with a minority stake. By the end of October 1996 the project was more than 75% complete, with work having started on

Fig. 10.8   The first phase of newly constructed industrial units on the former railway goods yard, now The Albion, Salford.

the final phase of construction of industrial units (Figure 10.8). There was no observable post-development stigma effect on either rental or sales prices achieved.

A number of different uses had previously existed on this site and the nature of goods stored in the rail yard was unknown. The site had been extensively fly tipped and a substantial area, the former railway cutting, had been filled to a depth of several metres. Part of the site was also a former gas works. The most appropriate highest risk use was therefore considered to be 'waste disposal site' and a 'very high hazard' assessment was ascribed to the site, which would certainly have been classed as contaminated. The treatment method used was excavation and removal of contaminated material. The fill material included a substantial amount of inert material, in the form of concrete and brickwork, which was crushed and used to re-fill the railway cutting. A 'low hazard' post-treatment assessment was used to allow for the remote possibility of any contaminated material remaining within the filled areas. The model as applied to this site is set out in Table 10.4.

Table 10.4 The risk assessment model applied to case study 10.5.

Comparable case study:	Former railway goods yard and gas works site	Model value adjuster
Present or past industrial use(s):	Uncontrolled waste disposal site, railway land	
Highest risk present or past use:	Waste disposal site	55.36
Pre-treatment risk assessment:	Very high hazard	90.38
Proposed or probable treatment method:	Group 1 and Group 2 Excavate and remove contaminated material from site, re-use inert material as fill	2.50
Post-treatment expected risk assessment:	Low hazard	7.05
Aggregate model value:		155.29
Expected stigma effect:		38.82%
Observed stigma effect:		55.00%

Conclusion

The case studies described in this chapter demonstrate that it is possible to redevelop contaminated sites from a variety of past uses to provide modern industrial developments. Furthermore, these redeveloped sites are considered to be acceptable by occupiers and funding institutions alike, although it is often necessary to provide both the users and financiers with information as to the types of activities previously undertaken on the site and the remedial measures used.

There appears to be little or no sign of any 'post-remediation' stigmatisation attributable to the former contaminative uses on any of the case study sites, but it must be remembered that in many industrial redevelopment situations the land element represents less than 25% of the completed investment value of the project. Nevertheless, if end users and financial institutions were really affected by the 'fear factor' they would not make the decision to relocate into, or provide finance for, developments on previously contaminated sites.

Although there was no real evidence of 'post-remediation' stigma, the same cannot be said in respect of the 'pre-remediation' situation. Industrial property developers are demonstrably cautious when it comes to the acquisition and redevelopment of contaminated sites. The same can be said about the providers of development finance. If there is any uncertainty involved, such as incomplete site operating records or inadequate site investigation reports, developers will either decline the development opportunity or demand a substantial discount to take account of their increased risk. Even when provided with detailed site investigations and recommended remediation strategies, complete with estimates of cost, developers will frequently expect 'stigma' type discounts. The ways in which negotiations between landowners and developers may be conducted, with fairness to both parties, is considered as part of the conclusions in Chapter 13.

Chapter 11
Redevelopment of Contaminated Sites: for Residential Use

The previous chapter described several case studies, where contaminated sites had been redeveloped for industrial uses, which were relatively insensitive in terms of risk perception as the redevelopment was simply a continuation of industrial use. Such 'recycling' of industrial land has long been accepted by developers and investors in the United Kingdom, although the contamination issue has only achieved prominence in recent years. To change the use of a contaminated industrial site to a use which, in risk perception terms, is regarded as being much more sensitive than continued industrial use may require a very different approach.

In any redevelopment of contaminated land many individuals and organisations will need to be convinced that the hazards involved have either been removed from the site or have been treated in such a way as to reduce the risks to an acceptably low level. It will be necessary for the developer to convince the planning officer, building control officer, environmental health officer and the National Housebuilders Registration Council (NHBC) inspector that the remediation programme is appropriate to the site and that any proposed standards are actually achievable. The Environment Agency may need to be involved, especially if the remediation work is likely to require a Waste Management Licence, or if there is any potential risk to controlled waters during or after the remediation programme. The bank or other provider of development finance will need to be satisfied, as too will the building society or any other institution which may be expected to provide long term mortgage finance to purchasers. Finally, but by no means least, the eventual purchasers or tenants of the new houses will need to be assured that they are being provided with a 'safe' environment for themselves and their families.

To satisfy all of these different parties, the developer will need to build in a 'comfort factor' as part of the project proposals. This may simply involve being open with prospective purchasers and supplying them, or their legal advisors, with a summary of the work which has been undertaken, or it may involve the creation of an attractively landscaped environment. As a general rule, all of the site remediation work should be completed before work starts on house construction and certainly before marketing commences. This will serve to reduce, or even overcome, any stigma effect which may remain from the previous use of the site.

Any action which the developer can take to reduce possible stigma effect will assist the development, although as time passes from the date when the contamination occurred, or was discovered, the stigma effect on value is likely to diminish. This assumes, however, that a programme of remediation has been undertaken. In the United Kingdom context of regenerating urban areas this is of considerable importance as, in many cases, it may be impossible to distinguish between a fall in value attributable to the presence of contamination and that caused by a general fall in value due to industrial decline.

It can be argued that it is pointless remediating a contaminated site when the surrounding area is made up of other similar sites and derelict or semi-derelict buildings. Such areas are frequently perceived as suffering from high unemployment and high crime rates, and those businesses which remain are quite often subsisting at the margin of economic viability. These perceptions can even continue to persist long after a site has been treated or a programme of urban regeneration has commenced. An area with a bad reputation may take a long time to lose that image, rebuilding is not always sufficient, professional and public perceptions of the area will also have to be changed.

The comprehensive treatment of a contaminated site within such an area may result in the land being improved to a standard far in excess of the general surroundings, without any significant increase in value, at least in the short term. Consideration must therefore be given as to whether the cost of treatment can be justified, given that it may not be possible to recoup the expenditure in full. Where a single site or building is concerned, within a run-down area, the decision may well be that the random or 'pepper pot' approach to regeneration cannot be justified. Landowners and developers may find that it is more beneficial to combine their resources in order to ensure the redevelopment of contaminated sites.

If the site is large enough, or can be made so by bringing together several ownerships to create a 'self-contained' environment within a wider area of deprivation, it can be argued that the cost of treatment is justifiable, even if the full expenditure cannot be recouped out of the initial project. Such developments may be seen as having a 'catalytic' effect on the surrounding area, from such simple actions as encouraging other landowners to tidy up or repaint their premises, to encouraging the commitment of substantial capital in new developments.

Bleich et al (1991), working in the United States, considered the impact that a 'bad neighbour' user might have on the values of adjoining, but uncontaminated, properties, specifically the impact of a landfill on a residential neighbourhood. Starting from the premise that 'it has always been assumed that buyers would pay less for a house in close proximity to a landfill' (Bleich et al, 1991), the researchers undertook an empirical study comparing house sales prices in a neighbourhood adjacent to a landfill with those on two other neighbourhoods situated one to one and a half miles, and three to six miles from the landfill. After analysing a total of 1628 transactions over a ten year period in the three neighbourhoods using regression techniques, the results of the research indicated 'that there is no significant difference in either current prices or in appreciation rates (and thus prices over time) over a ten-year period' (Bleich et al, 1991).

Although Bleich and his colleagues did not use the term 'stigma', they were considering the possible negative impact on property values which may be attributable to the existence of a potentially contaminative use. They argued that 'modern laws, restrictions and management techniques, however, make it possible to reduce or remove the negative impact of a landfill during its useful life' (Bleich et al, 1991).

Bleich was in fact prepared to go further as he has expressed the view, during a discussion with the author in March 1994 that, since completion of the study, values in the neighbourhood adjacent to the landfill had risen faster than values in the two control neighbourhoods. He was unable to produce any empirical support for his opinion but he had identified it as an area for further research. The landfill had by this time been closed and extensively landscaped. The neighbouring householders knew that the closed landfill would never be developed for any 'bad neighbour' use and that it was starting to provide an attractive environment, which had the effect of encouraging the residents to take a pride in the locality.

It is argued that, over time, the wider effects of treating the original contaminated site and bringing it back into full economic use through a quality development, may have the effect of not only removing any stigma effect but may also result in an enhancement of value above that attributable to the surrounding area. The stigma effect on property values would then be similar to that shown in Figure 11.1.

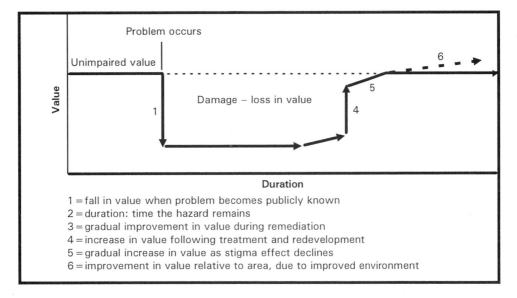

1 = fall in value when problem becomes publicly known
2 = duration: time the hazard remains
3 = gradual improvement in value during remediation
4 = increase in value following treatment and redevelopment
5 = gradual increase in value as stigma effect declines
6 = improvement in value relative to area, due to improved environment

Fig. 11.1 The impact of contamination on land value: through the cycle of discovery, investigation, treatment, development and subsequent re-use (after Mundy, 1992b).

The longevity of any stigmatisation following treatment of the contaminated site will depend upon a number of factors, such as the use to which the treated site is put, the treatment method used and its effectiveness, and general market conditions. It may be postulated that the less sensitive an end use the more likelihood there is that any impact on value associated with an earlier contaminative use will be short lived. But, so far as the United Kingdom is concerned, is this a reasonable assumption given the role of major financial institutions in the industrial and commercial property markets? Indeed, it may be that residential markets are less sensitive to site histories unless, of course, trees and shrubs begin to wilt, offensive odours pervade the development and the residents experience increased levels of illness. This reduced sensitivity could be due to relatively low value (and more numerous) property transactions on new residential developments compared to those found on commercial or industrial developments.

It is quite possible that experience in the United Kingdom will differ quite significantly from that in the United States, given the difference in size between the land area of the two countries and the pressures that may arise out of market demand for development sites in the former. Similarly, differing perceptions of contamination may result in different stigma effects and approaches to clean-up. The following case studies illustrate that contaminated land can be redeveloped for residential use, and they highlight some of the problems involved in redevelopment. As with the industrial and commercial redevelopment case studies in Chapter 10, tables in each of the case studies compare the expected and observed 'stigma effects' using the 'risk assessment' valuation model from Chapter 9.

Redevelopment case studies – residential use

Case study 11.1: A mixed use site in Manchester

This case study, originally published as part of Syms (1993) and subsequently revised, relates to an area of industrial dereliction immediately to the north of Piccadilly Station, Manchester's main line railway terminus. The area in general is bisected by the Manchester and Ashton Canal and includes the junction of that canal with the Rochdale Canal. A land use study commissioned by Manchester Phoenix Initiative, a private sector urban regeneration organisation, identified a site of approximately four acres (1.62 hectares) bisected by the Ashton Canal which, due to the fact that many buildings had already been demolished, could be developed at an early date.

At the time of the land use study, the site was in eighteen different ownerships, which included bodies such as British Waterways, Manchester

City Council and British Rail. The Canal was still in use as part of the Cheshire Ring of the leisure waterways, although it was in need of dredging. The canal structure, its walls and adjacent footpaths, was in an unsound condition and totally unsuitable for the new development. During the commercial lifetime of the canal, the two parts of the site had contained a total of three canal basins, but these had been filled in with contaminated material, some of which had been dredged from the canal (Figure 11.2).

Fig. 11.2 The canal basins had been filled with contaminated material.

Previous land uses had included canal warehousing, a timber yard, a cotton weaving shed, later to become a jigsaw puzzle factory, and stabling for the shunting ponies used by the railway company, with a beer house next door. Several terraced houses, mostly with the ground floor converted to shops, occupied one road frontage and a former chair factory had been destroyed by fire.

By the early 1980s most of the original uses had ceased and a number of other uses had taken their place. The warehousing had been demolished, replaced for some years by a scrap yard, then used for depositing canal dredgings, the jigsaw factory had been demolished with the concrete floor left in place and had been fly-tipped. The timber yard had closed and was also affected by fly-tipping, the stables had been demolished but, as the site was surrounded by a high brick wall, had not been seriously affected by fly-tipping. The beer house had closed and was occupied by a rag sorter. A number of the terraced houses had been demolished and were in use as a car sales lot, and the site of the chair factory remained derelict.

Contamination affecting the site consisted mainly of heavy metals and coal tars. The worst affected areas were the filled canal basins and the dredged spoil deposited on the north side of the site. The fly-tipped materials were found to be generally uncontaminated. Other than the material deposited on or within the site, the soil was found to be high in sulphates, probably due to fall out from the former town-gas works located near to the site.

An architectural competition was held to find a suitable concept and design for this important site. Reclamation of the site was carried out in 1988–89, prior to the introduction of the Environmental Protection Act 1990. Nevertheless the site was reclaimed in a controlled manner, with the contaminated material being removed to a licensed landfill. Thus a clean site option was chosen, so as to render the site suitable for any end use. Where contaminated material was contained in voids, such as old canal basins, these were excavated and either refilled with clean material or re-opened to the canal. Following reclamation, the ground was left with a high sulphate level, probably no different to that found in the surrounding area, due to the proximity of a former town-gas works, and sulphate resistant cement was used in the construction of foundations and ground floor slabs.

When the redevelopment project was conceived in 1987 the property development industry was fairly buoyant, but private sector funding on its own was not sufficient to ensure the success of the project. Public sector support was necessary to provide the right environment for urban renewal by overcoming the ground and water engineering problems, and a City Grant of £1.13 million was awarded to the project. This equated approximately to the estimated costs of reclaiming the site and the restoration works to the canal; the new development itself did not receive any commercial subsidy.

The project was initially designed to provide 125 residential units, 15 craft studios, 6 shops and 16 000 square feet (1 486 square metres) of office accommodation. During the course of construction a number of changes were made, which increased the number of residential units to 150 and omitted the craft units. The contractors for the site treatment work, rebuilding of the canal walls and the underground infrastructure works were appointed on the basis of a competitive tender. Construction, roads and landscaping work was undertaken by the joint venture company owned by the development partners.

Most of the land required for the development was either vacant or derelict, with all but one of the buildings having been demolished. All of the land acquisitions were undertaken by agreement, without any need for the use of compulsory powers by Central Manchester Development Corporation in whose area the site was situated. The total price paid for the land, excluding fees, was only £58 500 per acre (£125 600 per hectare). This relatively low price for land close to the city centre was attributable to the major changes in level which existed between the canal and the adjoining streets, the configuration of the plots themselves which made redevelopment extremely difficult and anticipated ground problems, which included contamination. At the time of the site assembly, prime industrial land in the Manchester area, with good road connections, was selling at between £309 000 and £370 500 per hectare (£125 000 and £150 000 per acre), with good quality residential development land in the suburbs fetching almost twice these figures. These figures are based on records maintained by leading Manchester estate agents.

Adams et al (1985) had undertaken a study of inner city land values in Manchester shortly before the site assembly commenced and this provides an invaluable means of comparing land values. Most inner city sites suffer from problems in respect of small plot sizes, inadequate road access, poor services and, in the case of Manchester in the mid-1980s, a declining industrial base. The study undertaken by Adams and his co-researchers examined land transactions in the inner city during a study period 1978–83. This included sites which had subsequently been redeveloped and those which had remained vacant.

Given the mixed commercial and residential nature of the development and its proximity to the city centre, it is reasonable to assume that if the site had been uncontaminated and available for sale in a developable state, it would have commanded a price between the highest recorded for a residential development site and the mean price for commercial sites. On this basis, an uncontaminated value for the site has been calculated at £183 470 per hectare (£74 250 per acre). The cost of site reclamation, including rebuilding of the canal walls and basins, was covered by the public sector grant aid without any private sector subsidy. Therefore the difference between the value indicated by Adams' study and the price actually paid, £38 918 per hectare (£15 750 per acre) may be regarded as the discount required by the developer over and above the cost of dealing with the site problems. This represents a 'stigma' effect of 21.21%.

Even in one of the worst markets for residential property, a good level of sales was achieved. During the eighteen month period following release of the first phase, a selling programme was maintained three to four months ahead of sales completions. Whilst the residential properties had to be priced at full market value, a requirement of the City Grant, they were fixed at a realistic level so as to attract purchasers into this previously untested part of the inner city. Prices ranged from £39 950 for a 'bedsit' and £50 000 for a one-bedroomed apartment, up to £140 000 for a four-bedroomed house. 'At these prices it is not difficult to understand why people are willing to consider moving back to the centre' (Hanson, 1991). Sales of the commercial properties were slower than the residential units, much more in line with market conditions.

The fact that the site was previously contaminated does not appear to have presented any significant problems and, so far as the development company is aware, has not resulted in any potential purchasers being refused mortgages. Information concerning past uses on the site and the treatment method used was made available to solicitors and building societies. The development was unique in terms of its waterside location, design, and proximity to the city centre. Selling prices of up to £1075 per square metre (£100 per square foot) were achieved on the development, compared to around £700 per square metre (£65 per square foot) for conventional housing developments, lacking the water aspect, approximately half a mile further from the city centre. It is therefore not possible to identify any post development 'stigma' effect and, so far as the developer is aware, no prospective purchasers were discouraged by the site's industrial

Fig. 11.3 Newly completed dwellings in an attractive waterside environment.

history. As an exercise in urban renewal the project has transformed a run down area of the city, and is starting to demonstrate a 'catalytic' effect in encouraging adjoining landowners to embark upon development projects.

As mentioned previously, many different uses had existed on this site. The use with the highest risk was that of 'scrap yard' and this determined the base value for the valuation model. The site investigation did not produce evidence of any highly toxic contaminants and since the most serious hazard was found to exist in relation to the sub-structures and services for the new buildings, the pre-treatment risk level was assessed as 'medium hazard'. A Group 1 excavation and disposal method was used to treat the site and the post-treatment risk assessment was 'low hazard'. A 'very low hazard' risk assessment was not applied to this site because the soil was left with a high sulphate level. Although appropriate measures were taken to protect the sub-structures and services, a residual risk of failure remains. The model as applied to this site is set out in Table 11.1.

Table 11.1   The risk assessment model applied to case study 11.1.

Comparable case study:	Mixed use site, Manchester	Model value adjuster
Present or past industrial use(s):	Warehousing, timber yard, scrap yard, textiles manufacture.	
Highest risk present or past use:	Scrap yard	39.89
Pre-treatment risk assessment:	Medium hazard	22.43
Proposed or probable treatment method:	Group 1 Excavate and remove contamination	2.5
Post-treatment expected risk assessment:	Low hazard	7.05
Aggregate model value:		71.87
Expected stigma effect:		17.97%
Observed stigma effect:		21.21%

Case study 11.2: Former engineering works; east Manchester

This 2.91 hectare (7.2 acre) site is located in an area which, until 1980, was totally dominated by heavy industry, especially engineering. Today virtually all of the industrial businesses have closed as a result of going out of business, a reduction in the number of plants or relocation to greenfield sites. They have left behind a legacy of redundant buildings, mostly vandalised and some cleared but contaminated sites.

The case study site was once the location of a long running industrial dispute in the early 1980s, when the workforce was locked out by the management. After many months of bitterness the matter was brought to an end, the factory was demolished and the site was eventually sold as a residential development site. Following the sale, site investigations revealed extensive contamination caused by the previous industrial use (Figure 11.4). Part of the site appeared to have been filled with waste materials from the former metal finishing operations, whilst other areas were filled with demolition rubble, some of which contained contaminants from the same source.

There was no recourse to the vendor. *Caveat emptor* applied and the purchaser had neglected to undertake any investigation work before entering into the contract. In time, the intending developer became the victim of financial difficulties and the bank stepped in as mortgagee.

After more than two years, and many abortive negotiations, the bank agreed to sell the site for a figure which was significantly below the price

Fig. 11.4 Green and level before redevelopment but containing several contaminated 'hot-spots'.

paid by the original developer and the Department of the Environment offered a City Grant of £765 000 to ensure the redevelopment of the site. The amount of grant exceeded the cost of site remediation and included an element of commercial subsidy, supporting the provision of new housing in a depressed part of the city. The private sector funding was provided from the internal resources of the developer, Maunders Urban Renewal, a division of John Maunders plc, and all of the design work, other than the site remediation, was undertaken by the in-house team.

The entire site was covered with demolition rubble and industrial wastes, up to three metres in thickness, over a layer of ash material on top of the natural clay. The site had been levelled following completion of the demolition work and banked along the road side to prevent fly-tipping and use of the site by itinerants, then left to naturally vegetate. A disused canal which formed the western boundary of the site had been filled with a variety of material of unknown origin and then landscaped (Figure 11.4).

Following a site investigation commissioned by the bank the fill material was found to be contaminated with a wide range of heavy metals and mineral oils. Most of the contaminants were at concentration levels below the trigger concentrations for domestic gardens, as set out in ICRCL 59/83 (1987), but elevated levels of lead, arsenic, copper, zinc, nickel and boron were found. For all of these contaminants the highest concentrations were found within two discrete areas of the site. The consultant engineer responsible for carrying out the site investigation for the bank was subsequently retained by the developer to supervise the remediation work.

The method of site remediation used for this site was based on the safe containment of a residue of contaminated material under the development itself, at concentration levels which were considered to be safe. Contaminated 'hot spots' were removed and the remaining contaminated fill material was regraded to fill the voids left by the 'hot spot' removal. This had the effect of lowering the ground level throughout the site and reducing the remaining contaminants to concentrations below ICRCL trigger levels. The site was then covered with one metre of clean clay and topsoil.

The alternative of removing all of the contaminated material to landfill, and 'backfilling' with clean material, was considered, but this would have cost in excess of £1.2 million. The level of grant aid required for this alternative would substantially have exceeded the Department of the Environment's aid guideline of one part of public money to four parts of private money (DoE, 1992b). The money could therefore have been more effectively used elsewhere and this site would not have received grant aid.

Most of the existing housing in the locality comprises two storey terraced houses of 55 to 70 square metres (600 to 750 square feet) floor area, built in the latter part of the last century. In good condition these houses sell for around £25 000 to £30 000; which is no more than the construction cost for similarly sized new homes, excluding land, profit and finance costs. The new development comprises terraced and semi-detached houses of similar size to the existing dwellings, developed at a density of 19 units per acre. These 'starter homes' are aimed to sell in the price range £35 000 to £42 000, excluding garage (see Figure 11.5).

According to the developer's market research, virtually identical homes in other parts of the Manchester conurbation unaffected by industrial dereliction were selling for prices up to 10% higher, and the older terraced houses also achieve similarly higher prices. The generally lower selling prices in east Manchester may not be due entirely to the possibility of contamination blight but may also, to some extent, be a symptom of the depressed economy in that part of the city. It is, however, very difficult to separate out the effects.

After taking account of the subsidy contained in the City Grant, the price paid by the developer represented a discount of at least 70% against the value of an uncontaminated site. Much of the reduction in the price paid was attributable to the expectation of lower selling prices in this de-industrialised locality, but at least part of the discount is attributable to the developer's perception of increased risk. The developer also considered that an increased marketing budget was

Fig. 11.5 Newly built starter homes on the reclaimed site, 'The Carriages', east Manchester.

required to overcome the possible stigma attaching to the previous use.

If the subsidy element of the City Grant is disregarded, the price paid by the eventual developer represents a reduction of 35% against the price paid by the original developer, who had not considered the possibility of contamination. The original selling price was substantially below residential development land values in other parts of the city, and no doubt reflected the industrial character of the locality. The further reduction is considered to be a discount to reflect 'stigma'.

Only one previous use was recorded for this site and, due to the nature of the waste materials buried in the ground, the pre-treatment hazard level was judged to be 'high'. The site treatment method involved the removal of contaminated 'hot-spots' and disposal off site of the most highly contaminated material. The remaining contaminated material was regraded and the site covered with clean fill, a Group 2 method. The post treatment risk assessment for the site was considered to be 'low', but some residual risk remains from the covered material. The model as applied to this site is set out in Table 11.2.

Table 11.2 The risk assessment model applied to case study 11.2.

Comparable case study:	Former engineering works	Model value adjuster
Present or past industrial (use(s):	Metal treatment and finishing	
Highest risk present or past use:	Metal treatment and finishing	46.97
Pre-treatment risk assessment:	High hazard	58.19
Proposed or probable treatment method:	Group 2 Partial excavation, cover and contain remaining contaminated material	8.00
Post-treatment expected risk assessment:	Low hazard	7.05
Aggregate model value:		120.21
Expected stigma effect:		30.05%
Observed stigma effect:		35.00%

Case study 11.3: Former tram and bus depot

This site has an area of approximately 1.80 hectares (4.37 acres) and was originally developed as a tram depot. Around 70% of the site area was covered by buildings, which were primarily used as maintenance workshops. Within the buildings were maintenance pits, extending over almost half of the total floor area, above which the trams were driven on rails supported by cast iron columns. The average depth of the pits was 1.5 metres.

When trams ceased to operate in the streets of Manchester and Salford the depot was converted for use by motor buses. The conversion involved filling the pits and constructing at least four groups of 'finger pits'. The origin of the fill material is unknown but is assumed to have comprised industrial wastes, mainly in ash or slag form, from nearby metal treatment and finishing works. Following closure of the bus depot, all buildings on the site were demolished down to floor slab level and some of the demolition material appears to have been used to fill the 'finger pits'.

The site was subsequently sold to a developer for the construction of a new housing scheme of 119 units. A site investigation was commissioned, and based on the information then available a City Grant was awarded by the Department of the Environment. The development was not started and the developer eventually went into receivership.

Four years later a second developer agreed to purchase the site, provided that grant aid was still available, and to carry out the original scheme. At this stage it was found that the original site investigation had not included any chemical testing of the fill materials and a second investigation was commissioned to identify the nature and extent of any contamination. This revealed that the fill material in the maintenance pits was heavily contaminated with heavy metals, including, arsenic, boron, chromium, mercury, nickel, lead, selenium and zinc, and with poly-aromatic hydrocarbons (PAHs). A formal, quantified, risk assessment subsequently classified the site as 'high risk'.

The site was adjacent to a river and was considered to be at risk from flooding on the basis of a one hundred year flood. The National Rivers Authority, now part of the Environment Agency, had recommended that the finished floor level of the ground floors of the dwellings be raised by at least one metre above the existing datum. A remediation strategy was evolved which required the removal of contaminated hotspots and the sealing of residual contamination within the original maintenance pits, with the entire site being covered with at least one metre of clean material (Figure 11.6). On completion of the work the risk assessment would be reduced to 'low risk'.

The entire cost of the site remediation and abnormal foundations work was covered by an offer of investment funding from English

Fig. 11.6   At the start of site remediation work it was necessary to break out the concrete which covered much of the site area and to remove many underground obstructions.

Partnerships and the developer agreed to purchase the site for a price which represented a discount of 21.42% against the price paid by the original developer. Reductions in the end value of the development, attributable to a fall in house prices, had been fully offset by a reduction in construction costs and therefore the whole of the reduction in site value is considered to be due to the stigma effect (Figure 11.7). The model as applied to this site is set out in Table 11.3.

Case study 11.4: Derelict site, Wigan

A site of 0.37 hectare (0.91 acre), surrounded on all sides by local authority housing was originally intended as informal open space but in reality it became a communal 'rubbish tip'. A site investigation revealed that the entire area of the site had been raised above its natural level by up to two metres and that the fill material was contaminated with arsenic, copper and nickel at concentrations which exceeded the guidance in ICRCL 59/83 (1987) for domestic gardens, allotments and areas in which plants are to be grown. The origin of the fill material was unknown but glass and paint industries had formerly operated in the area.

The site was owned by the local authority and, prior to the site investi-

Fig. 11.7 The first phase of new homes nearing completion.

Table 11.3 The risk assessment model applied to case study 11.3

Comparable case study:	Tram and bus depot	Model value adjuster
Present or past industrial use(s):	Tram depot converted to bus garage all buildings demolished, extensively filled	
Highest risk present or past use:	Fill materials of unknown origin, probably metal treatment and finishing	46.97
Pre-treatment risk assessment:	High hazard	58.19
Proposed or probable treatment method:	Group 1 and Group 2 Excavate and remove most highly contaminated material from site, re-use less contaminated and inert material as fill, clean cover	8.0
Post-treatment expected risk assessment:	Low hazard	7.05
Aggregate model value:		120.21
Expected stigma effect:		30.05%
Observed stigma effect:		21.42%

gation, a local house builder had agreed to purchase it in order to construct 18 low cost houses (Figure 11.8). It was agreed that the most suitable form of remediation was to remove the most severely contaminated fill material from the site, in order to enable a clean cover layer to be introduced. The total cost of treatment was covered by grant aid and a 25% reduction in the purchase price was agreed, so as to allow for stigma. The model as applied to this site is set out in Table 11.4.

Summary of case studies

As demonstrated by the four case studies in this chapter, it is possible to achieve successful redevelopment of contaminated sites for residential use. In three out of the four case studies some residual contaminants were left on site following remediation, and the soil on one site was left with a high sulphate level, requiring sulphate resistant concrete to be used in the foundations. It must be stressed, however, that in none of these cases had the sites been contaminated with seriously high concentrations of toxic metals or with known carcinogens.

In all four instances the developers endeavoured to create an

Fig. 11.8 New starter homes on an infill site which was previously used as a communal rubbish tip.

Table 11.4   The risk assessment model applied to case study 11.4.

Comparable case study:	Derelict site, Wigan	Model value adjuster
Present or past industrial use(s):	Open space within residential area	
Highest risk present or past use:	Industrial wastes from paint manufacture	50.11
Pre-treatment risk assessment:	Medium hazard	19.07
Proposed or probable treatment method:	Group 1 and Group 2 Excavate and remove contaminated material from site, import clean material as fill	8.0
Post-treatment expected risk assessment:	Low hazard	7.05
Aggregate model value:		84.23
Expected stigma effect:		21.06%
Observed stigma effect:		25.00%

environment within the development which was totally different to that which had previously existed on the site, or indeed within the vicinity. The developers also ensured that the site remediation works were carefully supervised, recorded and made available to prospective purchasers, their solicitors and building societies.

Two of the developments were intended to provide housing for 'first time buyers' and individual units were priced towards the lower end of the housing market. One development provided much needed private sector rented accommodation in a depressed area where the only private rented housing which had previously existed was generally old and in poor condition. This development attracted more than 800 applications for the 119 new units, with minimal advertising. In contrast to the other three case studies, the Piccadilly Village development, close to Manchester's city centre, was targeted at higher income purchasers, professional and business people working in the city or requiring a convenient location with excellent communications.

So far as is known, no potential sales or tenants were lost on any of the case study developments because of the industrial history of the site, or the fact that it had been contaminated. As with the industrial case studies, the land element attributable to each housing unit was relatively small and it was not possible to identify any significant reduction in price which could be attributed to 'stigma'. In some cases the prices were marginally lower than achieved on developments say two or three miles from the subject site but these were invariably more well established residential locations.

Grants and policy incentives

Although all of the case studies described in the previous section and in Chapter 10 relied upon grant aid to meet the physical cost of site remediation, no allowance was made in the example valuations in Chapter 9 in respect of any grants or other incentives which might be available towards the cost of dealing with contamination. This is in spite of the fact that Guidance Note 2 in the 'Red Book' makes reference to the need to reflect grants or other financial incentives in the valuation. The government has adopted the principle of 'polluter pays' (DoE, 1990a) and does not consider it appropriate to use public money in clearing up contamination resulting from industrial activities.

Even in situations where the property is no longer owned by the original polluter, the attitude is that land values should reflect the cost of dealing with contamination. This was confirmed by the Department in its City Grant Guidance Notes (DoE, 1992b), which states that 'if the site value is high it may be reasonable to assume that the land or buildings can be used or developed without grant' and that the appraiser 'will ask what the site is likely to fetch if sold now, in its existing physical condition ... on the assumption that grant will not be available. In many cases this value will be negligible.' (DoE, 1992b)

A similar approach to existing site values is being applied by English Partnerships, which has taken over responsibility for the grant regimes [formerly Derelict Land Grant and City Grant] which were administered by the Department of the Environment. Although

Government policy is clearly stated in respect of the 'polluter pays' principle, all of the case studies described in the previous section received grant aid from the Department of the Environment, the Welsh Office, English Partnerships or a development corporation.

In some cases, the application for grant aid was made, and the grant approved, before the stricter policy on base values was introduced in 1992. So far as other cases were concerned, the contamination originated from many sources, many of which could not be traced, although it could be argued that the site owner should have exercised greater control over operations on the site, or have kept it securely fenced so as to prevent fly tipping. With hindsight, it would have been far more cost effective for the whole of the north Wales colliery site to have been remediated at the time of the original development in 1985 but this would have involved additional expenditure at the time.

All of the case study developments in Chapters 10 and 11 produced 'hard' end uses in terms of new industrial units, offices and residential accommodation. They also fulfilled urban regeneration policy objectives relating to the creation of employment and housing in depressed areas. Piccadilly Village, in central Manchester (case study 11.1) received a MIPIM award as the 'best urban waterside residential development in Europe'. Most importantly, all of the case study projects have resulted in the remediation of contaminated sites.

The developers of these and other similar development projects tend to regard the grant aid as being the input required to overcome the contamination problems, although in reality the need for public sector support is appraised against the project as a whole (see Syms, 1994a) and not simply in respect of the abnormal ground conditions. Where applicable, the developers have regarded any commercial subsidy as a welcome bonus but there is no doubt that none of the case study projects would have been undertaken without public sector support. Whether any of the schemes would have proceeded if an alternative form of incentive, such as rental guarantees, had been available instead is doubtful. There may, however, be a case for arguing that direct grant aid should be limited to the cost of dealing with contamination, and possibly other abnormal ground conditions, with any required commercial subsidy taking the form of rental or other guarantees.

It is most unlikely that grant aid will, as a general rule, be made available to tackle the problems of land contamination, without the prospect of a worthwhile redevelopment project for the site.

> 'Nevertheless, the problem remains of what should be done about the pollution and contamination arising out of the activities of previous generations. To compel present-day owners of land to clean up after previous owners would seem to be inequitable, especially as those same owners may well be having to face up to the fact that the property, for which they paid the market price several years ago, now has a nil or even negative value. Even forcing businesses to reclaim land which has been contaminated over earlier years by the industrial processes of the firm may be counterproductive if it has the effect of forcing the company out of business.'
>
> (Syms, 1994a)

It is likely therefore that exceptions may have to be made in situations where the cost of treatment is significantly in excess of any development value which would accrue from the site, or in circumstances where environmental, as opposed to economic, benefits are the expected outcome of the treatment.

Different methods of appraising the need for government support were applied to the two grant aid schemes previously administered by the Department of the Environment and these are fully discussed in Syms (1994a). The essential differences were that applications for Derelict Land Grant were appraised on the basis of existing site value, treatment costs and future site value only, without the costs and benefits attributable to any new construction being taken into account, whereas the City Grant method considered the entire project and the grant was largely determined by the provision of 'hard end use', such as new jobs created or homes constructed. The two schemes have now been replaced by the 'English Partnerships Investment Fund', which places a far greater emphasis on partnerships between public, private and the voluntary sectors, including the taking of equity stakes in developments by the grant awarding body. The method of appraisal used in assessing the eligibility of projects is broadly similar to that used for City Grant, but a wider range of benefits is now considered to be acceptable. For example this might include the preparation of a site for development, without the actual provision of any buildings.

Section 4

Satisfying Users and Regulators

Chapter 12
Sale, Transfer and Insurance

All property acquisition, investment, and development decisions are based upon imperfect knowledge of the physical characteristics of the property and its market context. Quite often the final decision to acquire a property will be made for seemingly uncommercial, or non-market related, reasons and without the benefit of adequate research. For example, the decision to acquire a site for a new factory may be based on the fact that it is less than three miles from the managing director's home, or because from his new office window he will have a view of the hills in which he enjoys walking during his leisure time. The availability of public transport for the workforce and access to markets may receive only secondary consideration.

Similarly, a property developer may decide to develop a particular site simply because the project down the road has been successful, or because of a 'good feeling' about the site and its location. Market research might in fact have revealed that the earlier development had satisfied a pent up demand in the area and that the future 'take up' of space is likely to be limited. All too often such research is not undertaken, or at least not until after the developer has made a commitment to purchase the site and, even then, not with any degree of sophistication.

Property investors, especially investment fund managers, possibly represent the most sophisticated sector of the industrial and commercial property market (including development sites) and are more likely to commission market research in respect of development opportunities. The larger investors are probably also more likely to undertake due diligence enquiries in respect of their tenants, which should include enquiries into any manufacturing processes to be undertaken and/or materials to be stored in the premises. For the majority of landlords, however, status checks to determine the ability, or otherwise, of the tenant to pay the rent may be the limit of their enquiries.

If the possibility of contamination arises, even the most sophisticated investment fund managers, well versed in objective decision making, may simply refuse to consider the investment, regardless of the fact that a site may have undergone an extensive programme of remediation. The same applies to some very experienced developers and industrialists who, in spite of evidence of minimal risk levels and detailed reports, will not consider the development potential of a contaminated site.

At first sight such decisions may appear to be irrational, representing lost development opportunities, and even against the public interest as they increase pressure for the release of greenfield sites for development. Nevertheless, such decisions, made by investment managers and developers, are understandable when viewed against the changes in government policies which have existed throughout the 1990s.

Purchasers' safeguards

The solicitor acting on behalf of the prospective purchaser of landed property is under an obligation to take such measures as are necessary to protect the client's interests. It is therefore the practice of purchasers' solicitors to submit pre-contract or 'preliminary' enquiries to the solicitor acting on behalf of the vendor. These enquiries are normally phrased in such a way as to procure as much relevant information as possible.

Unfortunately, however, not all solicitors make adequate enquiries relating to environmental issues, including contaminated land. A study conducted by Miles Keeping (1996) at Oxford Brookes University found that whilst most of the larger London based and provincial legal practices made detailed enquiries into environmental issues, many smaller firms were not so thorough. The study comprised a survey of 105 commercial property conveyancing departments within a range of private sector legal practices, ranging from small provincial firms with fewer than eight partners, to larger London firms with more than twenty partners. Larger provincial firms (in excess of eight partners) and mid-sized London firms were also included.

Each commercial property conveyancing department was asked to provide details of the environmental preliminary enquiries which they made and these were examined,

'to assess whether purchasers' solicitors are asking appropriate pre-contract questions, so as to reduce the risk of their clients purchasing a contaminated site which has associated environmental liabilities'.

(Keeping, 1996)

The results of the study are set out in Table 12.1, from which it may be seen that there is considerable variation in the type and number of

Table 12.1   Indication of the range of preliminary enquiries made by conveyancers relating to contaminated land (source: Keeping, 1996).

Type of firm	Larger London (n = 26)	Midsized London (n = 22)	Larger provincial (n = 51)	Smaller provincial (n = 6)	%age all firms making each enquiry (n = 105)
Land use details					
Previous uses/ activities on site?	12	15	45	3	71
Uses/activities on adjacent land?	12	9	33	0	53
Reclaimed/filled site	9	12	36	0	54
Which processes carried out on site and are they prescribed?	18	15	24	0	55
Water abstraction?	9	3	9	0	20
Waste/effluent disposal on site?	21	15	48	3	83
Site storage					
Active/disused tanks?	18	12	36	3	66
Toxic/hazardous waste?	21	12	36	0	66
Prescribed and/or hazardous substances?	18	9	39	0	63

Table 12.1 *Continued.*

Type of firm	Larger London (n = 26)	Midsized London (n = 22)	Larger provincial (n = 51)	Smaller provincial (n = 6)	%age all firms making each enquiry (n = 105)
Environmental audits					
Site audits/studies/ sampling?	18	18	50	3	85
Aware of actual/potential leaching or migration?	9	3	21	0	31
Details of remediation undertaken on site	12	0	27	0	37
Confirmations					
Polluting matter entering water source	12	12	29	0	50
Licences and consents					
Details of relevant licences/consents	18	12	45	0	71
Confirmation of compliance	21	12	36	0	66
Environmental insurance	6	3	24	0	31
Complaints					
Complaints received	15	9	33	0	54
Actions or claims					
Due to pollution	18	12	50	3	79
Proceedings for Statutory Nuisance	21	9	36	3	69
Civil proceedings due to state of the land	12	9	27	0	46
Have the NRA/EA carried out or are they likely to carry out work?	9	3	18	0	29

questions asked by legal practices. Some firms of solicitors were found to have a thorough set of environmental questions extending to eight or more pages which were constantly updated, but some conveyancers were found to,

'follow practices which suggest that they are totally and woefully unaware of environmental issues as they do not make a single contaminated land enquiry during the conveyancing process'.

(Keeping, 1996)

All of the conveyancers who failed to make contaminated land enquiries were in the smaller provincial firms, and even those firms in this category which did make some relevant enquiries tended to seek very little detail.

One of the conclusions drawn from the study was that the smaller provincial firms of solicitors may not deal with properties in former or currently industrialised areas and therefore assume that contamination is not an issue; however, such a situation is unlikely. Conveyancers should consider whether or not land contamination is a possibility on any property, whatever its location, and this accords with current guidance from the Law Society.

Although many conveyancers seek to ensure that the pre-contract enquiries made in respect of a property are relevant, there is a tendency on the part of some to 'play safe' in respect of environmental questions and ask every conceivable question they can think of, regardless of relevance. This approach can be antagonistic to the vendor and his solicitor, provoking unhelpful responses. However, it is not simply the irrelevant, obscure or inappropriate nature of preliminary enquiries which causes vendors to provide blunt unhelpful responses, such as 'the purchaser must rely on his own enquiries'. The vendor is not legally bound to answer preliminary enquiries and, furthermore, if he is careless and answers in a way which misleads the purchaser, the latter may be able to rescind the contract. Rescission *ab initio* means that the purchaser will be restored to his original position, with the vendor having to repay the sale proceeds together with all of the costs and incidental expenses incurred by the purchaser; a costly outcome for a careless answer.

Notwithstanding the commercial pressures on the vendor to disclose information regarding land contamination (i.e. if he fails to do so the purchaser may become suspicious and withdraw from the purchase) the quantity and quality of information emanating from the vendor as to contamination at or around the site might be quite limited. The purchaser who wants to make an informed decision will therefore have to look to other sources of information, and these are numerous.

In essence, the prospective purchaser may find it necessary to embark upon a preliminary investigation or historical study, as described in Chapter 5. For the purchaser or solicitor to undertake this work in person, it is likely to be extremely time consuming and costly. It is therefore probably more appropriate to employ a specialist agent to undertake the work, although even this will result in additional expense and delay in completing the transaction. The purchaser may even decide that it is necessary to undertake a full or partial invasive investigation in order to be satisfied as to the condition of the land being acquired.

Vendors' obligations

In English law the general rule of sale is *caveat emptor* (Let the buyer beware) and, after carrying out surveys, investigations, preliminary enquiries, local authority searches etc., the purchaser takes the property at his or her own risk.

The justification for *caveat emptor* is that it allows vendors to use the proceeds of sale without worrying about being sued by the purchaser after completion because the property is found to be defective in some respect. Critics of the rule say that it limits the flow of information about sites and when faced with uncertain information, for example in respect of contamination, buyers may withdraw from the transaction.

The rule of *caveat emptor* was reviewed by the Law Commission in 1970, when the recommendation was that it should not be changed. In 1994, as part of the review of contaminated land liabilities (see Chapter 4), the Department of the Environment consulted interested parties on the question 'Do you consider that there should be no change in the principle of *caveat emptor* in land transactions as regards environmental liabilities?' (DoE, 1994a). The majority of the respondents thought that the rule should be retained because it 'underpins a clear transfer of responsibilities from seller to buyer at the time of completion' (DoE, 1994b).

The rule of *caveat emptor* is subject to a number of exceptions and where an exception applies, the vendor cannot argue that the purchaser acquired the property at his own risk – defects included. On the contrary, where defects are found to exist, the purchaser can take action against the vendor for the legal remedy of damages or rescission. Generally speaking, the case law shows that exceptions to *caveat emptor* apply where, by words or actions, the vendor has discouraged, frustrated or misled the purchaser in the inspection of the property. No relevant case has yet involved ground contamination at a site, but the underlying legal principles appear wide enough to apply in such cases.

The following exceptions are potentially relevant if a purchaser subsequently discovers contamination at the property:

- *where the vendor has acted fraudulently*; for example if the vendor has deliberately concealed a material fact about the property such as covering up the contamination, which could not therefore have been discovered by the purchaser during an ordinary inspection or survey,
- *where the vendor has caused the defect*; for example, by personally carrying out inadequate works, which might include a site remediation system which subsequently fails,
- *where the vendor has misdescribed the site in the contract of sale*; for example, if the site had been described in the contract as a 'greenfield' site whereas in fact it was a former industrial site which had been put to a potentially contaminative use,
- *where the vendor misrepresented a material fact which induced the purchaser to enter the contract*; an example would be where the vendor, during the course of negotiations, represented that 'contamination is not a problem'. Legal remedies could be sought under section 2(1) of the Misrepresentation Act 1967 and/or the common law of negligent misrepresentation,
- *where the parties have a fiduciary relationship*; (e.g. trustee and beneficiary, solicitor and client, director and shareholder) or where the contract is *uberrimae fidei*, where one party has a duty to disclose material facts to another, as in the case of members of a partnership.

The public consultation document in respect of the draft Statutory Guidance on Contaminated Land (DoE, 1996, Chapter 4), encourages vendors to provide information when prospective purchasers ask questions about possible contamination at a site. The vendor may be potentially liable to remediate because he has caused or knowingly permitted contaminative substances to be in, on or under the land.

Vendors may therefore be well advised to provide prospective purchasers with details of the site's history at the negotiation stage, and possibly also to undertake some investigative work, making the results available to interested parties. Such actions, sometimes referred to as 'decommissioning' or 'divestiture' audits have a number of advantages for the vendor:

- they establish a base line as to the condition of the site at the time of sale, which safeguards the vendor in the event of any future legal action regarding contamination at the site,
- the audit can be used to demonstrate that contamination was either not caused by the vendor, or to assess the extent of any contamination existing on the site at the time of sale,
- it enables the vendor to 'clean-up' or contain any contamination which could migrate off the site and in respect of which the vendor could otherwise remain liable,
- where the site is to be redeveloped for a more sensitive end use, it enables provisions to be inserted into the contract for sale, specifying the works of remediation to be undertaken by the purchaser,
- it avoids the situation where the purchaser undertakes a survey, without the vendor knowing what is likely to be found, and then claims that the costs of treatment are far in excess of those which were previously anticipated, thus placing the purchaser in a far stronger negotiating position,
- in disclosing the environmental report to prospective purchasers, the vendor will have put them on notice as to any contamination on the site, strengthening the vendor's position in the event of a future claim being made against the vendor as the original polluter,
- if the audit findings are favourable, then the vendor will be more inclined to disclose the information to prospective purchasers,
- the purchaser, and funding institutions, might be able to rely in contract law on the findings of the audit, if a collateral warranty is entered into by the consultant,
- disclosure may dispel, or at least mitigate, any suspicions held by prospective purchasers,

- disclosure of an audit undertaken for the vendor, coupled with collateral warranties, may reduce expenditure on the part of the purchaser, thus attracting a higher bid, and reduce the transaction timescale,
- disclosure may open up the 'selling with information' defence contained in the Environment Act 1995.

Therefore, notwithstanding the *caveat emptor* rule, the vendor may wish to weigh up the benefits of disclosing information to prospective purchasers. The Royal Institution of Chartered Surveyors has argued, in its evidence to the House of Commons Select Committee on the Environment (RICS, 1996), that if a purchaser receives a discount off the price of a property, then he accepts the situation and should be deemed to be 'knowingly permitting' if contaminants subsequently escape from the site. In this way the purchaser would become part of the liability group and any liability of the vendor would be reduced accordingly.

Although there are many good reasons for vendors to commission an environmental audit prior to sale, there are a number of arguments which go against its disclosure:

- the vendor would need to agree with the environmental consultant that the audit can be disclosed to a third party; this goes back to the subject of preparing briefs to consultants which was considered in Chapter 5,
- if the audit discloses adverse findings the vendor may wish to keep them confidential, but this may be a problem if prospective purchasers become aware that an audit has been undertaken and specifically request to see the report,
- purchasers with little or no experience in land transactions, or in dealing with contaminated sites, may be 'scared off' no matter how trivial the contamination might be. Considerable care must therefore be taken by the consultants in preparing their report, so as to reflect the true situation at the site and not present an overly dismal picture,
- if the vendor discloses the audit to prospective purchasers, there must be some concern as to whom that information may reach, which may be addressed by the use of confidentiality agreements.

On balance, however, it would seem to be appropriate for vendors to adopt a policy of disclosing information to prospective purchasers. It should strengthen the vendor's negotiating position, possibly result in an increased offer for the site, reduce the transaction timescale and potentially reduce the vendor's future liabilities.

Financing purchase and redevelopment

The first warnings about how environmental liability risk might strike UK lenders were delivered six years ago (see Sykes, 1995, pp. 127–155) and the passage of time has brought this into sharper focus. As a result, most lenders have reacted to the environmental liability threat by developing risk containment strategies and processes. A general exception to this, borne out by some of the research described in this book, would appear to be building societies, who mistakenly tend to believe that they are less exposed. Some lenders have acquired a good working understanding of environmental law and know how to manage the risks which they face. That said, there is no consensus amongst UK lenders and environmental risk practices may vary from lender to lender, even branch to branch.

There are three types of environmental liability exposures about which lenders need to be wary:

- **credit risks**; in respect of the costs and liabilities incurred by a borrower, in order to comply with environmental regulations and involving, for example, expenditure on advanced technology equipment in order to abate waste discharges, which then compromise its ability to pay off the loan,
- **security risks**; a contaminated site is poor collateral, and if the loan fails it can leave the lender without any assets to go against. The stigma effect (see Chapters 9–11) may also mean that any value which the secured lender is able to realise will be significantly below the cost of correcting the contamination,
- **direct liability risks**; this category of risk has provoked a great deal of concern in the UK banking industry. It considers the possibility of lenders being required to meet the cost of site remediation as the result of active participation in the business

occupying the site, such as the result of having a director on the board of the polluting organisation, or as mortgagee in possession.

Although the latter category of risk has been a cause of concern to bankers, there have been hardly any cases where banks have been sued or prosecuted in their capacity as lenders. There are however a number of practical measures which banks can adopt in order to protect their position. These include requiring an environmental assessment to be undertaken before advancing the loan, and by ensuring that the loan documentation is adequately drafted to cover the possibility of environmental risk through the use of warranties, conditions precedent, express covenants and indemnities by the borrower.

The lender may decide to monitor closely the activities of the borrower during the lifetime of the loan, requiring periodic environmental audits to be undertaken, and for the borrower to take appropriate actions to remediate contamination, or to comply with environmental laws. It can, however, be argued that if a lender, or indeed a landlord, seeks to monitor and control the use of a property too strictly, it may find itself placed in the position of having 'knowingly permitted', in the event that contamination with the potential to cause 'significant harm' is subsequently discovered on the site. Care must therefore be taken to ensure that the extent of any 'management' involvement by lenders in organisations which have the potential to cause contamination, is limited in such a way as to ensure that they do not become responsible for environmental liabilities.

Insurance

Environmental insurance has now become a major business agenda item for almost all organisations and particularly so in relation to contaminated land, property acquisition/divestment, and redevelopment. The impact is two-fold; firstly, because of the perceived risk brought about by legislation, organisations are acutely aware of their exposure to legal action from the acquisition of contaminated land and the effects which contamination may have on its asset value. This environmental risk exposure can to some extent be covered by adequate insurance protection, provided that the appropriate criteria, in respect of contaminative acts and treatment, are addressed before, during and after development. Secondly, with the absence of set standards as to what constitutes contamination or satisfies remediation requirements, combined with a move away from prescriptive legislation towards a more risk based approach, insurance is more frequently seen as an alternative to standards or as a 'comfort factor' to the purchasers of contaminated sites. This can extend over the reclamation, redevelopment and operational future of the site.

In order to establish the present situation regarding environmental insurance, it is necessary to trace its development in the UK from the late 1980s and early 1990s. This may assist in identifying the characteristics of environmental insurance and the way in which changes are likely to occur in the future.

The problem with environmental insurance relates to the situation which existed in the American 'insurance market' at the inception of environmentally related legislation in the 1970s and 1980s, and particularly with the introduction of the 'Superfund' or Comprehensive Environmental Response Compensation and Liability Act 1980 (CERCLA) legislation. When this came into effect, insurance underwriters perceived that they were over-exposed under their general liability policies to risks relating to environmental pollution. An immediate restriction of cover to 'sudden and accidental' incidents under a 'claims made wording' occurred in response. 'Claims made' wording means that a claim has to be made within the period for which the policy was in place for it to be covered. There was also a simultaneous growth in a specialist, environmental insurance market, known as the Environmental Impairment Liability (EIL) market. At its height this specialist EIL market saw boom activity with many risks being underwritten with no real expertise as to the risk involved or covered.

Generous interpretation of pollution situations by the American legal system soon became the norm and restrictions placed on general policy wordings to 'sudden and accidental' incidents only, were ignored in many instances. The acceptance under the American legal system of 'Retroactive and Joint and Several Liability' meant that many insurers found themselves liable under old 'losses occurring' wording of past policies placed and for incidents far larger and wider spread than was ever anticipated. 'Losses Occurring' wording used to be commonplace, and means that a claim can be made at any time after the policy has been instigated, even after the policy has been terminated, provided that it can be shown that the claim arose (i.e. was caused by an accident which occurred) during the period covered.

In this initial market, many insurers suffered very heavy financial losses and immediately withdrew cover. The number of active underwriters in the American EIL Market at this time fell from an estimated total of 80 at its height, to 10 underwriters only twelve months later. Many insurers who were part of the American EIL Market rise and fall were UK based and this was a contributory factor in the problems experienced by Lloyds of London.

With the American situation as a backdrop and as the only means by which to predict possible legislative and market responses and trends, the first inception of the EIL Market in the UK was somewhat more muted. In the late 1980s and early 1990s, the UK EIL Market could be characterised by the following characteristics:

- very few active underwriters – all American
- very restrictive cover
- all known pollution excluded from cover
- site specific cover only
- cover subject to environmental survey/audit
- cover based on 'claims made' wording
- only one year duration of cover, with initially no statement of intent to renew after first year
- initial cover restricted to third party off-site liability only
- limit of indemnity circa £1million
- high premium costs
- high requirements for self-insurance

The extreme difficulty in the placement of cover, together with the restricted nature of these early policies, was in direct contrast to the sophistication and variety of insurance cover which was available in the USA at the time. The rationale behind this was that in response to the earlier inception of environmental legislation and liability in the United States, organisations were now more sophisticated in their environmental risk management. They therefore constituted better risks than their United Kingdom counterparts. Until such time as UK organisations caught up, there promised to be little progression in the EIL market position in the UK.

With the United Kingdom, legislation creating the potential liability but then withdrawing in its actual implementation and an EIL market only providing cover for what was commonly perceived to be 'no risk' situations for a high premium spend, the situation was essentially at a stalemate. This existed until about early 1995. About this time, insurers found that there was an increased requirement for environmental insurance. In the first instance this tended to be required by the large multinational companies, which found themselves operating in a number of foreign markets, many of which were more environmentally sensitive than the United Kingdom.

To control and manage their exposure in multinational markets, active environmental management became a logical necessity, as too did appropriate insurance cover. Other large commercial organisations in the same market sectors came to recognise the need for improved environmental management, partly as the result of 'peer group' pressure, encouraging them to replicate their competitors' actions in order to at least maintain their market share.

Manufacturing industry is now experiencing a situation whereby all of these large organisations also require some form of conformance from their suppliers, as part of their environmental risk management system. In response to such demands from large business customers, as well as the subsequent peer group pressure created within their own area, many such supply organisations are now implementing their own environmental risk programmes and the impetus is passing down the 'chain of supply'.

Other drivers in the demand for environmental insurance include financial investment institutions and peer pressures among lenders, all of which are related in their effects and consequences. These considerations now outrank environmental legislation as stimuli to organisations to implement active environmental risk management processes. This, in turn, has generated a greater interest in environmental risk transfer mechanisms such as environmental insurance; which has consequently resulted in expanding the degree of sophistication and level of cover available.

The UK EIL Market can now be characterised by the following attributes:

- an increased number of active underwriters – in 1996, all American
- wider cover is available
- more complex environmental risks are underwritten
- cover is mainly still site specific – but some blanket cover products are available for specific industry sectors
- cover is still subject to environmental survey/audit
- the 'claims made' wording remains
- cover is for one year with a statement of intent to renew, subject to satisfactory annual survey
- a wider variety of insurance products is available including 'own-site', 'first party clean-up costs', 'capping of re-development/remediation costs', and 'business interruption as a result of environmental risk incidence'
- the limit of indemnity is now increased to circa £5–10million
- premium costs are reducing in some circumstances
- requirements for self-insurance are decreasing

Future trends are likely to see a greater delivery of available products and coverage at increasingly affordable premium levels. The market is likely to be further affected by the situation with regard to pollution cover under general liability policies, most of which still include some element of pollution cover for 'sudden and accidental' incidence only.

Since the very beginning of the EIL Market, it has been widely perceived that at some future date all pollution insurance under general policy covers will be withdrawn, forcing all such insurance for this type of business into the specialist market. For a period in 1995 it seemed as though this time had arrived, when the German speaking re-insurers were reported to be considering suspending all support for environmental insurance under general policies. This has not come to fruition and there is not expected to be any further change to United Kingdom wording under general policies, relating to pollution cover, in the near future.

How long the present situation will remain is unclear, but as specialist EIL products become better adapted to clients' requirements, it is anticipated that further developments and growth of this market can be expected. Whatever happens, it is quite clear that no commercial organisation can afford to ignore the issue of environmental risk and the potential liability exposures which it generates. In such a rapidly evolving and changing market place, the only protection available for the company to protect itself in the long-term is via a pro-active management regime.

With such an approach exposure is minimised, as is the level of required risk which it may be necessary to transfer via insurance. Without appropriate risk management procedures, the company is exposed to a maximum level and insurance under these circumstances is unlikely to be available.

Conclusion

Both buyers and sellers need to consider the need for environmental information when acquiring or disposing of property. The lack of adequate information may result in costly liabilities, which may not be recoverable from third parties. The legal profession is usually seen as an important means by which purchasers' interests are protected, but it would appear that not all members of that profession are sufficiently well versed in contaminated land issues, or they simply fail to ask the relevant questions.

Failure to disclose information on the part of vendors may result in an exception to the rule of *caveat emptor*, giving the purchaser the right to rescind the contract. Even if the sale is completed, suspicion on the part of the purchaser may result in the re-negotiation of the sale price, or delayed completion. In general therefore, it would seem appropriate for vendors to be open with prospective purchasers and make all relevant information available from the outset.

Insurance is available to cover many of the risks associated with contaminated land, but at the present time premium costs are fairly high, with a limited number of insurers in the market. From the developer's point of view, two insurance products are likely to be of great interest. Firstly, insurance cover to 'cap' the remediation cost of site preparation at a pre-determined level and, secondly, cover against future liabilities arising in respect of failure of the treatment method which causes harm to owners or occupiers of the buildings. Vendors are likely to be interested in insurance cover which crystallises any possible future liabilities which they may have, at the time of sale.

Checklist

- Valuers and solicitors need to understand their client's criteria when acting in the acquisition of contaminated property and ensure that their advice is relevant to those criteria.
- There should be a clear understanding between the parties as to the future use of contaminated sites.
- Pre-contract enquiries should be considered in accordance with the list in Table 12.1 and should, at least, include reference to previous uses, waste disposal methods, the presence of underground storage tanks, and compliance with any licences or consents, including water abstraction.
- Check whether or not there is any existing insurance cover in respect of site contamination, or contaminative processes used on site, and whether the benefit of that insurance is transferable on sale.
- Consider whether or not any additional insurance cover is appropriate.

Chapter 13
Conclusions and Recommendations

An important objective of this book has been to demonstrate that contaminated land is an important resource, even if that land is regarded, at least in the short term, as a liability. The findings of the research described in the book support a risk assessment approach which identifies the future potential of such land, informing the decision making process in respect of its redevelopment and valuation.

Land which has been used once can be used again for a wide range of uses and, with care, future contamination of land can be minimised. This can be achieved through the use of town planning and environmental controls, but it would be naive to believe that all future contamination can be prevented. Accidents do occur, from the stranding of supertankers on rocky shores to the leakage of an underground tank in a petrol filling station. Some industrial activities have the potential to create contamination in spite of the most stringent controls, and the disposal of domestic and industrial wastes is a fact of life. For the foreseeable future, in the United Kingdom, the use of landfill for the disposal of a significant proportion of these wastes can be expected to continue.

The excavation of contaminated sites and deposition of the excavated material in landfills is also likely to continue for some time to come, in spite of, or even because of, the Landfill Tax. Alternative methods are available to tackle the problems associated with land contamination but their adoption will depend upon many factors including economics, time scale and the personal perceptions of the individuals charged with the task of finding solutions. Site specific factors and the possible future uses of contaminated land are also important factors in the selection of treatment methods.

For all but the simplest forms of contamination presenting relatively low levels of risk, it is certain that the cost of remediating contaminated sites will be of major importance in the consideration of redevelopment proposals. In many cases it is likely that the costs involved will exceed any future economic value which may be derived from the land, thus throwing into doubt the entire redevelopment project. When this occurs a number of questions will have to be asked:

- does the present or previous owner, or the original polluter, have any legal liability in respect of the 'clean-up' of the site?
- does the contamination create an immediate risk to surrounding properties, ground and surface water and/or the wider environment?
- is the proposed development essential, requiring immediate treatment of the contamination, or can longer term treatments be considered?
- if longer term treatments are suitable, is there a cost saving associated with them and can the delay to the project be justified in economic terms?

These and other related questions have been considered as part of the redevelopment process. A 'risk assessment' model has been developed to assess the economic impact of contamination on land value and usage.

The true extent of land affected by contamination in the United Kingdom is impossible to verify and there are differences of opinion between government estimates and independent research. The government has attempted to limit the extent of land designated as contaminated through the use of definitions which are more narrowly worded than may be desirable from the environmental perspective.

The definitions of 'contaminated land' and 'significant harm', contained in the draft statutory guidance on contaminated land (DoE, 1996), appear to go almost full circle to the definition which was offered to the Select Committee by the Department of the Environment in its 1989-90 session. This defined 'contaminated land' as 'land which represents an actual or potential hazard to health or the environment as a result of current or previous use' (House of

Commons, 1990). Such a definition is in marked contrast to the wide range of 'potentially contaminative uses' listed in Annex C of the consultation paper on the s. 143 registers (DoE, 1991a).

The decision taken by the Department to define 'contaminated land' in the narrow manner apparent from section 57 of the Environment Act 1995 and the draft statutory guidance is understandable, given both the earlier attempt to limit the extent of contaminated land through definition and the opposition experienced in respect of the registers proposed under section 143 of the Environmental Protection Act. Whether or not the definition of 'significant harm' presently under discussion between the Department of the Environment and its advisors will eventually be adopted, remains to be seen.

It may, however, be appropriate for the legal definition of contaminated land to contain a form of limitation, so as to focus attention on the most severely affected sites. To do otherwise would undoubtedly stretch the human resources of the regulatory authorities to such a point as to be self defeating unless, of course, unlimited financial resources were made available to tackle the problem. The objective of seeking to give priority to the 'clean-up' of the most seriously contaminated sites is laudable, but it must be questioned whether the definitions will do much to remove the 'blighting effect' in respect of land which is less seriously affected by contaminative materials.

The total area of land which would be classed as contaminated by virtue of its potential to cause 'significant harm' is impossible to estimate, but it is probably far less than the area of land which is legally regarded as being suitable for its existing use, or intended use, even though it contains contaminative materials. Property investors, whether for owner occupation or income, and the providers of mortgage finance tend to take a long term view when making their investment decisions. These property market actors are therefore likely to question the future uses of affected properties. They will wish to take into consideration alternative uses for the land, as a precautionary measure, in case the present or proposed use was to cease.

If the land in question is not considered to be suitable for an alternative use, say the redevelopment of an industrial site for housing purposes, then the investment opportunity may be rejected, even though the site is not officially designated as contaminated. This will create a 'grey area' containing a whole class of properties which are not 'contaminated' in the strict legal sense of the word, as they are 'suitable for use', but nevertheless contain contaminants at concentrations which exceed recognised threshold levels. Uncertainty will exist in the market, which prospective purchasers of 'grey area' sites will find difficult to reflect in economic terms.

In order to assist market mechanisms in respect of contaminated or damaged land, three levels of definition have been suggested for adoption:

'derelict or redundant land – 'land so damaged by industrial or other development that it is incapable of beneficial use without treatment.'

> This retains the existing definition of derelict land but broadens its scope to include land situated within the curtilage of operational industrial premises but which is surplus to current requirements. Such land may contain contaminative substances but at concentrations which fall below the ICRCL threshold trigger levels, or the trigger levels in any similar or any replacement guidance.

land affected by contaminative substances – land which contains substances of a potentially contaminative nature, with concentrations in excess of ICRCL threshold trigger concentrations (or any similar or replacement guidelines) but where the source of the contaminative substances is no longer active, and where the contaminants do not constitute a threat of significant harm in respect of the present use, or currently proposed use.

> This would include land where receptors of the type most likely to be affected by the contaminants are not normally present, for example elevated levels of phytotoxins on industrial land which is mostly covered by buildings and service yards, and land where the contaminants are contained under a cover layer or by a containment barrier.

contaminated land – any land which appears to the local authority in whose area the land is situated to be in such a condition, by reason of substances in, on or under the land, that:

(a) significant harm is being caused or there is a significant possibility of such harm being caused; or

(b) pollution of controlled waters is being, or is likely to be caused.

This would include land so identified in accordance with the definition of 'significant harm' proposed in the draft statutory guidance but, it is suggested, this should be expanded to include land which may be suitable for use at the time of inspection but where the nature of the contaminants is such that they have the potential to migrate from the land to affect neighbouring properties, regardless of whether or not there is any likelihood of pollution being caused to controlled waters.'

(Source: Syms, 1996e)

Adoption of the three levels of definition would assist regulators, developers and land users alike. For example, a local authority or one of the environment agencies may investigate a suspected contaminated site and conclude that it is not contaminated in the legal sense of the word, although it does contain high concentrations of some contaminants. The basis of this assessment would be that the site is not causing, or does not have the potential to cause, either significant harm or the pollution of controlled waters whilst it remains in its existing use. At the end of that use substantial expenditure may be required to 'clean-up', reduce or contain that contamination, even if the site is to remain in some form of industrial use. The future liability to undertake works of a decontaminative nature would have to be reflected in asset valuations and, in due course, in appraisals to determine the redevelopment potential of the site. The suggested three levels of definition, with the maintenance of associated records, would provide an invaluable source of reference for valuers, lawyers, developers and occupiers.

The redevelopment and value of contaminated land

Personal fears as to the risks from contamination, and prejudices against former industrial areas, may prevent many property developers from using their skills in the redevelopment of contaminated land. Perceptions of the problems involved are also influenced by the views and attitudes of their professional advisors and the lending or investment policies of funding institutions.

The results of the first questionnaire survey described in Chapter 7 demonstrated clearly that investors and housing associations were perceived as being the most cautious actors in the development process, although for all actors a tendency to avoid innovative treatment methods was indicated. As investors play a major part in the financing of redevelopment projects, their attitudes must be taken into account in the preparation of valuations and development appraisals. This is reflected in the valuation model tested in Chapters 10 and 11. Workers on industrial and commercial developments, and shoppers using retail developments, were perceived as being the least sensitive to a history of land contamination.

There are many problems associated with the redevelopment of land contaminated by former industrial activities. No two sites are identical and the severity of contamination will differ according to the nature of the contaminants and their concentrations. Sites which have been used for the same industrial activity can present totally different degrees of risk, as was demonstrated by the case studies reported in Chapters 10 and 11. The severity of contamination will have been influenced by the working practices, both within the firms themselves and entire industries, in respect of the storage of raw materials and disposal of waste products. Several of the case studies illustrate the problems brought about by commencing redevelopment without sufficient knowledge of the extent and nature of soil contamination and the consequences of inadequately designed treatments.

The period 1991–96 has been very difficult in terms of the redevelopment and valuation of contaminated land, due to changes in government policies and the inadequacies of professional guidance. Nevertheless, sites have been redeveloped and valuations prepared, with developers and valuers dealing with problems on a site specific basis. In general, developers and their advisors have adopted a cautious approach to redevelopment. To some extent this approach has been influenced by the funding institutions, which have tended to request increasing amounts of information on environmental issues.

Developers now have to satisfy regulators as to the adequacy of the soil remediation works which they intend to undertake before they start redevelopment. This may involve negotiations with building control, town planning and environmental health officers employed by the local authority, and in more complex cases with their specialist consultants. It may also be necessary to obtain approval from the Environment Agency (or Scottish Environmental Protection Agency) in respect of the proposed works, especially where pollution of controlled waters may be an issue.

Consideration should also be given by developers and their advisors to the desirability of obtaining Environment Agency approval or sanction in respect of proposed works, even when it is not legally required. Confirmation from the Environment Agency that it considers the work to be adequate and appropriate to the contaminants and risks involved may be of considerable benefit, should the extent of site remediation be called into question at some future date.

Valuation effects

The case studies have confirmed that, consciously or otherwise, prospective developers expect to receive a price reduction against the development value of the land, which exceeds the cost of remediating the land and preparing it for redevelopment. In most of the case study developments there was a close correlation between the actual discount received by the developer and the expected discount produced by the valuation model.

Stigma has been proved to exist and to be quantifiable. Pre-development 'stigma' impacts on value were observed for all of the case studies, ranging from 21.21% to 67%. The 'risk assessment' model developed proved to be a useful tool in confirming an expected stigma range of 17.97% to 41.84%. The stigma effect observed in the case studies was similar to the range of 21% to 69% observed by Patchin (1994) in respect of his research in the United States.

In all but one of the case studies it was not possible to identify any post-development price reduction which represents the stigma effect. In the one exception the observed price discount may in fact reflect other factors such as the 'run-down' appearance of the surrounding area and the developer's desire to stimulate market awareness of a location which had not previously been considered for residential development.

It would appear that, whilst house builders and developers expect to see a substantial discount in the price paid for remediated former industrial land, only a small part of the reduction trickles down to the eventual home owners through a reduction of less than 10% in the price paid for new homes. It would seem that the purchasers of new homes, in at least the lower price ranges of the market, are relatively insensitive to the former industrial, and possibly contaminated, nature of the sites upon which homes may be constructed. Also, resistance caused by the history of such sites may be overcome by the use of quality landscaping and the creation by the developer of a 'self-contained environment'. The extent to which similar results may be obtained in respect of land redeveloped for 'higher value' housing remains to be tested.

So far as the non-residential case studies are concerned, once potential tenants and investors were satisfied in respect of the treatment methods, there was no adverse impact on the rental or investment values of the completed development. In one of the case studies the contaminated material was removed from site and replaced with clean fill, and in another only the contaminated content of the fill material was removed from site, with the remaining inert material being re-used. The other industrial use case studies utilised cover and containment methods. The acceptance of more sophisticated, or technologically advanced, treatment methods may have been slow but it is to be hoped that this will change in the light of research and pilot tests.

The implications for valuers and developers

It is essential for valuers of industrial land to have an understanding of the causes and effects of contamination arising from industrial activities. This applies whether the land is to remain in the existing industrial use or is to be redeveloped for industrial or other purposes. Valuers need to be able to exercise their professional judgement in determining whether or not the contamination is potentially harmful. In some cases this may result in the valuer having to obtain specialist advice in respect of the contamination issues but it is argued, in many instances, a valuer should be capable of making a preliminary assessment of the risks involved with a site.

The information and observations needed to arrive at an assessment of risk in respect of an industrial property are similar to those which would be required by a prudent valuer for normal valuation purposes. A valuer's assessment of risk is likely to be qualitative in nature and may fall short of the requirements of a formal 'quantitative' risk assessment, but Cairney (1995) has suggested the use of a semi-quantified risk assessment procedure. This approach would seem to be compatible with the functions of the valuer and should enable assessments to be made which adhere to the proposed definition of 'significant harm'. Petts (1996) has, however, cautioned that the chapter in Cairney's book,

> 'on risks to human health is contentious in suggesting that occupational health criteria in terms of allowable exposure limits can be used directly to consider exposure risks amongst residents and sensitive members of the population (e.g. the pica child)'.

She also expresses doubts as to whether the semi-quantitative method will 'be used robustly by some members of the property and consultancy professions' (Petts, 1996).

That there are differences in terms of perceptions of risk between valuers and other 'consultancy' professions was quite apparent from the results of the third phase of the perceptions studies. The responses to the question relating to the harmful factors of contaminated land (in the second questionnaire survey) confirmed a very significant perception difference, in terms of both 'known risks' and 'uncertainties', between valuers and their colleagues in other professions. Less significant, but nevertheless noticeable, was the difference between the perceptions of the valuers and non-valuers in respect of the property related environmental issues. Although the valuers and non-valuers demonstrated very similar perceptions in terms of the 'known risks', the valuers' perception of risk associated with 'uncertainties' was noticeably higher and more aligned to the perception of the 'general population'. So far as landfills were concerned, the valuers' perception of risk, for both 'known risks' and 'uncertainties' was higher than that of the non-valuers and closer to the perceptions of the general population.

The results from the psychometric tests might be regarded as an indication that the 'valuers' group has a better perception of environmental risk than the 'non-valuers', in view of the closer correlation with the 'general population' results. Such an outcome is unlikely in view of the range of expertise in the 'non-valuers' group. A more logical explanation is that the valuers are less well informed about the risks associated with property related environmental issues, such as contaminated land, than their counterparts in other professions. As a result of this lesser informed state, the valuers may tend to over compensate for their lack of knowledge in dealing with the issues.

Most of the professions in the 'non-valuers' group, especially the engineers and environmental consultants, have been dealing with the issues of land contamination for a longer period of time than the valuers and developers. Many members of these professions have been involved with the problems of soil contamination for a period of more than ten years and it is likely that the risk perceptions of the technical professions peaked several years ago. Those professions will have learned to deal with land contamination as a management issue and are able to provide clients with relevant advice.

Valuers, on the other hand, will inevitably experience problems in providing clients with advice on the subject of contaminated land, a situation which will exist until such time as the appropriate guidance is provided by both government and professional organisations. In the absence of such guidance, valuers will adopt a cautious attitude to the valuation of contaminated land, both before and after treatment, which will be reflected in the advice provided to their developer clients.

The valuers' view of contamination issues is likely to be closely associated with the general public's perception, because education and training in the profession tends to deal with environmental issues in a fairly superficial manner, and most valuers have not had engineering or environmental training. The research would seem to suggest that there is scope for a greater emphasis to be placed on environmental training for valuers and general practice surveyors. Whether or not this should occur at undergraduate level is debatable, given the diversity of subjects with which new entrants to the profession are expected to be conversant, including marketing, business management, and professional ethics, in addition to the traditional subjects of valuation, law, construction and economics.

It may be more appropriate for valuers to develop skills in relation to the valuation and redevelopment of contaminated land through post-graduate courses. Such a course may, for example, include the following topics:

- an introduction to environmental issues and concerns
- contaminated land, pollution and waste management
- environmental legislation in the UK and Europe
- environmental management systems, risk assessment, management and auditing.

Valuers and developers need to be able to distinguish soil contamination which is directly attributable to present or past industrial uses and the 'background' levels of contamination which may be found in industrial areas. One of the case studies described the problems associated with the redevelopment of a site through a joint venture between the chemical company owner and a property developer. In addition to contamination which had arisen from the industrial activities carried out on the site, the soil was also affected by very high sulphate levels. The high sulphate concentrations would have been extremely aggressive if allowed to come into contact with foundations or services but there was no apparent source for the sulphates from within the site. Following further investigations by environmental consultants, including testing soil samples from adjoining properties, it was decided that the probable cause of the sulphate contamination was the former town gas works, situated approximately half a mile from the site, and that all surrounding properties were similarly affected.

Research by Douglas et al (1993), in the same Manchester inner urban area, found elevated levels of lead in surface soil samples and established a relationship between the sampling location and proximity to major roads. The example illustrates the need for valuers to look beyond the boundaries of the site being valued when considering the likelihood of contamination, and to research adequately the industrial history of the area.

The implications for Government policies

Government policy proposals in respect of 'registers of potentially contaminated sites', the subsequent debate and the withdrawal of the proposals, undoubtedly contributed to a state of uncertainty among valuers concerning contaminated land. Most of the valuers interviewed in the second phase of the perceptions study were opposed to the registers, with almost half of the interviewees believing them to have been ill conceived. Opinions were evenly divided as to whether or not registers of all land uses, past and present, would have been preferable to identifying certain uses as 'potentially contaminative'.

Concerns over the effect the registers might have on an already weakened property market provoked some of the opposition to the proposal, although only 14% of the interviewees expressed concern over the potential blighting effect which the registers might have on property values. Most of the opposition to a system of registers centred on the bureaucracy involved and similar concerns were expressed in respect of the role of the environment agencies. Addressing the problems of contaminated land is only one of the many functions of the new environment agencies, whose responsibilities range from fishing licences to the control of pollution, and the priority level to be applied to contaminated land remains to be seen.

In mid-1994, in the interview phase of the perceptions study, almost 50% of the valuers questioned were unaware of the British government's intentions to establish 'environment agencies' and, of those who had some knowledge of the proposal, opinions were equally divided between those in favour and those opposed to the new agencies. Eighteen months later almost 90% of valuers were in favour of the new agencies, provided that they were equipped with the necessary powers to tackle the problems and were not overburdened by bureaucracy.

In both the interview survey and the second questionnaire survey there was clear support for government policies which encourage the redevelopment of contaminated and 'brownfield' sites in preference to 'greenfield' development. For the most part, opinions were in favour of the use of public sector funds to tackle the problems remaining from industrial activities but there was also a widely held view that the polluter should pay.

An environmental impairment databank – is this a possibility?

Given the difficulties involved in obtaining appropriate comparables each time a contaminated property is to be valued and the need to identify the applicable determinants, it has been proposed that a national databank of comparables be established (Syms, 1995a). Initially this would contain data relating to the sales and valuations of contaminated properties, but in future it could be expanded to include other forms of environmental impairment. It was suggested that the databank would include the information set out in Box 13.1.

The databank would be available to valuers for use in preparing valuations or development appraisals of properties affected by

Box 13.1 Proposed environmental impairment bank: information required for each case study property.

General information
  Address of the property
  Tenure
  Site area
  Floor area of buildings
  Age of buildings
  Present or immediate past use
  Previous use(s)
Contamination information
  Nature of the primary contaminant
  Nature of the secondary contaminant(s)
  Whether site investigation and/or risk assessment undertaken
  Date of site investigation/risk assessment
  Hazard level of primary contaminant
  Hazard level of secondary contaminant(s)
Treatment information
  Whether a programme of treatment has been undertaken or is proposed
  Main method of treatment undertaken or proposed
  Secondary treatment method(s)
  Post-treatment hazard level
Valuation information
  Unimpaired value
  Disposal price
  Uncompleted sales price(s)
  Treatment cost, actual or estimated
  The availability of grants or other incentives

---

contamination; information concerning the property to be valued, including its past and/or present uses and the nature of any contamination, would be used to identify the most appropriate comparables. The valuer would be provided with a computer printout detailing the comparables suggested for use (but probably not their precise addresses because of confidentiality restrictions) and a recommended 'value adjuster' which could be applied to the impaired value arrived at after deduction of the quantifiable costs caused by contamination. Regional variations would be taken into account if applicable.

Ideally the primary search field for the identification of comparables should be properties which have been used for similar purposes but, given the problems in obtaining information in respect of an adequate number of similar properties, it is anticipated that, at least in the short term, comparisons would have to be made on the basis of risk levels and types of contamination. As the number of records in the databank increases, the procedures used in identifying suitable comparables would be subject to revision, so as to improve the accuracy of the valuation method. In addition to being used for the assessment of stigma, the databank would be of considerable benefit in recording information as to the costs of dealing with the physical aspects of land contamination. Once fully tested and operational the databank could be expanded to assist research into other aspects of environmental impairment.

Conclusion

This book has attempted to synergise the technical and economic aspects of contaminated land. Research involving more than 130 professionals engaged in the valuation, redevelopment, funding or transfer of contaminated land has been described. The research considered the technical aspects of site investigations and soil treatment methods from the perspective of the valuer, the development surveyor and the developer. This is an extremely large subject area, which was expanding, in terms of both technologies and literature, during the research period. No attempt has been made to provide a critique in respect of treatment technologies, but instead the intention was to consider those issues which are of concern to valuers, and their clients, when it comes to the selection of appropriate treatment methods for the remediation of contaminated soils.

Whether or not valuers and surveyors become involved in site investigations and the design of soil treatments will depend on individual practitioners. However, industrial property valuers in particular need to take account of contamination issues and much of the information required for a preliminary site investigation will be relevant in enabling the valuer to provide his or her client with meaningful advice.

Three principal contributions to knowledge were produced by the research. Firstly, the development of a model by which the value of contaminated land might be assessed. The 'risk assessment' approach adopted in the model accords with the Department of the Environment's approach and that of the 'technical professions'. Secondly, the psychometric part of the perceptions study proved that the perceptions of valuers were markedly different to those of a mixed professional group of 'non-valuers'. Finally, the research confirmed that investors are the most averse to risk of all actors when it comes to consideration of the treatment and re-use of contaminated land.

Solutions to the redevelopment of contaminated land require a multi-disciplinary approach and an attempt has been made to provide a link between the technical and economic aspects of the problem. Further quantitative testing is required in order to test the valuation model and a computer program is being developed for this purpose. Testing would also benefit from a 'comparables databank' and the problems associated with the establishment of a databank are recognised, not least in terms of commercial confidentiality.

Further research has already commenced, to examine the perceptions of funding institutions and equity investors with regard to contaminated land. This research will compare the attitudes of actors in the United States and the United Kingdom. Valuers, developers and investors all need to be better informed about innovative soil treatment methods. This is largely an educative process but further research is probably required in order to convince people investing large sums of money, often for a period of many years, that they will not be faced with environmental problems at some future date.

Ivor Richards has referred to the 'Paretto Principle' in attempting to assess the extent of the contamination problem in the United

Kingdom (Richards, I. 1995) and concluded that, of all the industrial and former industrial land in Britain, only 20% is likely to have been damaged to such an extent as to justify use of the term 'contaminated land'. The Department of the Environment, the Environment Agency and the Local Authorities Association, in giving evidence to the House of Commons Select Committee on the Environment in September 1996, were all unable to provide a reasoned estimate as to the number of contaminated sites which may exist, let alone the total area of land which may have the potential to cause 'significant harm'.

If, however, the Paretto Principle is applied when seeking to assess the extent of land with the greatest potential to cause harm, the most severely affected area may be assessed as one fifth of the total area affected by contamination. Using Richards' argument, it would appear that the extent of land in Britain affected by contamination which could cause 'significant harm' may be around 2800 hectares (6900 acres). Thus, whilst the problem of contamination, and its economic impact in terms of redevelopment, is important, it is probably nothing like as serious as some commentators would appear to indicate. Practical solutions can be found and land can be re-used, although at a cost which is probably best regarded as being the joint responsibility of all in society.

References

Adams, C.D., Baum, A.E. & MacGregor, B.D. (1985) The influence of valuation practices upon the price of vacant inner city land. *Land Development Studies*, **2**, Land Development Studies Education Trust.

Adams, C.D. (1986) *The accommodation needs of small industrial users in Inner Manchester*, research paper, Department of Town and Country Planning, University of Manchester.

Alloway, B.J. & Ayres, D.C. (1993) *Chemical Principles of Environmental Pollution*, Blackie, London.

Applied Environmental Research Centre (1994) *Guidance on preliminary site inspection of contaminated land*, a report prepared for the Department of the Environment, London.

Armishaw, A., Bardos, R.P., Dunn, R.M., *et al.* (1992) *Review of Innovative Contaminated Soil Clean-up Processes*, Warren Spring Laboratory, Stevenage.

Bardos, R.P. (1993a) *The NATO/CCMS pilot study on research, development and evaluation of remedial action technologies for contaminated soil and groundwater*, Warren Spring Laboratory, Department of Trade and Industry, December 1993.

Bardos, R.P. (1993b) Process constraints on innovative soil treatment technologies. *Land Contamination and Reclamation*, **1**.1.

Bardos, R.P. & van Veen, J. (1995) Longer term or extensive treatment technologies. A concept paper, presented at '*In Situ and On-Site Bioreclamation' The Third International Symposium*, April 24–27, 1995, San Diego, California.

Barry, D. (1991) Hazards in land recycling. In: *Recycling Derelict Land*, (ed. G. Fleming), Thomas Telford, London.

Beckett, M.J. (1993a) Land contamination. In: *Contaminated Land: Problems and Solutions*, (ed. T. Cairney), Blackie & Son, Glasgow.

Beckett, M.J. (1993b) Trigger Concentrations: More or Less? *Land Contamination and Reclamation*, **1**.2 EPP Publications, Richmond.

Beckett, M.J. & Cairney, T. (1993) Reclamation Options. In: *Contaminated Land: Problems and Solutions*, (ed. T. Cairney) Blackie & Son, Glasgow.

Beckett, M.J. & Simms, D.L. (1984) The development of contaminated land. In: *Proc. Conf., Hazardous Waste Disposal and the Re-Use of Contaminated Land, London*, SCI, London.

Bell, R.M., Gildon, A. & Parry, G.D.R. (1983) Sampling strategy and data interpretation for site investigation of contaminated land. *Reclamation of Former Iron and Steelworks*, Doubleday, Durham.

Bleich, D.H., Findlay, M.C., & Phillips, G.M. (1991) An Evaluation of the impact of a well-designed landfill on surrounding property values. *The Appraisal Journal*, April 1991.

Bohm, K. (1992) A Thermal Treatment for Cleaning Contaminated Soil. In: *Contaminated Land Treatment Technologies* (ed. J.F. Rees), Elsevier Science Publishers, Barking, Essex.

Bord, R.J. & O'Connor, R.E. (1992) Determinants of risk perceptions of a hazardous waste site. *Risk Analysis*, **12**.3.

Boyle, C. (1993) Soils Washing. *Land Contamination & Reclamation*, EPP Publications, Richmond, **1**.3.

British Bankers Association (1993) Banks and the environment. A position statement issued September 1993, BBA, London.

British Bankers Association (1994) Response to *Paying for Our Past* April 1994, BBA, London.

BSI (1988) *Draft for Development Code of Practice for the Identification of Potentially Contaminated Land and its Investigation* (DD175:1988), British Standards Institution, London.

Cairney, T. (1987) *Reclaiming Contaminated Land*. Blackie & Son, Glasgow.

Cairney, T. (1993) *Contaminated Land: Problems and Solutions*. Blackie & Son, Glasgow.

Cairney, T. (1995) *The Re-use of Contaminated Land: A Handbook of Risk Assessment*. Wiley, Chichester.

Cairney, T. & Sharrock, T. (1993) Clean cover technology. In: *Contaminated Land: Problems and Solutions*, (ed. T. Cairney), Blackie & Son, Glasgow.

Chartered Surveyor Weekly (1991) *Beware, contaminated site*, a news report, *Chartered Surveyor Weekly*, 4 July 1991.

CIRIA (1995) *Remedial Treatment for Contaminated Land*, in twelve volumes. Construction Industry Research and Information Association, London.

Crowcroft, P. (1994) Contaminated ground investigation – matching techniques to site conditions. Paper presented at *The Institution of Water and Environmental Management symposium on 'Contaminated Land – from Liability to Asset'*, 7/8 February 1994, Birmingham.

Deelen, A. (1995) The Dutch Challenge: City of Maastricht. Paper presented at *5th International FZK/TNO Conference on Contaminated Soil*, Maastricht, The Netherlands, 30 October – 3 November 1995.

Denner, J. (1991) *Contaminated land: Policy development in the UK*. Published by Contaminated Land Branch, Department of the Environment, London.

Denner, J. & Bentley, J. (1991) *General Overview of Clean-up Technologies*. Department of the Environment, London.

Denner, J. & Lowe, M.F. (1995) UK Contaminated Land Policy Development. In: *Contaminated Soil '95, proceedings of the 5th International FZK/TNO Conference on Contaminated Soil*, (eds W.J. van den Brink, R. Bosman & F. Arendt), Maastricht, The Netherlands, 30 October – 3 November 1995, Kluwer, Dordrecht, NL.

Denner, J. Kasamas, H. & Hoppener, K. (1995) International ad hoc Working Group on Contaminated Land. In: *Contaminated Soil '95, proceedings of the 5th International FZK/TNO Conference on Contaminated Soil*. (eds W.J. van den Brink, R. Bosman & F. Arendt), Maastricht, The Netherlands, 30 October–3 November 1995, Kluwer, Dordrecht, NL.

Dixon, T. & Richards, T. (1995) Valuation lessons from America, *Estates Gazette*, no. 9529.

Dixon, T. (1995) Comment: Contaminated land and property, *Journal of Property Valuation and Investment*, **13**.5.

DoE (1986a) *Transforming our Waste Land: The Way Forward*, a report prepared by University of Liverpool, Environmental Advisory Unit, Department of the Environment, HMSO, London.

DoE (1986b) *Landfilling Wastes: a technical memorandum for the disposal of wastes on landfill sites*, Waste Management Paper No. 26, Department of the Environment, HMSO, London.

DoE (1988, revised 1995) Planning Policy Guidance Note 2, (1988, revised 1995) *Green Belts*, Department of the Environment, London.

DoE (1990a) *Contaminated Land*, The Government's Response to the First Report from the House of Commons Select Committee on the Environment, Cm 1161, Department of the Environment, HMSO, London.

DoE (1990b) *This Common Inheritance:* Britain's Environmental Strategy, Department of the Environment, HMSO, London.

DoE (1991a) *Public Registers of Land which may be Contaminated:* a consultation paper, Department of the Environment and the Welsh Office, May 1991.

DoE (1991b) *Survey of Derelict Land in England 1988*, Department of the Environment, HMSO, London.

DoE (1992a) *Environmental Protection*, a draft Statutory Instrument, schedule and letter, intended to bring into force Section 143 of the Environmental Protection Act 1990, Department of the Environment, London, 31 July 1992.

DoE (1992b) *City Grant Guidance Notes*, Third Edition, City Grant Team, Department of the Environment, London.

DoE (1994a) *Paying for our Past*, a consultation paper, Department of the Environment and the Welsh Office, London, March 1994.

DoE (1994b) *Framework for Contaminated Land*, outcome of the Government's review and conclusions from the consultation paper *Paying for our Past*, Department of the Environment and the Welsh Office, London, November 1994.

DoE (1994c) *Guidance on Preliminary Site Inspection of Contaminated Land* (2 volumes), a report prepared by Applied Environmental Research Centre Ltd., Department of the Environment, London.

DoE (1994d) *Sampling Strategies for Contaminated Land*, a report prepared by The Centre for Research into the Built Environment, Nottingham Trent University, Department of the Environment, London.

DoE (1994e) *Planning and Pollution Control*, PPG23, Department of the Environment, HMSO, London.

DoE (1995) *Survey of Derelict Land in England 1993*, a report prepared by Ove Arup and Partners, 2 volumes, Department of the Environment, HMSO, London.

DoE (1996) *Contaminated Land*, public consultation draft of the statutory guidance proposed under Part IIA of the Environmental Protection Act 1990, Part II of the Environment Act 1995, Department of the Environment, London.

Douglas, I. Al-Ali, J. & Clarke, M. (1993) Lead Contamination in Manchester, *Land Contamination & Reclamation*, **1**.3, EPP Publications, Richmond.

Dutch Ministry of Housing (1987) *Soil Clean-up Guidelines (Leidraad bodemsanering)*, Dutch Ministry of Housing, Physical Planning and the Environment, The Hague.

Elliot-Jones, M. (1995) *'Stigma' in light of Bixby Ranch, DeSario, and T & E Industries*, published by Foster Associates Inc., San Francisco.

Ellis, B. (1992) On site and in situ treatment of contaminated sites. In: *Contaminated Land Treatment Technologies*, (ed. J.F. Rees), Elsevier Science Publishers, Barking, Essex.

ENSR (1992) *A Guide to On-Site Remediation of Hydrocarbons*, a special report by ENSR Consulting and Engineering, Acton, Massachusetts.

Ferguson, C. (1993) Designing sampling strategies for contaminated sites. Paper presented at *IBC Conference on 'Site investigations for contaminated sites'*, 23–24 September 1993, London.

Ferguson, C. & Denner, J. (1993) Soil remediation guidelines in the UK – a new risk based approach. In proceedings of *Developing Clean-up Standards for Contaminated Soil, Sediment and Groundwater*, Washington DC, 10–13 January 1993.

Fleming, G. (1991) *Recycling Derelict Land*, Thomas Telford, London.

Fletcher, A.J. (1992) Contaminated Land. Paper presented at *Incorporated Society of Valuers and Auctioneers seminar on 'Contaminated Land – Implications and Solutions'*, 2 November 1992, London.

Graham, T. (1995) *Contaminated Land*, Jordans, Bristol.

Grant, M. (1992) Environmental legislation and regulation affecting the property market. *The Response of the Property Industry to Environmental Change*, papers presented at a series of technical seminars Spring 1992, Society of Property Researchers and the Royal Institution of Chartered Surveyors, London.

Haines, R.C. and Harris, M.R. (1987) Main types of contaminants. In: *Reclaiming Contaminated Land*, (ed. T. Cairney), Blackie & Son, Glasgow.

Haines, R.C. (1987) Policy planning and financial issues. In: *Reclaiming Contaminated Land*, (ed. T. Cairney), Blackie & Son, Glasgow.

Hanson, M. (1991) Manchester revives its city centre. *Estates Gazette*, **9120**.

Harris, M.R. (1987) Recognition of the Problem. In: *Reclaiming Contaminated Land*, (ed. T. Cairney), Blackie & Son, Glasgow.

Harris, M.R., Herbert, S.M. & Smith, M.A. (1994) *Remedial Treatment for Contaminated Land*, (12 volumes) Special Reports 101, 112, CIRIA, London.

Haughton, G. and Hunter, C. (1994) *Sustainable Cities*. Jessica Kingsley and Regional Studies Association, London.

Health and Safety Executive (1991) *Protection of workers and the general public during the redevelopment of contaminated land* HS(G)66, HMSO, London.

HMSO (1978) *Inner Urban Areas Act 1978*, HMSO, London.

HMSO (1990) *Environmental Protection Act 1990*, HMSO, London.

HMSO (1992) *Environmental Protection Act 1990* – Section 143 registers, draft regulations, July 1992, HMSO, London.

HMSO (1995) *Environment Act 1995*, HMSO, London.

Hobson, J. (1991) *Contaminated land*. Directorate of Pollution Control and Wastes, Department of the Environment, London.

Hobson, D.M. (1993) Rational Site Investigations. In: *Contaminated Land: Problems and Solutions*, (ed. T. Cairney) Blackie & Son, Glasgow.

Holdgate, M.W. (1979) *A Perspective of Environmental Pollution*, Cambridge University Press, Cambridge.

House of Commons (1990) *Contaminated Land*, First Report of the Select Committee on the Environment, HMSO, London.

House of Commons (1996) *Contaminated Land*, Second Report of the Select Committee on the Environment, HMSO, London.

Howard, M. (1993) Secretary of State for the Environment, Written Answer to the House of Commons, 24 March 1993.

ICRCL (1983) *Guidance on the Assessment and Redevelopment of Contaminated Land*, ICRCL 59/83 Inter-departmental Committee on the Redevelopment of Contaminated land, London.

ICRCL (1986) *Notes on the redevelopment of gasworks sites*, ICRCL 18/79 5th edn. Interdepartmental Committee on the Redevelopment of Contaminated Land, London.

ICRCL (1987) *Guidance on the Assessment and Redevelopment of Contaminated Land*, ICRCL 59/83 2nd edn. Inter-departmental Committee on the Redevelopment of Contaminated land, London.

ICRCL (1990) *Notes on the development and after-use of landfill sites*, ICRCL 17/18 8th edn. Inter-departmental Committee on the Redevelopment of Contaminated Land, London.

Ironside, C.D. (1989) Private sector funding for redevelopment of contaminated land, *Journal of the Institution of Water and Environmental Management* **3**(2).

Jaconetty, T.A. (1996) Stigma, phobias, and fear: their effect on valuation, *Assessment Journal*, **3**.1.

Jefferis, S.A. (1992) Remedial Barriers and Containment. In: *Contaminated Land Treatment Technologies*, (ed. J.F. Rees), Elsevier Science Publishers, Barking, Essex.

Kasamas, H. (1995) Contaminated Sites Programme in Austria. In: *Contaminated Soil '95, proceedings of the 5th International FZK/TNO Conference on Contaminated Soil*, (eds W.J. van den Brink, R. Bosman & F. Arendt), Maastricht, The Netherlands, 30 October – 3 November 1995, Kluwer, Dordrecht, NL.

Keeping, M. (1996) An analysis of the *caveat emptor* principle as applied to contaminated land. Paper given to *RICS Cutting Edge Conference*, University of the West of England, Bristol, 20–21 September 1996.

Kelly, R.T. (1979) Site investigations and material problems. Paper presented at '*RECLAN' Conference*. Published in *Reclamation of Contaminated Land*, Society of Chemical Industry, 1980.

Kinnard, W.M., DeLottie, J.W., Geckler, M.B. & Noble, B.H. (1995) The impact of widespread, long-term soil contamination of residential property values: a case study. Presented at *Annual Meeting of the American Real Estate Society*, Hilton Head, South Carolina.

Kivell, P.T. (1987) Derelict land in England: policy responses to a continuing problem, *Regional Studies* 21(3).

Kruus, P., Demmer, M. & McCaw, K. (1991) *Chemicals in the Environment*, Polyscience, Quebec, Canada.

Laing, N. (1992) Putting a Price on the Problem – Valuation Issues, conference paper, Drivers Jonas, London.

Lizieri, C. & Palmer, S. with Charlton, M. & Finlay, L. (1995) *Valuation Methodology and Environmental Legislation: a research project for the RICS Education Trust*, Discussion Paper Series, City University Business School, London.

Local Authority Associations (1996) Written submission of the Local Authority Associations, given in evidence to the House of Commons Select Committee on the Environment.

Lord, A. (1991) Options available for problem solving. In: *Recycling Derelict Land*, (ed. G. Fleming), Thomas Telford, London.

Lord, D.W. (1987) Appropriate site investigations. In: *Reclaiming Contaminated Land*, (ed. T. Cairney), Blackie & Son, Glasgow.

McEntee, J. (1991) Site investigation. In: *Recycling Derelict Land*, (ed. G. Fleming) Thomas Telford, London.

Martin, I. & Bardos, P. (1996) *A review of Full Scale Treatment Technologies for the Remediation of Contaminated Soil*, EPP Publications, Richmond.

Morgan, M.G. & Henrion, M. (1992) *Guide to dealing with Uncertainty in quantitative risk and policy analysis*, Cambridge University Press.

Mundy, B. (1992a) Stigma and Value. *The Appraisal Journal*, January 1992.

Mundy, B. (1992b) The Impact of Hazardous Materials on Property Value. *The Appraisal Journal*, April 1992.

Mundy, B. (1992c) The Impact of Hazardous and Toxic Material on Property Value: Revisited. *The Appraisal Journal*, October 1992.

Murley, L. (1995) *NSCA Pollution Handbook*, National Society for Clean Air and Environmental Protection, Brighton.

Parry, G.D.R. & Bell, R.M. (1987) Types of contaminated land. In: *Reclaiming Contaminated Land*, (ed. T. Cairney) Blackie & Son, Glasgow.

Patchin, P.J. (1988) Valuation of Contaminated Properties, *The Appraisal Journal*, Jan 1988.

Patchin, P.J. (1991a) Contaminated Properties – Stigma Revisited. *The Appraisal Journal*, April 1991.

Patchin, P.J. (1991b) The Valuation of Contaminated Properties. *Real Estate Issues*, Fall/Winter 1991, **16**.2.

Patchin, P.J. (1994) Contaminated Properties and the Sales Comparison Approach. *The Appraisal Journal*, July 1994, **LXII**.3.

Pearl, M. & Wood, P. (1994) *Review of Pilot and Full Scale Soil Washing Plants*. A report by AEA Technology, National Environmental Technology Centre (NETCEN), for the Department of the Environment, AEA Technology, Abingdon.

Petts, J. (1994) Contaminated sites: Blight, public concerns and communication. *Land Contamination & Reclamation*, **2**.4.

Petts, J. & Eduljee, G. (1994) *Environmental Impact Assessment for Waste Treatment and Disposal Facilities*, John Wiley & Son, Chichester.

Petts, J. (1996) Review of *The Re-use of Contaminated Land: A Handbook of Risk Assessment*, by T. Cairney (1995) *Land Contamination & Reclamation*, **4**.1.

RCEP (1984) *Tackling Pollution – Experience and Prospects*, Royal Commission on Environmental Pollution 10th Report, HMSO, London.

Redhead, B. (1992) *Months in the Country*, Ebury Press, London.

Richards, I. (1995) Lands of opportunity, *Estates Gazette*, London, **9536**, 130–131.

Richards, T. (1995) *A Changing Landscape: The Valuation of Contaminated Land and Property*, The College of Estate Management, Reading.

Richards, T. (1996) Contaminated land stigma. Letter in *Estates Gazette* 9614, The Estates Gazette, London.

RICS (1993) Valuation Guidance Note 11, (VGN11), Environmental factors, contamination and valuation, *Manual of Valuation: Guidance Notes*, Third Edition, Royal Institution of Chartered Surveyors, London.

RICS (1995a) *Contaminated Land: guidance for Chartered Surveyors*, Royal Institution of Chartered Surveyors, London.

RICS (1995b) *Environmental Management and the Chartered Surveyor*, Royal Institution of Chartered Surveyors, London.

RICS (1995c) Valuation Guidance Note 2, in the *RICS Appraisal and Valuation Manual*, Royal Institution of Chartered Surveyors, London.

RICS (1995d) *RICS Appraisal and Valuation Manual*, Royal Institution of Chartered Surveyors, London.

RICS (1996) Evidence to Select Committee on Environment: draft Statutory Guidance on Contaminated Land, October 1996, Royal Institution of Chartered Surveyors, Policy Unit, London.

Sanden, J. (1995) Planned legal regulations on soil conservation and rehabilitation of contaminated sites in the Federal Republic of Germany. In: *Contaminated Soil '95, proceedings of the 5th International FZK/TNO Conference on Contaminated Soil*, (eds W.J. van den Brink, R. Bosman & F. Arendt) Maastricht, The Netherlands, 30 October – 3 November 1995, Kluwer, Dordrecht, NL.

Sappänen, A. (1995) Contaminated soil sites in Finland, Present situation and policy goals. Paper presented to *5th International FZK/TNO Conference on Contaminated Soil*, Maastricht, The Netherlands, 30 October – 3 November 1995.

Sax, N.I. & Lewis, R.J. (1989) *Dangerous Properties of Industrial Materials*, 7th edn. Van Norstrand Reinhold, New York.

Scottish Enterprise (1993) *Requirements for contaminated land site investigations*, Scottish Enterprise, Glasgow.

Simm, G. (1992) Problems for the valuation surveyor. Paper presented at *Seminar on 'Environmental Assessments'*, Sheffield City Polytechnic, 5 March 1992.

Slovic, P. (1992) Perception of Risk: Reflections on the Psychometric Paradigm. In: *Social Theories of Risk* (eds S. Krimsky & D. Golding), Praeger, Westport, Connecticut.

Smith, M.A. (1985) In *Contaminated Land*. Report of the NATO/CCMS pilot study on contaminated land, Plenum, New York.

Smith, M.A. (1987) Available reclamation methods. In: *Reclaiming Contaminated Land*, (ed. T. Cairney), Blackie & Son, Glasgow.

Smith, M.A. (1990) *Memorandum of evidence*. Report of the Environment Committee (Volume II), HMSO, London.

Smith, M.A. (1991) Data analysis and interpretation. In: Fleming, G. (ed) *Recycling Derelict Land*, (ed. G. Fleming), Thomas Telford, London.

Smith, M.A. & Harris, M. (1994) Available guidance on Risk Assessment and the use of Guidelines and Standards. Paper presented to *'A Risk Management Approach to Contaminated Land'*, a Clayton Environmental Consultants seminar, 12 October 1994, London.

Smith, M.A. (1994) Options for Remediation. Paper presented to *'A Risk Management Approach to Contaminated Land'*, a Clayton Environmental Consultants seminar, 12 October 1994, London.

Soundarajan, R. (1992) Organic Stabilization/Solidification – theory and practice. In: *Contaminated Land Treatment Technologies*, (ed. J.F. Rees) Elsevier Science Publishers, Barking, Essex.

Sutherland, E. (1994) Environment's impact on construction practice. *Chartered Surveyor Monthly*, January 1994.

Sykes, S. (1995) Environmental Liability: practice in the UK. In: *Environmental Liability for Banks*, ed J. Norton, Lloyds of London Press, London.

Syms, P.M. (1986) *Incentive policies and land use responses: a study of the industrial property market in the Manchester conurbation and the impact of enterprise zones*, M.Phil thesis, Victoria University of Manchester.

Syms, P.M. (1992) Valuation of Contaminated Land and Buildings. Paper presented at *Incorporated Society of Valuers and Auctioneers seminar on 'Contaminated Land – Implications and Solutions'*, 2 November 1992, London.

Syms, P.M. (1993) Piccadilly Village, Manchester: a case study in waterside urban renewal. In: *Urban Regeneration: property investment and development*, (ed. J. Berry, S. McGreal & B. Deddis) E. & F.N. Spon, London, 307–321.

Syms, P.M. (1994a) The funding of developments on derelict and contaminated sites. In: *Industrial Property policy and economic development*, (ed. R. Ball & A.C. Pratt) Routledge, London, 63–82.

Syms, P.M. (1994b) The Post Remediation Values of Contaminated Land. Paper presented at *The Institution of Water and Environmental Management symposium on 'Contaminated Land – from Liability to Asset'*, 7/8 February 1994, Birmingham.

Syms, P.M. (1995a) Environmental impairment: an approach to valuation. In *Proceedings of the RICS 'Cutting Edge 95' Research Conference*, University of Aberdeen, Royal Institution of Chartered Surveyors, London.

Syms, P.M. (1995b) The Valuation of contaminated land: the problems caused by lack of accessible data in the United Kingdom. Paper presented to the 'Brownfields Working Group', Great Lakes Environmental Finance Center, Cleveland State University, Cleveland, Ohio, 20 October 1995.

Syms, P.M. (1996a) The effects of industrial contamination on residential land values in the United Kingdom. *Land Contamination and Reclamation*, EPP Publications, Richmond, **4**.1, 1–8.

Syms, P.M. (1996b) A question of evidence. *The Valuer*, ISVA, London, **65**.2, 12–13.

Syms, P.M. (1996c) Dealing with contaminated assets. *Estates Gazette*, London, **9612**, 124–5.

Syms, P.M. (1996d) Contaminated land and other forms of environmental impairment: an approach to valuation. *Journal of Property Valuation and Investment*, **14**.2, 38–47.

Syms, P.M. (1996e) Memorandum of evidence to the House of Commons Select Committee on the Environment, October 1996.

Syms, P.M. (1996f) *The redevelopment and value of contaminated land.* PhD thesis, Sheffield Hallam University.

TEGOVOFA (1988) *Valuation of land subject to soil pollution*. Background Paper BP19, The European Group of Valuers of Fixed Assets, London.

Thomas, K. (1981) Comparative risk perception: how the public perceives the risks and benefits of energy systems. *The assessment and perception of risk*, a Royal Society discussion, The Royal Society, London, 35–50.

TIAVSC (1990a) *The effect of environmental factors or pollution on the valuation of fixed assets for financial statements*. Guidance Note 15 (draft), The International Asset Valuation Standards Committee, London.

TIAVSC (1990b) *The consideration of environmental factors and pollution in the valuation process*. Background Paper 15 (draft), The International Asset Valuation Standards Committee, London.

Tromans, S. & Turrall-Clarke, R. (1994) *Contaminated Land*. Sweet and Maxwell, London.

Turner, N.J.K., Gronow, S.A. & Pritchard, P. (1994) Assessing the environmental risks of property investment portfolios, *Journal of Property Finance*, **5**.4, 68–83.

USEPA (1994) *Superfund Innovative Technology Program: Technology Profiles*, 7th edn. United States Environmental Protection Agency, Cincinnati, Ohio.

van Dyke, E. (1995) The contaminated sites policy in Flanders. Paper presented to *5th International FZK/TNO Conference on Contaminated Soil*, Maastricht, The Netherlands, 30 October – 3 November 1995.

Waters, J. (1993) Site investigation for clean up design. Paper presented at *IBC Conference 'Site investigations for contaminated sites'*, 23/24 September 1993, London.

Weihs, St. (1995) The Austrian Register of Contaminated Sites. In: *Contaminated Soil '95, proceedings of the 5th International FZK/TNO Conference on Contaminated Soil*, (eds W.J. van den Brink, R. Bosman & F. Arendt), Maastricht, The Netherlands, 30 October – 3 November 1995, Kluwer, Dordrecht, NL, 103–103.

Welsh Development Agency (1993) *The WDA Manual on the Remediation of Contaminated Land*. Report prepared by ECOTEC Research and Consulting and Environmental Advisory Unit, Welsh Development Agency, Cardiff.

Wilbourn, P. (1995) Chartered surveyors and land quality statements. *Estates Gazette*, London, **9509**, 311–313.

Wilbourn, P. (1996) Contaminated land stigma. Letter to the *Estates Gazette*, London, **9614**, p28.

Wilby, T. (1987) Sweetening the land. *CSW Refurbishment Supplement, Chartered Surveyor Weekly*, London, 29 October, xi–xii.

Wilson, A.R. (1994) The Environmental Opinion: basis for an impaired value opinion. *The Appraisal Journal*, **LXII**.3, 410–423.

Wilson, A.R. (1996) Emerging Approaches to Impaired Property Valuation. *The Appraisal Journal*, **LXIV**.2, 155–170.

Index